Iconic Events

Media, Politics, and Power in Retelling History

Patricia Leavy

LEXINGTON BOOKS

A division of
ROWMAN & LITTLEFIELD PUBLISHERS, INC.
Lanham • Boulder • New York • Toronto • Plymouth, UK

LEXINGTON BOOKS

A division of Rowman & Littlefield Publishers, Inc.
A wholly owned subsidary of The Rowman & Littlefield Publishing Group, Inc.
4501 Forbes Boulevard, Suite 200
Lanham, MD 20706

Estover Road
Plymouth PL6 7PY
United Kingdom

British Library Cataloguing in Publication Information Available

Library of Congress Cataloging-in-Publication Data

Leavy, Patricia, 1975–
  Iconic events : media, politics, and power in retelling history / Patricia Leavy.
    p. cm.
  Includes bibliographical references.
  ISBN-13: 978-0-7391-1519-0 (cloth : alk. paper)
  ISBN-10: 0-7391-1519-7 (cloth : alk. paper)
  ISBN-13: 978-0-7391-1520-6 (pbk. : alk. paper)
  ISBN-10: 0-7391-1520-0 (pbk. : alk. paper)
  1. Collective memory—United States. 2. Psychic trauma—Social aspects—United
States—Historiography. I. Title.
  HM1027.U6L43 2007
  302.230973'0904—dc22
                                                    2007006895
Printed in the United States of America

To my daughter Madeline Claire
and in loving memory of my grandmother Aina Smiltens

Contents

Acknowledgments

In the work toward this book I am grateful to many. At Boston College I have to thank professors Stephen Pfohl, Eve Spangler, David Karp, and Seymour Leventman. Stephen, my endless gratitude to you for your extensive feedback on this project, as well as all of your feedback and support over the years. You have influenced not only this work, but my thinking, writing, and teaching in general. Eve, I can't thank you enough for your many readings of this work, and unfailing support through the long journey of putting this book together. Thank you for believing! Thank you to everyone who contributed to the editing and revising, particularly Elwood Watson for your generous review. Thanks to Harvard University professor Steven Biel for meeting with me to discuss my ideas. Thank you to my colleagues at Stonehill College for the support and encouragement. I also have many research assistants from Stonehill who have contributed to this project. First and foremost, thank you to Nathan Regan for searching for references, formatting, and seeing the manuscript through to the end. Thank you to Kim Foley, Michael Gennarro, Kathryn Maloney Kristina Nicastro, and Paul Sacco for your assistance collecting data and literature. A spirited thank you to all the folks at Lexington Publishers involved with the publication of this book, and particularly my editor Joseph Parry. And of course, much appreciation to my family and friends. Mom and Dad, thank you for your love, support, and friendship. Mom, thank you so much for always encouraging me to write. To my daughter, Madeline Claire, I dedicate this work to you. In the story of my life, you have provided the greatest memories and the purest love. You have shared your childhood with this work, and I am forever grateful. Finally, I also dedicate this work in loving memory of my grandmother, Aina Smiltens, who provided me with the most splendid childhood memories one could hope for.

Permissions

Front page of *Woman's Journal*, April 1, 1911, "The real triangle: rent, profit, interest." Reprinted with permission from The Schlesinger Library, Radcliffe Institute, Harvard University.

Front page of *Woman's Journal*, April 27, 1912, "Votes for Women to the Rescue. When women cannot vote the ship of state is like the steamship Titanic." Reprinted with permission from The Schlesinger Library, Radcliffe Institute, Harvard University.

Chapter One

Iconic Events:
Public Imagination and Social Memory

It had not yet been a full year after the attacks of September 11th when I found myself watching television and a commercial came onto the screen. Not really a commercial, but a *public service message*—in which, children, one by one recited the following:

> I helped kill a judge.
> I helped kill a police officer.
> I help terrorists.
> I help bomb buildings.

The screen went **black** and the announcer said:
> "Drug money supports terror. Talk to your children."

The American viewer is left with an image of 9-11, an image now linked to the twenty-year ongoing political anti-drug campaign—a campaign addressing the drug trade in Colombia and far removed from our current "conflict" in the Middle East. What is this commercial *really* about? What social phenomenon are we seeing? What are we *not* seeing? How can we make sociological sense of this

phenomenon and its connection to other historical event "uses" that have occurred over the past century?

A commercial came on the screen—a public service message. But what was
actually being projected onto that screen? What process does it reveal? Was it
new? Should we be concerned?

Introduction

Iconic events are used to sell products, spin ideology, and legitimate war. It can
be argued that in recent years, when it comes to the business of recycling history, no one has consumed more than Americans. Events deemed important are
used as the subject matter of film and television and have also quickly become
embedded in products for sale including memorabilia and a range of everyday
commodities. The selling of iconic events extends far beyond the commercial
realm of bumper stickers and terrorist trading cards, into political culture: the
sphere in which "a way of life" is determined, justified and challenged. In short,
throughout the past century powerful American special interest groups have
appropriated various events towards forwarding political agendas that are not
inherently linked to the actual events being used. These same events have also
been inserted into popular culture, where commercial stakes are high, with certain events being transformed into entertainment for mass audiences. The co-
opting of such "events" occurs in ways that are insidious and appear natural
serving to reinforce the dominant agenda while silencing counter-dominant and
otherwise resistive narratives.

Political groups do not act alone in the appropriation of tragic events. The
American media also plays an integral role in this process by seizing upon certain events and marking them with historic significance. My central tenet is that
the American press plays a major role in deciding which events are to become
staples in collective memory, also influencing *how* these events are interpreted.
Furthermore, the press constructs very particular and limited narratives about
these selected events, providing interpretations that are often built on simplified
mythical concepts (such as patriotism, martyrdom, heroism and evil) that are
later available for transplant into a range of political causes and cinematic
scripts. Events that do become the focal point of political action and subject matter for film and commodities become legendary within the society and are therefore assumed to be major moments in the history of the nation.

I am concerned with the process by which American journalists narrate historical events for the American public, how other political groups appropriate
the media narrative for their own ends, and how the events are eventually co-
opted into commercial culture. Within the commercial enterprise that is American news reporting, the press has a vested interest in capturing the public's

imagination and legitimizing their spin on events for which they claim interpretive ownership.[1] Journalists thus rely on standard scripts as they represent events to citizens. This base-line collective memory is then ritualistically appropriated by special interest groups into a variety of political agendas and commercial enterprises. This often occurs in ways that appear natural and thus, legitimate.

Historical events are at the center of American collective memory practices, that is, shared narratives about American history. These events are not "historical" per se (in the sense I mean) when they first occur, but rather are current events deemed to be of an extraordinary nature and, through a cultural process they come to acquire "historicity." Every society has methods for creating and communicating ideas, values, norms, and morals. These ideas may be about the time and space in which its citizens live, ideas about right and wrong, normality versus deviance and may include cultural meanings attributed to status characteristics like race, class and gender, as well as a range of other topics that impact individual and collective identity. Events serve as vehicles by which a range of ideas and social meanings are communicated to society. Some events, which seem to acquire a mythic status within the culture, come to dominate the cultural landscape through a proliferation of representations which flood the public space. It is these "iconic events" that constitute the subject matter of this book. The mass media are central to the construction of these *iconic* events, which once legendary, can then be used to further political and/or corporate agendas. The explicit use of 9-11 in an anti-drug commercial is merely a glimpse into this much larger multi-faceted phenomenon which impacts both political and consumer culture in ways that are ultimately tied to social power and national identity.

Iconic events take shape in different ways. From the moment they occur, certain events seem to occupy a disproportionate space in the culture. The media fixates on these events which in turn, alerts the public to the event's unique significance. The press thus engages in a tautology: the event is historically exceptional and it gets endless coverage, thus reinforcing its historical exceptionality. "Saturation coverage," in the media age, is the constant bombardment of representations of a particular event. Whenever you pass a newsstand or turn on the television, you are exposed to representations of the event. This in itself affords the event a "turning point quality."[2] Due to the constant repetition the event becomes larger than life. While this may appear to be naturally occurring or organic, it is actually the result of a series of actions taken by the press. The 1999 shootings at Columbine High School are an example of this kind of saturation coverage. From the moment the event occurred it was transmitted to the public through a non-stop barrage of television coverage. Columbine monopolized television for weeks through live-feeds, interviews, pre-recorded footage, and political and other "expert" commentary. CNN and other news networks covered the story exclusively in a 24-hour-a-day loop, for several days. Many of the Columbine funerals were broadcast live with normal programming suspended, on the major television stations. This, in and of itself, marked the event with importance. Furthermore, Columbine filled U.S. newspapers and other print venues for weeks. More recently September 11th was the subject of saturation coverage where, for example, images of the collapsing World Trade Center Towers were repeatedly broadcast for weeks. It has been suggested that the saturation coverage (repeated images of the towers collapsing) had the effect of "déjà vu" raising concerns that the "reality principle," itself, had been destroyed.[3]

In addition to the press' initial intense coverage, some events seem to continually "resurface" within the public space. These events are repeatedly rewritten, remembered and used as organizing tools to talk about *other* events and *other* social issues. These signature events occupy a special space within the culture, not necessarily because of their actual lived social significance, but based on the breadth of cultural meanings that come to be associated with them. Titanic is a clear example of this kind of event because it never seems to go away—it is continually revisited and re-emerges in new forms, despite having little long-term impact on social life beyond shipping laws. This was evident in 1997 when the film *Titanic* was accompanied by a flood of Titanic books and commodities and again in 1998 when new explorations of the ship's remains, influenced by the making of the film, provided new information about the role of social class in the Titanic experience. Pearl Harbor is another example of a national event that regularly re-emerges in the news or popular culture, though differing from Titanic it is widely considered to be a nationally significant event, a turning point. Likewise, it often emerges as a tool for talking about *other* events or contemporary social issues. This was clear when September 11th occurred and Pearl Harbor became the most evoked historical metaphor through which journalists contextualized 9-11 reports.[4] This raises several sociological questions.

When historical events are revisited, what is the nature of their reinterpretation(s)? How do social changes, such as contemporary conceptions of race, class and gender change the way we interpret these events? How do changes in technology and information flow impact new representations? How do dominant and resistive narratives challenge each other over a period of time? Are relations of social power transformed through these staple events in collective memory? Within consumer culture, how do we commodify these "special events," brand them nationally, and thereby turn history into a product for sale or entertainment to be consumed? How are iconic events appropriated by special interest groups to serve their own political agendas? By examining the social processes that construct and reconstruct iconic events, we can attempt to answer these questions.

Ultimately, I define an iconic event as: *an event that undergoes intense initial interpretive practices but also becomes mythic within the culture through its appropriation into other political or social discourses and its eventual use within commercial culture.* An iconic event attains mythical status within the culture and also comes to serve as a representational vehicle for a host of purposes. An iconic event, though sufficiently compelling, undergoes a social process whereby, in addition to the inherent quality of the "pure" event, it takes on "layers," serving as a representational vehicle and attaining mythic status. It is difficult to tease out the cultural process from the quality of the "pure" event in that all of the events under exploration *are* historically unique. In other words, while all of the events in this book are of a tragic nature involving at minimum, the loss of human life and may also be unique, at least, in magnitude, it is important to maintain a focus on the underlying premise of the book. In this vein the goal of the book is an attempt to denaturalize the process by which certain events have become iconic in American culture. It is not a matter of whether these events are "worthy" of special status, clearly they are; however, there is nothing natural about the manner in which we come to normalize the significance of these events, how we come to understand them and assign meanings to them, their use in political agendas often far removed from the actual event, and their adaptation into popular entertainment (which is itself a culturally unique phenomenon). In this book Titanic, Columbine, Pearl Harbor and September 11th are explored as events that have gone through a similar social process to become iconic, despite differences in the kinds of events they are and the difference in their social significance (as measured by lives impacted, physical destruction and economic impact). What these events have in common is that they have all *undergone hyper-representation, been appropriated into ongoing political agendas, transformed into commodities, and adapted into popular entertainment.*

Even at first glance, when beginning to think about this set of commonalities, it becomes evident that something potentially significant is happening within the society. Consider the following: when events are initially hyper-represented are other events of (inter)national interest overshadowed? If so, on what basis does this occur? What are the ethical, political and social implications of using over-exposed, tragic events as political platforms? How is this phenomenon linked to social power, national identity, and the democratic process? When historical events are transformed into products for sale or popular entertainment to be consumed during leisure time, how do citizens distinguish between history and entertainment? How do we make sense of commercializing traumatic parts of national history for profit? In this context, how do citizens come to share collective memories that may influence their social consciousness, political activity, and economic reality? When looking at what iconic events have in common, these are merely the initial issues to be exposed. Returning to some of these topics later, it is safe to say that the events chosen have, for reasons I will explore in-depth, captured the public imagination in an intense and prolonged manner.

In making this argument it is also necessary to consider a negative case. In this vein the 1911 Shirtwaist Factory Fire (the "Triangle" Fire) is explored as an event that could have become iconic within the culture but failed to do so, in order to gain a better understanding of the social processes that transform some events into signatures within collective memory instead of others. The Shirtwaist Factory Fire is an event that many Americans, particularly young Americans, have never heard of and yet it meets the criteria of the other events in this book in that it was a historically unique event when it occurred, at least, in terms of scope. Why didn't this event capture the public's imagination in a prolonged and meaningful way, despite its long-time presence in worker health and safety literature?

In this chapter, this project is situated within the interdisciplinary collective memory literature, showing how an examination of iconic events extends our current body of knowledge. Then in addition to my methodology, I review the selection of particular events in American history. Finally, I outline the three-part process that this book reveals—the process whereby events are transformed into historical markers and are appropriated for political and commercial ends. The last section touches on the social significance of iconic events and why it is important to understand how cultural practices of collective memory bear directly on politics and consumerism in powerful ways.

Events and Collective Memory

All societies engage in practices of collective memory. These are normal interpretive practices through which a society creates meaning surrounding local, national, and international events and happenings of relative import, while negotiating and renegotiating its national identity. Likewise, every society has cultural memories of national events which extend beyond a person's own experience. These memories are enshrined in the material representations that helped create them, later acting as sites of recollection and remembrance. For example, newspapers, books, archives, statues and monuments are a few of the material forms in which collective memories are created and contained at particular sites. At times, entire landscapes within cities or special cemeteries may serve as sites of collective memory (consider Washington D.C., Tiananmen Square or the Wailing Wall). Through exposure to these material sites citizens are made aware of dominant aspects of collective memory. People adopt social memory by storing concepts that are easier to remember than "full representations"[5] such as victory, loss, heroism or defeat. Collective memory is not "natural" or existent only in the mind of individuals, but is rather the result of social processes that result in material forms outside of the human subject that engages with them. Michael Schudson defines collective memory as "social memory, referring to the ways in which group, institutional, and cultural recollections of the past shape people's actions in the present."[6] Collective memory impacts how people remember the past, how they understand the past with respect to the present, and how they imagine the future. Most simply, collective memory can be thought of as a repository of shared cultural images, narratives and visions of the past. The representations that comprise collective memory are reductions of lived history. Furthermore, the term "shared" does not imply consensus. National memory is a site of social tensions, resistance, and political conflicts over meaning.[7, 8] For example, the different feelings in the United States about the Viet Nam War are interwoven into collective memory of the event and resurface at critical moments where that memory is called on, such as during the controversial planning and execution of the Viet Nam Memorial Wall. Nonetheless, every society has a dominant collective memory, meaning, a central set of legitimated ideas regarding the past, though individuals or groups may respond differently to that version of social history. Dominant and resistive visions of the past often operate in conjunction or in tension with each other although dominant forms, produced by those with the power to write history, monopolize the cultural landscape. The conflicts that help shape collective memory also show that it is not stagnant but can be contested and revised. Current events are first interpreted and represented when they occur, but some, particularly those viewed as markers in the national past, continue to be rewritten as time passes.

Rituals of collective memory are a normal and even mundane component of every society. They are part of a daily interpretive process whereby we attempt to gain a sense of our environment. In order to understand the present, individuals contextualize the present-moment with explicit reference to the past and implicit reference to the future. When a child scolds herself with hot water, memory of the event may then cause her to jerk her hand back before sticking it under a running tap in the future. Though individual memory differs greatly from social memory, a parallel can be made. For example, the Titanic sinking and Challenger exploding are both evoked as "warnings" against ritualized deviance and unwavering faith in technological progress. The present, and our place within in, is understood and experienced relationally. In this way, all points in time are on a continuum and the present is lived both temporally and spatially. With regard to social memory, the past is actively remembered through commemorative practices in order to help contextualize the present. Anniversaries are a common time for preplanned remembrance and commemoration. While collective memory has a relationship to history, the two concepts have not always been linked in the ways they are now. The relationship between memory and history is of critical importance in the contemporary world which is perhaps why it has received so much attention from scholars over the past three decades. Patrick Hutton asserts that it is now clear that memory has a history and history is (effectively) memory.[9] French sociologist Pierre Nora has been at the forefront of theorizing about the relationship between history and memory in the modern era. Nora coined the term "lieux de memoire" to demarcate the sites of memory that have come to fill the void left by the eradication of "real" memory by history or historiography (the scholarly practice of historicizing our understanding of the past which involves revision and therefore assumes an incomplete or inaccurate historical record).[10] Positing that the main tenets of historiography are antithetical to memory (which Nora romantically views as spontaneous) he explains how the critical practice of history has created a disjuncture between memory and history. Lieux de memoire, such as archives and memorials, result from the will to remember, the *intention* to remember. The concept of "lieux de memoire" reemerges later in this book when contemplating how different groups, including the press, the government, special interest groups, and commercial industries, intentionally activate particular memories for their own purposive ends.

Regardless of how precisely one theorizes the relationship between history and memory in contemporary society, most agree that it was during print culture that history became blurred with collective memory creating new methods and mediums for forging collective memory (and consequently, national identity). Technologies of print culture such as the printing press allowed for the high-speed dissemination, reproduction and repetition of temporally ordered knowledge. Newspapers are a prime example of this kind of time-ordered knowledge intended for mass distribution. For example, daily newspapers allow the same events to unfold over time, creating a recorded account of the chronology of events. Print culture both textualized and contextualized social memory by creating chronological "records" not only available, but also *intended* for future inspection.[11] Acts of memory in the present, such as newspaper reporting, created "records" taken *as* history in the future, or at least as part of the public historical narrative. As modern collective memory practices are an integral component in the building of national identity the state has a vested interest in what these "records" reflect. Accordingly, the communications systems that developed in media culture propelled the administration to instate several strategies, such as weekly press conferences, for ensuring their message remained dominant within documented media forms. Daniel Boorstin labeled many of these state-sponsored events "pseudo-events" to distinguish them from spontaneous events.[12] The state is not alone with its interest in how memory practices play out in the media. The advances of print culture not only historicized social memory but also propelled the transformation of history into a commodity. As a commercial enterprise, the news underwent the same rigorous attention to packaging as did other commodities. The transition from print culture to media culture, in which consumers can get the news from many different highly stimulating sources, has amplified the impact of the commercial imperatives that dictate how journalism is practiced. Television news outlets and network executives have to contend with remote control fingers and a short attention span ready to change the channel at the precise moment of boredom. As a result there is great pressure on broadcast news to keep stories short, fast-paced, relatable and eye-catching, complete with sensational headlines, graphics, and sound bites.

Newsmakers and Collective Memory

The commercialization of the news that began during print culture and has grown with the era of media culture affords the press a very particular space within collective memory practices. This section provides an overview of the key dimensions of how newsmakers shape the collective memory of events. The major issues discussed are 1) how the commercialization of the news creates memory professions, 2) why journalists are particularly interested in "hot moments" (traumatic events), 3) the concept of journalistic objectivity central to journalistic practice in the United States and how it creates a particular format for creating meaning and connecting with citizens through human interest perspectives, 4) the frames journalists typically employ and conventions in the narrative process they engage in, and 5) how connotations are created through a process of signification or symbolism.

The commercialization of the news impacts our ideas about current events and their role in national identity and public policy, and places journalists at the center of memory practices. In terms of national identity, when current events became saleable during print culture, collective memory was provided with an immediate mass audience. A current event such as a major fire or criminal act that historically may have been considered relevant to only a localized audience, now finds a national audience (if deemed newsworthy). This process helps to solidify a sense of national identity by uniting a mass of geographically separate people through awareness of a common event and through the manner in which the event is narrated which may evoke currents of patriotism, ideas about democracy, or other values linked to nationhood. The event can then serve to create meanings and a sense of history that is shared by many who would otherwise be disconnected from each other. Beyond national identity, the commercial component of narrating current events also empowers the press as a particular community of memory makers.

Newsmakers are at the forefront of packaging and distributing collective memory. In Michael Schudson's language, there are "memory professions" and a "memory industry" within which other interest groups reside.[13] These groups have a vested interest in constructing "successful" and "binding" collective memories. In the media age, collective memory practices often begin with journalists and result in a repository of shared images and narratives. As Bellah et al. explain, the press has a significant role in creating "communities of memory."[14] The formation of these groups ultimately dictates the extent to which a particular collective memory will be revisited over time in service of political or other agendas. In this process the press often use events as vehicles for memory practices, because they present a focal point through which a society can represent and reinterpret itself.[15] In this regard iconic status can be viewed as the result of "successful" press narratives that inspire continued renegotiations over meaning. In this context, what kinds of events do memory-makers focus on?

"Hot moments"[16] or "critical incidents"[17] can be particularly fruitful for the construction of collective memory for their perceived journalistic and commercial value.[18] These are events that are anomalous. When these events occur, claims are quickly made by the press and officials as to the singularity of the event. Events said to be of this caliber become the subject of extended journalistic focus because, they appear to warrant considerable attention. Events are able to occupy a primary space in the public sphere simply because they have taken on a "turning point" quality. This provides extraordinary possibilities for journalists to legitimize themselves individually, and to legitimize the special place that their profession occupies within the society. These events may be viewed as an "acute" or "chronic" crisis.[19] An acute crisis is when an unscheduled event causes a sudden disruption of the normal course of events and is perceived as shocking. A chronic crisis differs in that it is the result of some persistent failure in the social system. Arguably, some events are labeled by officials as shocking social disruptions despite resulting from a struggle over power, foreign or social policy problems, or systemic failings in the criminal justice system.

Journalists are taught that unfolding disaster stories may be "*the* story" (career-making) because they continue to have audience appeal and can be written from many angles including "the who, what, where and when" as well as "human interest" pieces that may serve as sidebars to larger "substantive" pieces.[20] Human-interest pieces are critical for reporters because they provide additional writing material and can legitimize a journalist through his or her coverage of a particular event. More importantly with regard to iconic events, human-interest writing connects the consumer to news stories. Sociologist Iwona Irwin-Zarecka[21] explains that giving a story a "human face" engages memory consumers on an emotional level. Journalism textbooks are quite blatant about this. One book aimed at aspiring American journalists purports that in disaster reporting "as in most good reporting, the human element is entwined with the news."[22] Part and parcel of a commercial enterprise, and the need to validate themselves as a major interpretive community, the press are trained to "hook" readers and this requires going beyond the "who, what, where, when, and how." By drawing on human interest appeal, the journalist is able to keep the story fresh for a longer time, itself marking the event with significance. Furthermore, the emotional connection citizens make in relation to the event as a result of this kind of writing is a part of how collective memory becomes established. Critical incidents are therefore appealing to news media because they carry with them avenues for indefinite emotional appeal.

Pearl Harbor, Columbine, and 9-11 were all immediately classified as "critical incidents." The events that undergo extensive interpretive practices are always presented as socially significant, though this happens largely through a process of "rhetorical legitimacy." To summarize, it can be said that these kinds of events are quickly afforded an exceptional historical quality (nothing like this has ever happened, something has changed forever, this is unusually significant) and this allows the press to continue to put forth representations of the event. Arthur G. Neal[23] explains that "national traumas" are likely subjects for memory work. Such events are social disruptions and as a result their "newsworthiness" seems authentic and is likely to go unchallenged. Furthermore, traumatic events bring collective grief, anger, sadness, and fear, making them, in Neal's estimation, particularly prone to extensive memory practices. The social disruption that accompanies traumatic events, such as Columbine, 9-11, the Southeast Asia Tsunami disaster, the 2005 London Bombings or more recently Hurricane Katrina, leave citizens confused and often scared. It is under these conditions that people are most vulnerable, looking to make sense of what has happened, to try to understand what is going on. The social disruption and sense of betrayal that accompany the trauma, points to the contingency of social life and challenges the popular notion of order, predictability, and consistency.[24] In this way traumatic events open up a social space in which to reevaluate social life. They also create a space for political action.[25] Citizens are also unlikely to notice or care if an event is dominating the public sphere, they may in fact have been primed to want it. Ross[26] explains that "shared narratives" help people cope under traumatic conditions. As a primary interpretive community, the commercial press knows this well. The question then becomes: how does the press represent these selected traumatic events to the public? Moreover, what specific techniques are employed to construct and convey meaning during tense times?

In order to understand how the press narrates traumatic events it is important to bear several things in mind. There is a common belief in the United States that journalists are objective and so they are classified as reporters as opposed to narrators or interpreters. Despite the romantic post-Watergate image of American journalists "out there" getting "the scoop" and sniffing out "the truth" via secret sources, journalists actually operate under social, political and economic constraints which always effect and may even conflict with their efforts at journalistic integrity.[27] "Objectivity" for journalists, per their professional training, is equated with disavowing personal feelings of human compassion and not "becoming the story" or getting too close by allowing themselves to become emotionally engaged.[28] Furthermore, the nature of the questions and even broader lines of inquiry, provide a framework for their stories, and already contain built-in assumptions as to how stories are to be told.[29] In other words, the avenues that journalists pursue, correspond to the formats that they are accustomed to using. Journalists are trained to write in a particular format that affords the story a built-in dimension of authenticity.

In addition, media writers use certain frames to capture the public's imagination and make their stories more convincing.[30] The press as the major American interpretive community, has a stake in whether or not the public buys their version of social reality, using world events to contextualize and legitimize their authority.[31] Events are a vehicle through which journalists authenticate themselves through the canonization of significant moments in American history.[32] In fact, despite operating under the umbrella of "reporting" and "objectivity," half of all journalists openly contend that their interpretive role is significant.[33] In order to create and maintain their "journalistic authority," media writers put forth compelling event narratives for public consumption and are reluctant to change their stories unless evidence of errors emerge or other highly visible journalists change the original interpretation of the same event. Much like the state, journalists who also operate within institutional settings are reluctant to admit error and generally stick to their stories, and in the event that changes are made, initial mistakes tend to be entirely glossed over. When journalists do change the content of their stories, the same narrative frame is often reused, creating continuity with the original reporting on the same event. Within this context, what kind of "frames" do the media co-opt in their meaning-making processes?

Event reporting can be thought of as a story-telling or narrative process. As any other type of storytelling, journalism is a form of fiction with its own constraints, assumptions and conventions.[34] The press constructs a narrative about something that is happening or has happened in order to report, explain and contextualize events deemed important. Narrative is the technique whereby collective memory is created, shaped, and reinforced, how meaning is imparted. Narratives are essentially stories that document unfolding events.[35] Here we can see the merging of two cultural practices: memory practices and narrative.[36] " . . . Memory and history are concepts, while objects and narratives are forms for expressing or distilling concepts."[37] The journalistic authority that legitimizes the press as the major information-bearing community is also dependent on the fusing of collective memory and narrative.[38] Not just any narrative form will necessarily capture the public's interest so considerations are made and conventions used. The press ultimately aims to tell a story that resonates with cultural beliefs and assumptions.[39] The mass media is a commercial enterprise that reinforces dominant ideology. This occurs in ways that bear directly on the event such as what information is taken as fact, how the (geo)political or economic roots of the event are covered, and how an event may be depoliticized. It also bears indirectly on how the press reports an event, in terms of the kinds of social norms, values and socially constituted morality that are reinforced through their reporting (such as ideas about race, gender, or nationhood). For example, prevailing stereotypes about race or gender are a part of the language reporters use as they narrate current events and thus these stereotypes may be indirectly communicated as a part of normal event reporting.

The government has unparalleled access to the press and thus, through weekly press conferences and other conventions such as preplanned addresses, are able to use the media to not only communicate "the facts" but also to normalize their version of events as they see fit. The government deploys the media and other societal institutions (such as public education) in the construction of an "official story" that is consistent with national identity[40] or imagined national identity. Somewhere at the intersection of the professional incentives for writing compelling narratives and the spinning of dominant ideology, media writers employ narrative frames. They ultimately use these frames selectively to focus on particular elements of a story and construct a specific understanding of social reality.[41] In other words, the media use particular packages to frame world events. Furthermore, some packages have sponsors that not only advocate certain narratives but also actively promote them. It is arguable that both journalists and the government have a stake in spinning world events in particular ways and as a result social history may, as Irwin-Zarecka explains, undergo a "beautification process."[42] The burden of identifying and communicating the facts, when they fall outside of the "official story"—providing the public with an alternative narrative strain—this responsibility rests with resistive groups and not the mainstream press.

The selection of a narrative frame through which stories are told, is a process of signification. Narratives contain a host of symbols that communicate meaning and are meant to evoke particular conclusions. Schwartz explains that frame selection operates in conjunction with the process of "keying."[43] The process of framing and keying shows that memory is a "recognizing and pairing links accomplishment."[44] Keying is a communicative act that pairs experiences to public symbols of the past.[45] In other words, when using particular frames as story-telling vehicles, the press also creates connotations between the past and the present. For example, at the Super Bowl following the events of September 11th actors were used to recreate two images on the field prior to the game; the flag raising at Iwo Jima and the flag raising at Ground Zero (the site of the destroyed World Trade Center Towers in NYC). This did not appear strange to the American public who were already accustomed to comparisons between Pearl Harbor and 9-11, linkage that appeared frequently in politics and the media.

When using symbolism and metaphor to suggest meanings, journalists maintain a focus on capturing the audience and therefore emphasize the human-interest aspects of their writing. Media writers need to draw on shared social meanings while also connecting with people on an individual level. To this end, more conventions are employed. One standard narrative form, referred to academically as "psychocultural narrative," operates through a blend of nationalism and human-interest writing. For example, the "United We Stand" mantra promoted by the press (as well as the state) merged imagined ideas of patriotic community with extreme images of loss and bereavement. Psychocultural narratives[46] are grounded in worldviews with which citizens are familiar, but also rely on emotionality to hook the consumer. Towards this end, the narrative needs to be compelling, that is why standard frames whose resonance has previously been established within the culture, are employed. Meaning is then created not just through what is told, but *how* it is told. As Ross contends, "It is the images and organization of narratives that give them their power, not the facts."[47] The content and form of collective memory cannot be treated separately if we are to understand how a dominant version of social reality is constructed and a collective memory, established. This is especially true in the case of iconic events that are later employed in the service of political and commercial enterprises.

Special Interest Groups and Collective Memory

Events that have received extensive press coverage may then be transplanted into political or commercial realms. The collective memory of the events becomes activated by interest groups, typically in conjunction with the media. When a particular collective memory is activated for a directed political use it can be understood as a "memory project."[48] By "memory project" it is meant that interested parties activate initial press memory in a purposeful way.[49] For example, there are numerous instances of filmmakers activating particular repositories of Holocaust collective memory in order to bring certain aspects of the Holocaust into the public's eye, to challenge previous understandings, to fill a gap in our knowledge about the event, to contemporize the event, and so forth. This leads us to a vital question: who creates memory projects?

There are many different "communities of memory" that all have different interests in a particular event and different communications avenues with financial resources available for creating their memory project. When thinking about communities of memory there are two major genres in which groups tend to fall. First, there are those with organic ties to the event, itself. These groups may include event survivors, the bereaved who lost loves ones in the event, and the perpetrators of the event. These groups may be particularly interested in how the event is first marked with significance (by the press and state) and then, how the event is "officially" commemorated—which may include national remembrance, memorials, and the like (and often involves a state response that is publicized by the press). These groups may activate the collective memory of the event for any number of memory projects. For example, groups may commemorate the event at the local level and also lobby for national recognition such as publicly supported memorials, remembrance on the anniversary, and so forth. Official kinds of commemoration involve human energy and the investment, perhaps for an indefinite amount of time, of financial resources. Consider for example, the emergence of the Titanic Historical Society which includes its own museum and store. The allocation of human and financial resources is part of why some events remain iconic in the culture while others, like the Andrea Doria, seem to be rendered invisible shortly after their lived experience. Survivors of the Columbine High School shootings as well as the bereaved have organized to raise funds (with the goal of one and a half million dollars) to establish a permanent memorial to the victims. These fundraising efforts are directly tied to personal experience and loss. The collective will to remember thus drives some events to iconic status and also dictates the way in which the event is remembered.

The communities of memory that I am primarily concerned with, fall into the other genre, and are those that are not organically linked to the event, those for whom interest in using the event extends beyond honoring a loved one or traditional national commemoration. These kinds of communities of memory, which may activate a repository of collective memory for political purposes, are special interest groups or sponsors which either reside in the media sphere or have access to it. Some events seem to have sponsors or "interested parties" from the outset, that are ready and able to co-opt the event for particular purposes. These groups invest capital and human labor into keeping the event in the public domain in some form or another. The use of Titanic by anti-suffragists and the exploitation of September 11th by the pro-life lobby are two examples. In-depth examples of the memory projects created by these kinds of groups are reviewed in chapter three.

Some press narratives lend themselves more readily for use in later memory projects. Specifically, simplistic narratives are more easily adapted to frame other events or issues. These simplistic narratives must also be compelling enough to be transferred to other issues; generally, good versus evil biblical narratives are employed to serve these purposes. Additionally, journalistic stories that contain reduced mythical concepts or broadest common denominator characterizations such as heroism, martyrdom, villainy, and patriotism are easily appropriated because interested parties can take one or more of these simplified concepts and implant them into a different public discourse. In this regard, I can not but, be influenced by the work of Roland Barthes[50] who viewed mythical concepts as political propositions that have been emptied of the history that constructed them. Consider for example the unprecedented public display of American flags after September 11th. Flags hung from windows at private residences and businesses, and were attached to antennas on cars. Wal-Mart reported selling out of flags only days after the event. Many of those directly and indirectly touched by the events, used the flag during their process of coming to terms with the event but as Jenny Edkins points out[51] may have done so because no other symbol was available to them. Furthermore, the flag carries with it a complex and dynamic set of meanings that in the time period just after 9-11 underwent a reduction with the flag, ending up signifying for many, only the horror of that one day.

To argue that the two kinds of communities of memory are clearly distinguished would however in large part be false. In actuality the different kinds of groups with direct or indirect interest in an event may all come together intentionally or otherwise to contribute to a memory project. With this said, chapter four takes up memory projects primarily orchestrated by communities of memory not directly tied to the event through personal loss.

Selection of Events

Given the nature of this project, the events chosen as case studies needed to be first and foremost, "iconic" within American culture. Put differently, the events needed to have attained some sort of mythic status within the culture. Citizens ought to feel a familiarity with, and be interested in these events, implying that they have some kind of general appeal, draw, or that they evoke fascination. Ultimately, the events must have captured the public's imagination for a prolonged period. Given the role of the press in the construction of iconic events, and eventual political appropriations of these events, it was also necessary to select events that received unusual amounts of press or media coverage. Iconic events are subject to extensive real-time reporting, often in the form of saturation coverage. In addition to immediate reporting, the event continues to circulate in press narratives for weeks (if not months or years). This appears natural as journalists circulate more than "who, what, where and when stories" by adding human-interest stories, update stories, anniversary stories (which may occur much more frequently then annually) and so on. Iconic events seem to be represented in a way that may be disproportionate to the event itself, or, disproportionate in comparison to the representation of other world events. Sometimes, however, the event is itself imbued with historicity, so effectively that citizens may not notice it is being disproportionately covered because the volume of coverage seems to be inherently warranted. For example, in the process of reading much about collective memory in preparation for writing this book I was struck by how widely it was assumed that Columbine was a "turning-point" event and how frequently it was categorized with the same status as the Viet Nam War, Pearl Harbor, and other globally relevant events.

As the literature in this field suggests, "traumatic" events are often the subject of this kind of cultural representation. The iconic events in this book are all traumatic "surprise" events that were disruptive of the normal cycle of events and resulted in the loss of life. Furthermore, the disruption of the normal course of events allows for the disruption of the normal flow of news in a way that appears legitimate. I will discuss this later. Over and above selecting social disturbances, the events under investigation also represent spaces of ambiguity and uncertainty. This eventually leads to social questioning and continued investigation. I argue that events that become mythic within the culture, tend to not only be traumatic but also, be problematic in some way (not knowing the root cause of the event, not knowing how the event unfolded, and so forth). For example, the conflicts over the Viet Nam War and its commemoration received more public attention then the war itself. The assassination of John F. Kennedy, another iconic event in American memory, is surrounded with uncertainty and skepticism resulting in its continued reemergence in the public sphere. Questions surrounding the assassination fuel continued explorations which result in new scholarly publications, popular books, films and more, including new and enhanced video footage from the shooting, which has recently been broadcast on the news. When discussing the persistence of Marilyn Monroe as a pop culture icon author S. Paige Baty explained that her mysterious suicide created a space for the constant rewriting of her story.[52] In other words, because Monroe's death has been contested over time (whether it was really suicide or murder and in either case—the reasons why), her story is able to be rewritten, and like JFK's assassination, has been ritualistically reconstructed over time. As later chapters show, the process of revisiting events has also occurred with regards to all of the iconic events in this book. For example, it wasn't until 1998 that technology and a concerted funded effort revealed that the steerage gates remain locked, as Titanic disintegrates on the bottom of the Atlantic Ocean, lending credence to the long contested claim that third-class passengers had been prevented from trying to escape and thus, allowing for Titanic to again be a lead news story as well as the subject of a host of new books.

In addition to being markers in collective memory and national history, it is necessary for analytic purposes to distinguish between *contained* and *diffuse* events. A contained event is one that occurs at a particular time and place (reporters may note where an event occurred and offer a time frame for when it began and ended). There are also iconic events which can be thought of as "sprawling" or diffuse events. For example the Great Depression and the Witch Craze are certainly "iconic" by my definition, though each occurred over a sustained period of time. Like the events in this book, the Great Depression and Witch Craze have also been used for political ends and turned into commodities (consider the persecution of independent women via accusations of "witchcraft" and the more recent commodification of this process via Halloween kitsch items including witch costumes, figurines, and cauldron trick-or-treat baskets). While it is important to study the process by which diffuse events are remembered, activated, and "used," for the purpose of this book I have focused on the process by which contained events become iconic. The process by which events acquire special status may differ for contained versus diffuse events and each project warrants proper attention. Moreover, I have not included natural disasters because while they often cause the greatest loss of life and material destruction, these events tend not to be memorialized in the same way as other kinds of events even when initial reporting is extensive such as with the 2004 South East Asia Tsunami and 2005 Hurricane Katrina on the Gulf Coast of the United States. In the concluding chapter I do, however, suggest how researchers could go about studying diffuse events and natural disasters in order to understand how they do or do not acquire mythic status.

Finally, the project necessitates a time dimension. More specifically, the cases selected, span the past century which allows for the examination of how changes in technology and systems of mass communication impact the representation of an event. This includes looking at the shift from print narratives to images, the advent of television and "live news," the Internet, and modern cinema. How do changes in systems of mass communication impact the speed by which an event is represented and reconstructed? How does technology impact the circulation of resistive narratives (their breadth and duration)? For example, how has blogging changed the circulation of resistive accounts? When mainstream narratives incorporate or respond to resistive accounts, how does the process differ in print versus media culture?

With respect to the cases under investigation, this time dimension is two-fold. First, it is important to examine the construction of an iconic event at the beginning of the twentieth versus twenty-first centuries. Second, by using Titanic as the primary case, I also examine how representations of Titanic have changed over time, influenced by technology and overall social context. For example, there are no recorded images of the sinking of the ship; however, from the 1950s onward, the sinking has been reconstructed in audio-visual form with increasing technological capabilities. Additionally, the ship's discovery in 1986 also allowed for photographic and further audio-visual images of the sunken ship. How do these developments impact collective memory of the event?

Titanic

It has been claimed that Titanic is the third most written about event in human history, following the life of Jesus Christ and the assassination of President John F. Kennedy. Similarly, some Titanic authors claim Titanic to be the third most recognizable word worldwide, following "God" and "Coca Cola." While these claims are shocking, given the unbelievable wealth of data I found when researching the event, these extraordinary claims may very well be true. The 1997 film *Titanic* is to date the highest grossing film in history, and was accompanied by a large-scale resurgence of interest in the Titanic remains as well as the rewriting of Titanic history by scholars and other experts. All of this indicates that though it did not change the course of human history in meaningful ways such as by impacting national priorities, changing public policies, or altering the daily lives of Americans that were not directly involved with the ship and/or its passengers, Titanic has, notwithstanding, captured the public's imagination.

Titanic is a *sociologically* significant event because, for nearly a century it has been systematically remembered creating a large repository of representations. When the film *Titanic* was released in 1997, I was immediately struck, not just by the extraordinary success of the film, but by the wealth of other Titanic representations that seemed to surface. Bookstores placed Titanic books, both new and old, in prime locations and even sold reprinted newspapers from 1912 alongside current newspapers (at an inflated price of approximately $5.00 per copy). Titanic memorabilia, including games, puzzles, postcards, jewelry, statues and kitsch items were everywhere and Titanic websites flooded the Internet creating virtual communities of people interested in the century-old wreck. Moreover, Titanic was making news with stories about how finally, evidence was discovered that the third-class passengers were, in fact, prevented from trying to save themselves. In short, the extent to which Titanic had resurfaced in the public imagination was intriguing, but perhaps, the repository of Titanic collective memory was always there, ready to be activated.

My surprise at the extent to which Titanic was occupying public space owes mainly to the nature of the event, itself. Titanic was certainly a tragedy, but that being said, this was not an event that changed the course of global or even American history. The British even question whether Titanic has a real place in American history at all or whether it has been co-opted for its commercial value.[53] While most Titanic historians and others who write about the event support the place of prominence it has in our collective past, I would say that Titanic was really a "middle-range" event. This is an event that is surprising to most and undoubtedly newsworthy when it occurs, and also has some degree of social significance (such as multiple lives lost and is perhaps viewed as preventable), but at the end of the day is not an event that significantly impacts the world on a global scale such as a war, nuclear explosion, biological warfare, health epidemic, ecological catastrophe, or severe economic depression. Giving this some thought, I realized that certain other iconic events might also be considered middle-range. This is not to imply that they all have the same social significance as middle-range events exist on a continuum ranging in social, economic and political significance. For example, both Titanic and Columbine can be viewed as middle-range events despite a huge difference in lives lost and material destruction. Bearing all this in mind, I selected Titanic as the primary case and several other events, ranging in significance, beyond the bounds of this "continuum" and occurring at different times over the last century, as secondary cases.

I have chosen Titanic as the primary case study because its representations span almost a century. This is important for three reasons. First, by tracing Titanic narratives one is able to witness how changes in technologies of mass communication impact processes of collective remembering. This becomes particularly important when thinking about how different groups with varying degrees of social power have been able to, or not as the case may be, construct event narratives. For example, how has television (ranging from live news to newscasts that include reproducible event images, to docudramas and the like) impacted how events are narrated and remembered? More recently, how has the Internet impacted the production of counter-dominant or otherwise resistive versions of history (from alternative websites to blogging)? How has the advent of independent film impacted the content of cinematic representations of history? These are just some of the questions surrounding how technology influences the (re)writing of history. Secondly, the fact that all Americans are, to varying degrees, familiar with Titanic, means that the event must have captured the public imagination. Additionally, our general familiarity with the event will help illustrate how as we are all a part of the process of creating a collective memory, we are active participants, and therefore, may challenge the political and commercial appropriation of events as we deem fit. Lastly, Titanic is admittedly a bit of an anomaly, even among other iconic events, as it is one of the most written about subjects in human history—being ever-present to varying degrees, within the culture. The hyper-representation that Titanic has undergone has also produced a wealth of narratives in multi-medium forms that make it a very compelling subject for investigation.

The nearly unparalleled production of stories and images is remarkable, given that Titanic was ultimately an industry accident that occurred nearly a century ago. Again, while it was a tragedy, on its merits alone, it hardly seems to warrant the kind of attention it receives—even over other events such as war. Of course the mythic status of some events in the culture is a result of the meanings associated with them, that serve to create a mythology around the event, regardless of how important the event may have been, in real-time. This peculiarity strengthens the case that it is iconic while simultaneously raising serious social questions about which events get remembered and which do not. The same is true of the 1999 shootings at Columbine High School which, while tragic, ultimately resulted in the loss of fifteen lives, two by suicide. And yet, it was presented to the American public through "saturation coverage" (a never-ending news loop) trumping even the war in Kosovo (the largest bombing in that war occurring on the same day). In short, the ratio of degree of attention and interpretation, seems disproportionate to that of the event itself—leading one to think about how it is that historical significance is determined in the first place, by whom, and toward what end(s). The historicizing of events and the ascribing of certain events with a "turning-point" quality, becomes particularly contested when looking at the example of September 11th. This is discussed at length, later in the book.

Pearl Harbor, Columbine, September 11th and the Shirtwaist "Triangle" Fire
With Titanic in place as the primary case study, Pearl Harbor, Columbine and September 11th were selected as the secondary cases. These are events of varying significance, all having captured the public imagination, and all being iconic. Not only are they "familiar," and are thought of as *defining* moments in U.S. history, (albeit in different ways), but they have also been intentionally co-opted as political tools and have been transformed into commodities and popular entertainment. Additionally, because these are different kinds of events that, at times might not *seem* to have a common thread: an industry accident, criminal violence (transformed into a site of moral panic), a military attack and a terrorist attack—the focus of this book is on interpretive processes. In other words, be-

yond the particular nature of the event, what is the overall cultural process by which it becomes a part of national collective memory?

The shootings at Columbine High School were a tragic event for the people involved and the community in which it happened, and they were the largest school killing in U.S. history and accordingly, certainly newsworthy. With this said, in terms of the total loss of life and material destruction, Columbine could be viewed as a relatively insignificant event in comparison with other events that resulted in many more deaths and changes to social life that are felt by many. Furthermore, unlike the other events in this book Columbine was not, in any respect, considered to be a global event, but solely a part of contemporary American history. Columbine is therefore an example of how the press seizes an event, marking it with significance while allowing other groups to follow suit, keeping the event visible in the public domain. Columbine was presented through saturation coverage in all media, much like the coverage that September 11th would later receive, a comparison which in and of itself indicates that there is a cultural process at work, one that is greater than the inherent importance of the particular event.

Pearl Harbor and September 11th compared to the other events in this book, are (events) of greater significance. Both resulted in more loss of life and material destruction, public policy changes, changes in national priorities, and impacted people in and outside of the United States who were not directly involved with the events (or, perhaps not in ways commonly attributed). Interestingly, what really makes these events most significant is what has been most abstracted from them. I lump these events together because they have been categorized popularly as "surprise attacks on U.S. soil" and have served as the formal impetus for U.S. involvement in war; however, the real thread between these two very qualitatively different events is that both are the result of chronic political and foreign policy failures and yet have been viewed as contained and "shocking" events. In other words, what they most have in common is that they are really nodal points in a larger picture, having both been emptied of their historical and social underpinnings, so that both are looked at as being "surprise attacks." This resulted in a further commonality, namely, the extent to which both have been depoliticized. They are also useful to study as iconic events because of the mythology that has grown around them, the symbolism and imagery developed to denote them, and the American perception that they are "sacred." This runs counter to their endless use in political crusades not directly tied to the events as well as commercial films which serve to turn them into objects of entertainment.

It is also necessary to have a negative case study—a middle-range event that was reported, receiving initial attention, but then somehow never having captured the public's imagination to become a signature event in collective memory—despite appearing, in many respects, to have the qualities of one. A colleague suggested that I consider the Shirtwaist Factory Fire of 1911 because it happened around the time of Titanic, resulted in ten times the loss of life as Columbine, and seemed to have disappeared from public recollection. At the time I had not heard of Shirtwaist, so indeed, it did not appear to be iconic. After researching the event, I became fascinated with its failure to be transformed into a signature event, given the way that other middle-range events have been deemed iconic.

The next chapter provides a detailed sketch of each event (often contradicting popular perception). It is however, worth briefly summarizing Shirtwaist so that its failure to acquire iconic status within the culture becomes noteworthy from the outset.

On March 25th 1911 one hundred and forty six people died in what was at the time, the worst industry fire in American history. The majority of the dead were female immigrants, primarily in their teens and twenties, that were employed in the factory. The high casualty rate was suspected to be the result of fire doors having been locked, thereby preventing employees from escaping. The factory owners Max Blanck and Isaac Harris, later referred to as "the Shirtwaist Kings," reportedly locked the doors to prevent unauthorized breaks and stealing. Blanck and Harris were indicted for first and second-degree manslaughter, but by April 1911 were acquitted of all charges. In 1914 Blanck and Harris were ordered to pay $75 to each of the twenty-three families who had sued them in civil court. In fact, comments made on the book jacket of *Triangle: The Fire That Changed America* referred to September 11th as the worst workplace disaster since the Shirtwaist Fire of 1911.[54] Shirtwaist is a middle-range event in American history. Given the historic nature of the event (then the largest industry fire in U.S. history), the loss of lives, and the organizations that continue to commemorate the event annually, why did it not become a marker of American collective memory that spawned public interest, films, and the like?

Methodology

This book explores multiple interpretations of events over time. Newspapers, television news, magazines, journals, commercial films, documentary films, and products are all sampled and presented (as applicable to each event). Chapter three consists of an analysis of press narratives including print and television news, as appropriate.

It is not possible to understand how a particular event comes to be presented as "spectacular" without considering the social, historical context in which the event occurs. For example, would Columbine have been presented on a 24-hour news loop if it occurred a few days after September 11th? It is necessary to consider "simultaneity" or "synchronicity."[55] Before looking at newspaper representations of the events, I collected newspapers from the day prior to each event in order to gain a sense of the journalistic landscape prior to each event in an effort to know which other stories were competing for journalists attention (ie: what else was going on in the world at the time and the extent to which these other events and issues may have ultimately been displaced as a result of the emerging iconic event). This kind of context also provided insight into the politics of the time, becoming especially important in chapter four.

In order to analyze press representations, I conducted a content analysis of newspapers for a two-week period following each event. For all of the events, the newspapers analyzed for a two-week period were: *The New York Times* (as the national paper of record) and the *Denver Post* (as the major paper in the Columbine area). Both newspapers reported on all of the events in this book, all of this material being available on microfilm. Furthermore, they have significantly different circulation rates and are produced in different geographic regions. The *Denver Post* also regularly includes cartoon illustrations of current events or issues which provide some interesting analytical material. I first looked at each day's paper in its entirety in order to get a sense of overall coverage and breadth of scope. Then, I assessed the composition of the newspapers including front-page stories, lead stories, headlines and photos examining how stories are placed, in relation to each other. For example, when looking at a page of *The New York Times* after the events of September 11th, what different kinds of 9-11 stories are placed near each other and what other stories, if any, appear on the same pages as 9-11 stories? I also looked at individual articles which were coded thematically. In addition to these two newspapers, I looked, though in a less formal manner, at a wide range of newspapers from around the country.

The data from newspapers is presented in chapter three, through a thematic analysis of journalists' narratives, exploring two central components in journalistic representation: the *content* of representations and the *narrative forms* used. What are the major themes that journalists covered in their reporting of these events? Which themes dominate the newspaper coverage? What narrative techniques are employed (such as the construction of heroic and villainous figures)? What contradictions emerge within articles, within newspapers and across newspapers? In analyzing newspaper reporting of the events, the central concern is with how the event came to be historicized during the initial weeks of reporting, thus being integral to how an event becomes iconic within the culture. In this vein, several aspects of press reporting are examined: the use of language such as superlatives which help to mark the event with a turning-point quality; how social, political and historical context is provided; the way in which historic significance is presented; as well as how key players are identified, written about and at times imaged (such as heroes, villains, and martyrs). I also pay careful attention to representations of race, class, gender and technology. In the cases of Columbine and 9-11, television news coverage is considered in a similar manner. Finally, differences occurring across cases that speak to changes in press reporting resulting from the shift from print culture to media culture, are also noted.

Chapter three describes in detail, how journalists used similar narrative frames in the reporting of all of the iconic events. The press relied heavily on standard frames of good versus evil which were already resonant within the culture, staying in synch with the "official" state sponsored narrative. Likewise, in all of the positive cases, journalists immediately noted the historic quality of the event by giving it saturation coverage, using superlatives and focusing on certain kinds of historical comparisons while ignoring others. Contradictions and even factual inaccuracies abound within initial representations. Furthermore, journalists focused on the human story as a method of engaging readers and often juxtaposed such stories with politically imbued interpretations of the event. In addition to press representations, cinematic versions of these events are also reviewed.

Chapter five presents a sample of historical films that portray each iconic event. As Titanic and Pearl Harbor have produced an abundance of films I selected the major commercial films produced since the event (such as 1958's *A Night to Remember* and 1997's *Titanic*). I also include what I consider to be "outliers." By this I mean narrative films that were produced within a highly specialized medium or by a particular group that may have had a counternarrative to tell. For example, in the case of Titanic there is a propaganda film produced by the Nazi Party. In addition to narrative films, I also sampled documentary films which are abundant in the cases of Titanic, Pearl Harbor, and September 11th. Once selecting a sample of films, I watched each film in its entirety, noting the major plot line and themes. I then coded each film using scene change as my unit of analysis. I coded for image, dialogue, sound and color, paying attention to questions such as: What is the primary narrative conveyed? Are there sub-narratives and if so, what are they? From whose point of view is the story told? Who are the main characters and how are they portrayed? How is music used to evoke emotion or punctuate scenes? How is color used to denote or create mood? How are personal stories created and presented? How does fiction serve the narrative? What does a viewer take away from this film? In addition to films, chapter five includes a brief discussion of commodities of all kinds (from puzzles to T-shirts to trading cards).

This book is ultimately concerned with how some events come to dominate the cultural space and what kinds of competing narratives help to formulate our collective memory about a particular event. Therefore, when studying the representations of each event particular attention is paid to contradictions within or across narratives, changes in dominant interpretations over time, and silences or voids in particular representations (points of view that have been left out). The interplay between dominant "official" narratives and counter-dominant or otherwise resistive versions of the events is also emphasized. For example, how do film narratives challenge official memories and how then are official memories revised to accommodate new ways of looking at the past?

The Life of an Iconic Event: The Press, Politics, and Popular Culture

This book ultimately reveals a three-part process whereby some historical events are transformed into iconic events. The process is as follows: 1) intense initial interpretive practices by the press, 2) directed political uses by special interest groups, and 3) the transformation of history into a commodity to be offered on the open market and/or as a form of popular entertainment. Chapters three, four and five, use the case studies to detail each phase of this process.

Chapter three focuses on the press' coverage of the case studies. The intense initial representation of events that constitutes the first phase toward an event becoming iconic is merely an extension of a normal social process. All events deemed newsworthy undergo initial interpretive practices and from Titanic to September 11th, the events under discussion all warrant reporting. Current events are reported and represented in whatever media forms are technologically available. This is a mundane practice. It is during these initial interpretive practices, that the represented event begins to emerge. A body of widely available representations is eventually produced, including items such as newspaper stories, photographs/illustrations and television accounts. Together these representations create a *mediated version of the event* which I call the *represented event*. Generally, events are first interpreted and filtered to the public in dominant venues such as commercial news, television and magazines. The American public first becomes familiar with social events through the reporting done via these media outlets. The questions in this chapter are: Which ideas do the press spin for the culture, as they create initial event narratives? What narrative frames do journalists employ as they create event narratives?

Chapter three shows that dominant press narratives are presented as "fact" and "truth" but bear contradictions from the outset while simultaneously representing a particular worldview that is inseparable from political power. All future versions of events are built on and mediated by these initial press interpretations making their structure and content all the more significant. In short, the represented event acts as a mediator or filter for all future representations of the event, and iconic events are necessarily reinterpreted over time. The press has a stake in this process because, as shown in chapter three, they legitimize their own authority as a valuable interpretive community, through creating authoritative event narratives which they then become motivated to support and even defend. The press does not create these narratives alone. As we will see, many event narratives have sponsors, groups interested in disseminating particular kinds of narratives. The state plays an integral role in the process as evidenced by the interplay and at times fusing of the press' narratives and government's "official story." In this way the press and government often legitimize each other by sticking to certain kinds of storytelling and using a host of conventions including saturation coverage, historical metaphors, superlatives and so forth.

Initial representation helps create a baseline collective memory but does not itself equate with an event acquiring mythic status. Chapter four presents a review of the process by which special interest groups appropriated narratives and transplanted them into a variety of political agendas in ways that were purposeful and intentional. This level of representation is not normative and extends beyond the mundane interpretive rituals that construct initial memory. Here, the event is intentionally co-opted into an ongoing political agenda that may be far removed from the event itself.

For example, consider the case of Titanic and the Women's Suffrage Movement. Titanic was directly used as a weapon against suffragists who were fighting for the right to vote, and gaining momentum. It may seem surprising now, but at the time this appeared natural to those willing to accept it as such. The argument employed, was that women were better off with chivalry than with equality as evidenced by the Titanic sinking. The appearance of a "natural" connection between this event and the issue of women's suffrage was a direct result of the press' Titanic meta-narrative which focused on the saving of women but neglected to address the role of social class and ethnicity in the ultimate death count. Another example is how Columbine was introduced into debates over: gun control, school surveillance, family values, popular culture and censorship, to name just a few. In addition to the direct appropriation of Columbine into these ongoing political discourses, the intensive focus on this particular event overshadowed other events and issues of import such as the War in Kosovo as well as the overall decrease in American school violence during that same time period. I review these examples along with the use of 9-11 in an anti-drug campaign and many other appropriations of these events. In addition to looking at the process by which these events were appropriated, it is necessary to account for resistance to such appropriation.

Through the process of extensive press coverage and political appropriation, events may become mythic within the society, then appearing normal to the public to see them pop up all over popular culture as well. It is not surprising in this context, that iconic events are often turned into products for sale or transformed into subjects of mass entertainment—including narrative films, television movies, and books. In chapter five, the commercialization of iconic events is detailed.

The ways that iconic events appear in popular culture impacts the public's understanding of the event, keeps the event in the public domain thus transmitting versions of the event across generations, and normalizing its national significance while renegotiating national identity. Films are perhaps the primary source through which generations that did not live at the time of the event, come to learn about it. Historical films and other commercial narratives play a powerful role in the process of how selected events become a part of national identity and how that identity is then negotiated over time. Popular culture is also a cultural space in which resistance to dominant views on social reality visibly emerge. In academia, this is referred to as the "oppositional" possibilities of popular culture.[56] As such, it is in the commercial realm of films, books, and products that we can see most clearly how collective memory is revised over time to reflect contemporary needs and understandings. More specifically, collective memory is revised in order to account for new information about the event, as well as, more generally, new views on social reality (ie: norms about race and gender which change over time), new ideas about national identity, new national priorities, and changes in public and foreign policy (if applicable). A cursory glance at some of the cinematic versions of the events illustrates this point.

Titanic has been the subject matter of many films including the first 1929 sound film *Atlantic*, a controversial Nazi propaganda film in the early 1940s, a Hitchcock attempt that was thwarted by shipping industry insiders, 1958's *A Night to Remember*, and the highest grossing film of all time 1997's *Titanic*, and many others over the years. Each film tells a very different story of what happened aboard Titanic, who was to blame, and how social class and gender impacted the events. Pearl Harbor has also been the subject of many films, most notably *Tora, Tora, Tora* and *Pearl Harbor*. Despite a popular conception that September 11th is too sacred within American culture to be commercialized, less than four years after the event occurred there have been four 9-11 movies released. The first 9-11 theatrical release titled *September 11* came out in 2002, only a year after the events, and was an episodic film that included short films from eleven directors from different countries that all cinematically "responded" to the event in some way, in an eleven minute and nine second scene filmed in one frame. Two of the other films, one made for television and one a theatrical release, focused on the events that reportedly occurred on board United Flight 93 when it crashed in a field in Pennsylvania because of the efforts of passengers to regain control of the plane. The fourth film *World Trade Center*, by Oliver Stone, focuses on two of the police officers rescued from the rubble at ground zero.

Some films emerge explicitly to present a counter-dominant understanding of the event or to explore the political and social issues perceived by some groups as having caused or enabled the event. Both Michael Moore's *Bowling for Columbine* and Gus Van Sant's *Elephant* used the events at Columbine High School as a vehicle to challenge the mainstream interpretation of that event and to raise a host of political and social questions.

Historical books and films are a form for storytelling and follow conventions of narrative (much like newspaper articles which are shorter storytelling forms). Accordingly, films present new narratives about the event, which essentially involve new plot sequences, characterizations, different information, and perhaps even, different context, all of which has the effect of altering understanding. Iconic events however are also transformed into commodities, actual products for sale, that unlike books and films, rely on the transfer of distilled finite concepts and not descriptive narratives. Titanic products have been available for sale since almost immediately after the sinking and include games, puzzles, statues, posters, salt shakers, jewelry, memorabilia, reprinted documents, and many other items. These products have been sold consistently for almost a century having, at peak moments, flooded the market. Most recently the 1997 film *Titanic* was accompanied by the mass production of many Titanic items. This also occurred in 2001 when the film *Pearl Harbor* was released, despite the film's ultimate box office failure. Despite the strong currents of patriotism surrounding the events of September 11th, this event was also quickly commodified into a range of apparel items, products bearing the American flag or images of the Twin Towers, statues, terrorist trading cards, and even jewelry made from bits of rubble, just to name a few. This phenomenon raises several questions: what is the relationship between national identity and consumerism in America? How are concepts in historical event narratives implanted into products for sale?

In short, chapter five considers the overall role of commercial culture, and historical film in particular, in the making and "life" of an iconic event.

Conclusion: The Significance of Iconic Events

Iconic events are a major source through which a collective memory of the past is established and national identity is formed and contested. As they are written from different perspectives and by groups with different professional, political, commercial and personal interests, the different stories circulating within our understanding of each event tell us not only about the events themselves, but also about how we as a society make sense of current and historical events, how some ideas are naturalized from the outset, and how other ideas are challenged over time. The field of collective memory has exploded over the past two decades and there are many books that consider some of the events that this book explores. Most of the texts on collective memory and American events focus on one aspect of the collective memory process. For example, some books focus on how traumatic events produce disruption and solidarity. Other books emphasize the role of journalists in the process of writing history, some focus on films and collective memory, and still others focus on memorialization and politics. This book considers all of these aspects of collective memory with regard to events that have captured the public's interest in prolonged and powerful ways. By following each event through its journalistic, political, and commercial interpretations, we can begin to understand what, culturally speaking, the events that become mythic in the culture all have in common—beyond their status as trauma events. Furthermore, focus remains on the varied realms in which collective memory practices occur and not on the events themselves.

In order to be able to make any kind of commentary regarding journalistic interpretations of these events, how the events were used by different political groups, and how cinematic and other popular versions of the events reinforce or challenge earlier understandings, it is necessary to have some base-line understanding of the actual events. The following chapter takes on the task of outlining these events, including relevant background information and some of the event's direct aftermath. Presenting factual historical sketches is both necessary and impossible. The impossibility is two-fold. First, there are often discrepancies between the different sources from which we get information about these events. In order to deal with this, I have used multiple sources for my accounting of each event; however, there are, no doubt historians and other experts who might take issue with certain particulars in these accounts—despite a concerted effort at focusing on widely corroborated accounts. Second is the issue of determining what counts as "relevant" contextual information. For example, where one begins and chooses to end the event narrative, already implies a choice, or perspective. This can hardly be avoided though it does need to be recognized. For example, presenting a time-line of the events at Pearl Harbor without providing any context as to what lead up to the event would be misleading and would not serve our understanding of this event and its later representation. With that said, where one chooses to begin the narrative might be read as a more American or more Japanese sympathetic view of the event and what lead up to it. Furthermore, concluding a timeline with the end of the attack on Pearl Harbor, and not including at minimum, the President's response to the event, as well as the declaration of war, would not make sense. This becomes even more complicated when considering the events of September 11th which are viewed largely (in American culture) as a spontaneous attack devoid of political underpinnings (though this is an American-centric view, having the effect of depoliticalization). How does one determine a beginning and ending point for the event without appearing pedantic? Moreover, much of what is considered relevant context for understanding the event, is only viewed as such with the benefit of hindsight. For example, understanding New York building safety and fire prevention regulations in 1911 is vital to understanding the Shirtwaist Factory Fire; however, the laws one might now consider vital to know about only appear as such as a result of the fire and passing of time.

With all of this said, the following chapter does not attempt to rewrite the history of any of these events or to provide the most detailed and thorough account of the event or even to be critique-free. The point of the chapter is merely to provide some understanding of each of these events so there is a base-line from which to examine later representations. In fact, some disputes in accounts of the events does not seriously impact the larger goal of the book which is not about rewriting the actual events, but rather, to look at the mediated forms of the events that have permeated political and commercial culture. Additionally, the iconic status of these events within American culture is the primary reason that a straightforward rendering of the events is necessary. A mythology has grown around each of the events in this book and it is therefore necessary to try and distinguish between myth and reality whenever possible. Chapter two begins by unraveling the myths surrounding Titanic, the "ship of dreams."

Notes

1. Barbie Zelizer, *Covering the Body: The Kennedy Assassination, The Media, and the Shaping of Collective Memory* (Chicago: University of Chicago Press, 1992).

2. Daniel Dayan and Elihu Katz, Media Events: *The Live Broadcasting of History* (Cambridge, Mass: Harvard University Press, 1992).

3. James Der Derian, "9/11: Before, After, and in Between," in *Understanding September 11*, ed. Craig J. Calhoun, Paul Price and Ashley Timmer (New York: The New Press, 2002), 82.

4. Betty H. Winfield, Barbara Friedman, and Vivara Trisnadi, "History as the Metaphor Through Which the Current World Is Viewed: British and American Newspapers' Uses of History Following the 11 September 2001 Terrorist Attacks," *Journalism Studies*, 3, no. 2 (April 1, 2002): 289–300.

5. James Fentress and Chris Wickham, *Social Memory* (Cambridge, Mass: Blackwell Publishers, 1992), 32.

6. Michael Schudson, *Watergate in American Memory: How we Remember, Forget, and Reconstruct the Past* (New York: Basic Books, 1992), 3.

7. Iwona Irwin-Zarecka, *Frames of Remembrance: The Dynamics of Collective Memory* (Somerset, N.J.: Transaction Publishers, 1994), 67.

8. Martita Sturken, "Memorializing Absence," in *Understanding September 11*, ed. Craig J. Calhoun, Paul Price and Ashley Timmer (New York: The New Press, 2002).

9. Patrick H. Hutton, *History as an Art of Memory* (Lebanon, N.H.: University Press of New England, 1993).

10. Pierre Nora, " Between Memory and History: Les Lieux de Memoire," *Representations*, 26, Special Issue: Memory and Counter–Memory (Spring 1989).

11. Hutton, *History as an Art*, 19.

12. Daniel J. Boorstin, *The Image: A Guide to Pseudo–Events in America* (New York: Harper and Row, 1964).

13. Schudson, *American Memory*, 211.

14. Robert N. Bellah and Richard Madsen, eds., *Habits of the Heart: Individualism and Commitment in American Life* (New York: Harper and Row, 1985).

15. Schudson, American Memory, 14.

16. Claude Levi-Strauss, *The Savage Mind* (Chicago: University of Chicago Press, 1966).

17. Zelizer, *Covering the Body*.

18. Zelizer, *Covering the Body*, 169.

19. Arthur G. Neal, *National Trauma and Collective Memory: Major Events in the American Century* (Armonk, N.Y.: M. E. Sharp, 1998) 7.

20. Brian S. Brooks and George Kennedy, eds., *News Reporting and Writing 5th Edition* (New York: St. Martin's Press, 1996).

21. Irwin-Zarecka, *Frames of Remembrance*.

22. Brooks and Kennedy, eds., *News Reporting*, 236.

23. Neal, *National Trauma*; Arthur G. Neal, *National Trauma and Collective Memory: Extraordinary Events in the American Experience* (Armonk, N.Y.: M.E. Sharp, 2005).

24. Jenny Edkins, *Trauma and the Memory of Politics* (Cambridge, U.K.: Cambridge University Press, 2003), 5.

25. Edkins, *National Trauma*, 216.

26. Marc H. Ross, "The Political Society of Competing Narratives: September 11 and Beyond," in *Understanding September 11*, ed. Craig J. Calhoun, Paul Price and Ashley Timmer (New York: The New Press, 2002).

27. Robert C. Manoff and Michael Schudson, *Reading the News: A Pantheon Guide to Popular Culture*, (New York: Pantheon Books, 1986), 5.

28. Brooks and Kennedy, eds. *News Reporting*, 218.

29. Manoff and Schudson, *Reading the News*, 5.

30. Amy Binder, "Constructing Racial Rhetoric: Media Depictions of Harm in Heavy Metal and Rap Music," *American Sociological Review* 58, no. 6 (December 1993).

31. Zelizer, *Covering the Body*.

32. Zelizer, *Covering the Body*, 13.

33. Winfield, Friedman, and Trisnadi, "History as the Metaphor," 290.

34. Manoff and Schudson, *Reading the News*, 6.

35. Ross, "Political Society," 304.

36. Jens Brockmeier, "Introduction: Searching for Cultural Memory," *Culture and Psychology* 8, no. 1 (March 2002), 8.

37. James Peacock, "Memory and Violence," *American Anthropologist* 104, no. 3 (September 2002), 961.

38. Zelizer, *Covering the Body*, 190.

39. Schudson, *American Memory*.

40. James V. Wertsch, *Voices of Collective Remembering* (Cambridge, U.K.: Cambridge University Press,), 68.

41. William A. Gamson and Andre Modigliani, "Media Discourse and Public Opinion on Nuclear Power: A Constructionist Approach," *American Journal of Sociology* 95, no. 1 (July 1989).

42. Irwin-Zarecka, *Frames of Remembrance*, 109.

43. Barry Schwartz, "Memory as a Cultural System: Abraham Lincoln in World War II," *American Sociological Review* 61, no. 5, (October 1996).

44. Schwartz, "*Cultural System*," 909.

45. Schwartz, "*Cultural System*," 911.

46. Ross, "Political Society."

47. Ross, "Political Society," 317.

48. Irwin-Zarecka, *Frames of Remembrance*.

49. Irwin-Zarecka, *Frames of Remembrance*.

50. Roland Barthes, "Myth Today," in *A Barthes Reader*, ed. Susan Sontag (New York: Hill and Wang, 1982).

51. Edkins, *National Trauma*.

52. S. Paige Baty, *American Monroe: The Making of a Body Politic* (Los Angeles: University of California Press, 1996), 26.

53. Stephanie Barcezewski, *Titanic: A Night Remembered* (New York: Hambledon and London, 2004).

54. David Von Drehle, *Triangle: The Fire That Changed America* (New York: Atlantic Monthly Press, 2003).

55. Steven Biel, *Down With the Old Canoe: A Cultural History of the Titanic Disaster* (New York: W. W. Norton and Company, Inc., 1996).

56. Stuart Hall, "Notes on Deconstructing the Popular," in *People's History and Socialist Theory*, ed. Rapael Samuel (London: Routledge and Keegan Paul, 1981).

Chapter Two

Historical Sketches of the Events

Introduction: Unraveling Myth

It has been claimed that Titanic is the third most written about event in human history, following the life of Jesus Christ and the assassination of President John F. Kennedy. Similarly, some Titanic authors claim Titanic to be the third most recognizable word worldwide, following "God" and "Coca Cola." It is hard to believe, that the sinking of Titanic could possibly be one of the most discussed and historicized subjects in all of human history. Though I initially found these claims to be absurd, after doing the research, they seem more plausible. There seems to be an endless supply of Titanic books all purporting to "finally" tell the truth and dispel the myths surrounding the voyage and sinking. Therein is part of the point of this book. The fact that there are so many books written about Titanic that it may well be one of the most analyzed events in recorded history, shows the extent to which this event has captured people's imaginations. This creates two dilemmas involved with the writing of this book.

Though many Titanic historians claim to dispel myth, thereby validating yet another book on the subject, many if not most of these books ultimately succumb to and perpetuate myth. This occurs in many ways, including the recasting of certain figures as heroes and others as villains, and also the standard discussions regarding gender and social class which, more frequently than not, simply legitimate earlier myths. The goal here, however, is not to poke holes in earlier accounts and thus present another version of Titanic history. Nevertheless, the major commonality in Titanic books is the naturalization of the mythic status of the event itself. In other words, nearly all (if not all) of the Titanic authors I have read, take it for granted that Titanic is inherently deserving of the attention it receives. This basic assumption goes completely unchallenged even by the authors who criticize the wealth of "inaccurate" books on the market. The point here is not to discredit Titanic's historical importance, but rather, to question this unacknowledged assumption. The same is true for the events of September 11th 2001 which are certainly fresher in people's minds and continue to directly impact many families and are thus, out of all the events covered in this book, perhaps the hardest to denaturalize. It is difficult for many, to imagine why one would even question the significance of the event. The intent of this book is not to make claims regarding the importance of these events, but rather to analyze the social processes by which some events acquire special status within the culture.

Returning to Titanic, the widespread naturalization of the social importance of the event is vitally important to understanding the different kinds of Titanic representations people have been exposed to in literary, political and entertainment culture. In the case of Titanic, as will be evidenced in regards to all of the events, the use of extraordinary language such as superlatives, biblical concepts of good and evil, and simplistic polarizing accounts such as "the most avoidable and most inevitable event", all serve to naturalize its unparalleled significance and thus perpetuate myths even when authors seem genuinely interested in debunking them. For example, one Titanic author who opens her book, *Titanic: A Night Remembered*, critical of James Cameron's 1997 blockbuster film soon thereafter writes:

> I also readily grasped the key to its overwhelming popularity. The tragedy that befell the *Titanic* on the night of 14 and 15 April 1912 is one of the most fascinating single events in human history. It is a story of how much human ingenuity can achieve and how easily that same ingenuity can fail in a brief, random encounter with the forces of nature... Above all, what continues to compel our interest in the *Titanic* story is that it is at its heart a story that reminds us of our limitations. Whenever human beings . . . start to feel themselves masters of their universe, the memory of *Titanic's* fate serves to jolt them from their complacency . . . God, nature or fate, with a gesture that was almost disdainful, swept aside something in which humanity had vested immense pride.[1]

Also naturalizing the significance of the event with superlatives and the language of myth, Titanic author Daniel Butler explains the "compelling power" of Titanic by claiming the event to be so unbelievable that it is even outside of the scope of fiction.[2] In this vein Butler marks the event with unparalleled meaning by claiming "No other disaster in history could have been more easily avoided or was more inevitable."[3] If that statement was put into another context it could arguably have been written about many different historical events including those covered in this book. In the midst of asserting that he will avoid a "revisionist account" that has a moral or social agenda, he writes a story about "courage and heroism" (which of course, despite his contradiction, are claims of morality).[4] My intent is not to pick on these particular Titanic authors, who have both written very useful historical accounts of the event. I merely use them as illustrations of the ways that most Titanic authors take for granted, the social significance of the event and thus by extension, uniformly serve to legitimize it. Of course, in fairness, it is perhaps unreasonable to expect to find an author that would question the importance of the very topic that has captured their personal imagination. Beyond the uniform naturalization of the status of the event, the wealth of accounts alone, while showing the event is iconic, also creates challenges with regards to this project.

The abundance of texts on the subject all staking their claim to "the truth" make it very difficult to provide an accurate historical sketch of the event itself. In this vein I have relied on commonalities across Titanic books and other sources (such as the Titanic Historical Society). The historical sketch provided in this chapter is thus undoubtedly incomplete but is meant to serve as necessary background information in order to understand later processes of press interpretations, political appropriations, and commodification.

I begin this chapter with a detailed historical sketch of the building, voyage and sinking of Titanic, situated within a larger discussion of the shipping industry of which it was a part. I then move into briefer outlines of Columbine, Pearl Harbor, September 11th and the Shirtwaist Factory Fire, all of which are presented in timelines.

The Origins of Titanic[5]

The building and excessive advertising of Titanic is best understood when placed in the larger context of the growing shipping industry and in particular cross-Atlantic travel. In the early 1900s, the shipping industry was growing exponentially as a result of significant increases in immigrants coming to New York as well as more and more wealthy travelers, able to travel for both business and pleasure. It was clear to businesspersons that the building of fleets of ships had unprecedented potential for financial success. In particular, large and luxurious ships would maximize financial profit by catering to both the growing immigrant market as well as the wealthy. The major competition in the International shipping trade was between British, German and American companies.

The Cunard line had been the most successful line of Atlantic ships until 1869 when Thomas Henry Ismay began the White Star Line. Cunard ships were known primarily for their speed, so in order to develop a competitive edge White Star focused on technological advances, luxury and size (though White Star was not alone in emphasizing these features). More specifically, size was important for catering to increasing numbers of immigrants and luxury benefited all social classes (while advertised for the wealthy the more luxurious ships of the time also had nicer third class accommodations than other ships).

During this time, a wealthy American entrepreneur named J. Pierpont Morgan, began buying shipping companies. In 1902 he purchased White Star and created a consortium called International Mercantile Marine. The result of this huge deal was the merging of American capital and British technology.[6] Henry Ismay's son, Bruce, retained control of White Star Line. As it turned out, Morgan cancelled his passage on Titanic at the last minute but the younger Ismay was a critical passenger on her only trip (and a controversial survivor as will be discussed in later chapters).

In 1907 Cunard revealed two monstrous ships: Lusitania and Mauretania. These Cunard ships, constructed with some government subsidies, were the largest and fastest ships that had ever been built. White Star decided that it needed to compete with these two ships, known for, among other things, their speed; however, since White Star could not compete with speed they decided instead, to focus on size and luxury. It is worth noting that the pressure to create larger ships did not only come from wealthy consumers but also from increased immigrant populations that now, also had more travel choices. Canadian born William James Pirrie was a partner at Harland and Wolff and agreed to partner with White Star to build giant liners. In the summer of 1907, Pirrie and Bruce Ismay met, under the direction of Morgan, and decided to build three massive ships (Pirrie sketched the ships with Ismay insisting on three, to outdo the two Cunard ships).[7] The three ships were to be launched in 1911, 1912, and 1913. Olympic was the first, followed by Titanic, and eventually Britannic (originally named Gigantic). Within six months, the Olympic was being constructed and early problems with it impacted the building of Titanic and also foreshadowed problems with these huge liners. Titanic was originally supposed to set sail in February of 1912 but the building of Titanic was twice postponed in order to put needed workers on the Olympic project (as the weather directly impacted the eventual collision, this change of date is important).[8] In addition to the two postponements, a 1912 coal strike also nearly delayed the voyage. As it was, White Star had to take coal from some smaller ships so that Titanic would have enough for the voyage.

The second problem that Olympic faced was a lost propeller blade which would again slow work on Titanic. The first problem, which with hindsight also seems to foreshadow later events, is the collision of Olympic with a smaller Cruiser named Hawke. The smaller ship Hawke was directly in the path of Olympic and the giant liner was unable to turn in time to avoid a collision resulting in damage to the ship. Some people in the shipping industry were concerned that these new larger ships couldn't be maneuvered swiftly and that, when faced with an obstacle, these ships might not be able to turn in time to avoid a collision (which was in fact the case when Titanic hit an iceberg). What's more interesting is that Captain Smith, who would later command Titanic, was the Captain of Olympic when it had its accident with HMS Hawke. Crew members, Lightoller and William Murdoch, who both worked on Titanic's only voyage, were also aboard Olympic when it struck Hawke. An admiralty court found that Captain Smith was to blame for the collision as Olympic was too close to HMS Hawke (and unable to sufficiently maneuver in time). White Star appealed the verdict which was ultimately upheld.[9]

Pier space also became a problem when Olympic and Titanic were built. The ships were destined for New York but there simply wasn't enough pier space there to accommodate them. Initially the New York Harbor Board wouldn't allow International Mercantile Marine to expand White Star Line piers to accommodate these new ships.[10] Given the economic benefits associated with these ships, representatives were sent to Washington DC where the War Department quickly gave International Mercantile Marine permission to lengthen their piers.[11] Olympic and Titanic were ultimately launched, without being christened, in Belfast Harbor. The docks were filled with people who had purchased tickets to watch the launch. The proceeds from the ticket sales benefited two local children's hospitals. The ships had been systematically touted as symbols of modern progress which clearly, generated public interest.

Beyond competition with Cunard (who later took over White Star), many have argued that Titanic and her sister ships represented technological achievement, modern progress and were thus symbolic of the American and Victorian dream(s). Author Wyn Craig Wade wrote: "The Gilded Age had pushed the Victorian Dream well beyond anything imaginable in 1851. The new palace had been designed to float."[12] It is clear from White Star's own 1911 advertisements of Olympic and Titanic that these ships were imbued with tremendous symbolic value: they were portrayed as symbols of modernity, of progress, and of capital. Also striking in the publicity booklet produced by the White Star Line is the racialized language employed in conjunction with the superlatives used to mark these ships with social importance. The seventy-two-page packet begins as follows:

The advent of these Leviathans of the Atlantic coincides very appropriately with the most important development of modern times- the movement of the

British and American people towards the ideal of international and universal peace. Of all the forces contributing to this great and desirable consummation, commerce has been one of the most potent, and as the growth of international trade is largely due to the progress in shipping, **it is impossible to over-estimate the service rendered to the Anglo-Saxon race by the enterprise of our Shipowners and Shipbuilders.** No better instance of this spirit of enterprise can be produced than the building of White Star Liner "Olympic" and "Titanic" . . . [they] mark a new epoch in the conquest of the Ocean, being not only much larger than any vessels previously constructed, but also embodying the latest developments in modern propulsion.[13]

The promotional booklet concludes with similar language.

...they [Olympic and Titanic] **stand for the pre-eminence of the Anglo-Saxon race on the Ocean**; for the "Command of the Seas" is fast changing from a Naval to a Mercantile idea, and the strength of a maritime race is represented more by its instruments of commerce and less by its weapons of destruction than was formerly supposed. Consequently, **these two Leviathans add enormously to the potential prosperity and progress of the race** . . .[14]

The clear linking of American and British progress and prosperity is vitally important as some Titanic authors have argued that Titanic has been co-opted by Americans and legitimately belongs to the British. Critics like Stephanie Barczewski[15] argue that Titanic was viewed as a national tragedy in Britain and not America, Titanic has a British heritage, and Americans have appropriated the event for entertainment purposes. The broader issue of event ownership and commodification will be addressed later in this book, as will the American press' response to the event which clearly indicates the event was viewed as a national tragedy. For now, it is important to realize that before the tragic events that led to the historicity of Titanic had unfolded, it was clear that Titanic owners viewed the ship materially and symbolically—as a joint venture. New books that claim otherwise, lack empirical evidence and reek of the desire to say something new about a tirelessly written-about topic. Furthermore, while there were inquiries into the incident in both the United States and Britain, the ship's seagoing rules were *written in the United States.* Returning to the promotion of Titanic, two further issues are important: the technological aspects of Titanic, as well as its unprecedented luxury.

Technologically, Titanic was an achievement; however, contrary to popular belief it was not the first ship to have watertight compartments. In fact, the Mauretania which was launched in 1907 was also advertised as "practically unsinkable." Titanic had the two largest reciprocating engines ever built. Additionally, the ship had sixteen watertight compartments that were connected by watertight doors. Two to four of the compartments could flood and the ship would stay afloat, if any more flooded then it would sink. The major deficiency of the compartments was that they did not close off at the top so that when filled, as with the Titanic sinking, the compartments flooded quickly one to another much like water flows from compartments of an ice-tray (a metaphor used by the Titanic Historical Society). White Star advertised Titanic rigorously as "practically unsinkable" but over time the qualifier "practically" fell away and popularly people came to believe the ship to actually be unsinkable (though White Star never claimed it to be). Architect Thomas Andrews oversaw the construction of Titanic in Belfast and on its only voyage he was the one to inform the Captain that the ship was sinking. Andrews was the Managing Director of Harland and Wolff.

Although popularly characterized as a luxury liner Titanic was legally classified as an "Emigrant Ship." The Board of Trade, the division of government that oversaw merchant shipping, categorized all ships carrying an excess of fifty steerage passengers from Britain to ports outside of Europe, as emigrant ships. These liners were accordingly subject to government-conducted inspections, ensuring the ship's safety and compliance with government mandated standards for life-saving equipment. A ship could only sail after passing inspection and receiving a clearance certificate. Titanic successfully completed these government procedures. Titanic was later criticized for not providing lifeboat capacity for all of the people on board, yet with lifeboat capacity for over fifty percent of the ship's passengers it was significantly above regulation at the time (which was later changed as a result of the sinking). At the time, lifeboats were seen as a method for transporting passengers from one ship to another and only truly viewed in this "lifesaving" capacity after the Titanic sinking, which of course helps explain the seemingly lax regulations. The ship's capacity was designed as follows: accommodation for 735 first class passengers, 674 second class passengers, and 1,026 third class passengers (commonly referred to as steerage passengers). On the only voyage, the ship carried passengers as follows: 337 first class (mainly wealthy Americans), 271 second class (mostly Anglo-Saxon), and 710 third class (mostly immigrants). The ship also carried 892 crewmembers.[16]

Like all passenger ships at the time, Titanic was divided by class. Steerage consisted of immigrants who underwent a mandatory health inspection prior to boarding. United States immigration regulations required that there be gates in third class separating steerage from the rest of the ship's passengers (this becomes a critical and often ignored factor in who died and who survived the wreck). Contrary to popular myth that states that no black people were aboard Titanic there was one black, Haitian-French family on the ship, staying in second class, the Laroche family. Servants of the first-class stayed in second-class. Prior to departure the second-class passengers were allowed to tour first class, an opportunity those in steerage were not given. The many luxurious features of first class included a gymnasium, a reading and writing room, the well advertised "Turkish baths," crystal chandeliers and the most famous feature of all: the "Grand Staircase." Located in the center of this magnificent staircase was a wood panel with a clock in the center and a classical figure on each side symbolizing "Honor and Glory." Among the noted names who occupied first-class were John Jacob Astor, Benjamin Guggenheim, William Stead, George Widener and Isador Strauss. John Jacob Astor was the wealthiest person on Titanic. Ironically, he owned a yacht, famous for its collisions.

The third-class accommodations were reportedly nicer than on most ships of the time. The rooms were in the lower parts of the ship and the steerage passengers were not allowed to use the second or first class stairwells. Of the 2,200 people aboard Titanic 710 were steerage passengers making immigrants the largest single contingent aboard, other than crew. The third class shared two bathtubs. While third class families roomed together, single men had to stay at the bow of the ship while single women stayed at the stern. This gendered division in the third class was particular to White Star ships.

The Voyage and Sinking

On April 10, 1912, at 12:00 noon Titanic set sail for what would be its only voyage. Approximately 100,000 people watched the ship depart. Passengers on deck were photographed joyfully waving good-bye. Only a moment after departing Titanic nearly collided with a smaller ship called the S. S. New York. This near miss caused a one-hour delay, again changing the departure time of the ship. Ironically, minutes into the trip passengers were reportedly overheard discussing whether or not such a large liner could be maneuvered in time to avoid a collision. Just as with the Olympic accident, these incidents were not taken seriously. Only a few days later these concerns would be confirmed when Titanic's inability to maneuver quickly would ultimately result in the deaths of over 1,500 people.

Captain Edward J. Smith has been repeatedly written about as one of the central figures of the Titanic event and interpretations as to his role vary tremendously. It is therefore difficult to accurately gauge his culpability in the events that unfolded. That said, some things are reasonably known. Smith was planning his retirement from the White Star Line after twenty-five years of service. Titanic's maiden voyage was to be his last trip (and it was, as he went down with the ship). Some have argued that because of his ability to socialize with the rich and famous Smith was known as the "Millionaire's Captain" and it is for this reason that despite his inexperience with the newer breed of large ships he was chosen as Titanic's commander. However, as others have noted, these larger ships were in fact new and thus even veteran captains had, at best, limited experience with them. Moreover, Smith had captained Olympic (when it hit HMS Hawke). Other than the incident between Olympic and Hawke, Smith had a perfect seagoing record. Also noteworthy, Smith seemed quite enamored with this larger fleet of ships. In 1907 he was quoted in an industry publication saying: "I cannot imagine any condition which would cause a ship to founder. Modern shipbuilding has gone beyond that."[17] This statement can of course be interpreted in many ways. Some have argued that Smith "took chances" such as increasing speed because he was all too enamored with the technological advances that made Titanic, perhaps in his mind, unsinkable. Others have said that these kinds of conclusions are ridiculous, as a veteran Captain Smith surely didn't believe the ship to be unsinkable but had reasonable confidence in modern shipbuilding as perhaps many or all Captains at the time did. As later chapters will show, while Smith has been written as a hero in popular interpretations that comprise collective memory of the event, the Titanic Historical Society holds Smith responsible for the unfolding of events (as much as any individuals are blamed), citing what they deem as his incompetence at multiple critical junctures.

There were two transatlantic routes available for ships, the Southern and the Northern corridors. Titanic took the Southern route (which was subsequently moved further south). Icebergs were considered to be the most serious danger in Atlantic travel at the time. Accordingly, Titanic had six specialist lookouts which was more than any other ship at the time. The lookouts worked in pairs, in rotation. Each pair worked for two hours and then had four hours off. They did not have binoculars (which they referred to as "night glasses") which the senior surviving officer Lightoller later claimed would have made a difference. Due to the Southampton (non)-incident Titanic was late arriving in France where more passengers, many of whom were American, boarded. On Thursday April 11th, the Titanic arrived in Queenstown harbor, on the South coast of Ireland, to pick up more passengers. New York was intended to be the next and final stop. The following events continue to be debated to this day so I will review what is reasonably known and note where major interpretive conflicts exist.

According to reported survivor accounts, Sunday April 14th was a lovely day. White Star had planned a morning lifeboat drill, customary on their ships, but that drill was cancelled by Captain Smith. It is unclear why Smith cancelled the drill. Some speculate that he didn't think it was necessary due to his belief in the ship, others claim that Smith didn't want passengers to realize how few lifeboats there were. There were no mandatory regulations regarding lifeboat drills at that time, even though ships were now carrying the largest passenger loads in history. In first-class, Captain Smith presided over a church service while simultaneously Father Thomas Byles gave a catholic mass in second-class. Then Father Byles gave a mass in steerage. At 1:40pm Titanic received a message from another ship warning of icebergs and large quantities of field ice.[18] This message was promptly given to Captain Smith who then gave it to Bruce Ismay.[19] Allegedly, Ismay glanced at the message and placed it in his pocket. Reportedly, Captain Smith later retrieved the message from Ismay. Several ice warnings were sent to Titanic that day but only one was posted, making the crew aware of only one warning. While all ice warnings were supposed to be taken seriously, this was a highly normalized form of deviance within the liner industry at that time.[20] Due to the high number of ice warnings received by each ship in the Atlantic passenger trade during that time of year, warnings were regularly disregarded in order to save time and resources.[21]

It has been written many times that Titanic passengers enjoyed a breathtaking sunset, the evening of April 14th.

As the ship was getting closer to Newfoundland, the speed was increased to over twenty-two knots. While much has been made of the speed increase, and it being problematic during evening hours when traveling near icebergs, it is still well under the speed with which some ships traveled. Critics have argued that Bruce Ismay strong-armed Captain Smith into increasing the ship's speed so that they could arrive early and impress the world with Titanic's performance. Some authors even claim that after checking the boilers Ismay said, "We will beat the Olympic and get in to New York on Tuesday."[22] Such claims are likely erroneous and highly influenced by the American press' treatment of Ismay (reviewed in the next chapter) and not fact. It is illogical to claim that there was a desire to get the ship in ahead of time and inconvenience the many passengers who had made hotel reservations or other personal arrangements, and there is no credible evidence to support such claims. Furthermore, Smith was the Captain of the ship and as the Titanic Historical Society asserts, under no circumstances would Smith have been taking orders from Ismay regarding the ship's speed. Nonetheless, to this day many accounts make such claims.

The air was now getting colder, indicating that the ship was nearing icebergs. At 6:00pm when a new officer began his look-out shift, Officer Moody told him that they would be reaching the icebergs at approximately 11:00pm. Detecting icebergs in the dark is very difficult because they may not appear white but rather transparent. Additionally, the weather was calm, making breaking water at the base of bergs almost nonexistent. At 7:30pm Titanic received another ice warning. At 7:35pm an officer noticed the temperature had dropped four degrees in half an hour.[23] This sort of severe weather change would typically alert a ship's officers that icebergs were near. An hour later it was almost freezing.[24]

At 8:55pm Captain Smith arrived on the bridge after socializing with several prominent guests.[25] With the increasing competition in the Atlantic passenger trade this sort of ritualized socializing was widely accepted and informally endorsed as a part of his job. He commented on the cold and lack of wind and left the bridge at 9:20pm. At 9:30pm the lookout officers were instructed to watch for ice. Shortly after, Titanic received another ice warning that it was heading straight towards a large rectangular ice field.

At 11:30pm lookout Fleet mentioned a slight haze to lookout Lee. Minutes later Fleet saw a black object in their path and shouted, "There is ice ahead." He rang the bell three times signaling that something was directly in their path. He then picked up the phone and when asked what he saw Fleet shouted the now famous line, "Iceberg, right ahead!" Despite swift efforts to decrease speed and turn the ship Titanic struck the iceberg less than one minute after its sighting.

At 11:40pm Titanic's watertight compartments were sealed. This had been the feature that was thought to make Titanic nearly "unsinkable." It was during a discussion with architect Thomas Andrews that Captain Smith and Bruce Ismay learned that Titanic would sink in approximately an hour and a half, maybe two hours. Allegedly, they were shocked. Andrews explained that too many of the compartments had been flooded and the ship couldn't stay afloat. Smith ordered the wireless operator to send urgent messages reporting that the ship was going down by the head, and help was needed. The Carpathia was the ship nearest to Titanic, yet it was four hours away. Officials knew it would be too late. Titanic only had enough lifeboats for slightly over half of the people aboard. Captain Smith and other officials knew that many people would die. While many have ignored the impact of this knowledge on the actions of Smith one must wonder how this knowledge affected Smith's decisions. Furthermore, if he was pondering the end of his own life, could this too have distracted him?

At 12:05am, approximately 25 minutes after the collision, Smith ordered that a distress signal be sent, the lifeboats be uncovered, and the passengers brought up to the deck. Smith ordered that "the rule of the sea" be invoked, meaning "women and children first." The under-filling of lifeboats was later explained by some crew, claiming they believed it was "women and children only" though this excuse remains highly contested. The crew was also ordered to try and avoid a mass panic. The passengers in the first and second classes had no idea what was going on. Many passengers were already asleep for the evening and some others experienced a jolt of sorts but had no indication of the severity of the situation (the passengers probably felt the vibration of the engines as they were turned off but not the collision with the berg). Crewmembers knocked on the doors of the first and second-class passengers asking them to come to the deck wearing their life vests. Many passengers tried to resist, clearly as a result of a lack of direct communication regarding the actual situation. Third class passengers were informed without the delicacy afforded the upper classes. Their doors were pounded, vests were tossed into rooms, and crewmembers shouted that they should get up. Due to their location in the ship it is assumed that third class single men were the first passengers to know there was real trouble because the part of the ship in which they traveled, was filling with water.

While there are many descriptive accounts of the mayhem between this point and the sinking, which offer windows into what the experience may have felt like for some people, there are two main facets of the actual event that are reviewed for my purposes: 1) the firing of rockets and the "ghost ship" the Californian, and 2) the filling of lifeboats.

It has been reported that there was a ship nearby Titanic that did not respond to Titanic's distress calls. Furthermore, this mystery ship has repeatedly been blamed for the deaths of so many. This raises two interconnected issues: whether or not this ship existed and how the Titanic crew handled the distress calls.

While some Titanic authors simply call this a "ghost ship" that doesn't really exist, and claim it to be an easy scapegoat, others emphatically insist that this ship did, in fact, exist, allowing for such a grave loss of life. The ship is not really a mystery ship, as the Californian has been named the ship that did not respond. Surviving crewmembers claimed that they saw the ship in the distance, stationary. The Californian was a passenger ship (without passengers) traveling from London to Boston and pioneered by Captain Lord (who was vilified in the American and British official inquiries). Some authors have mapped out the position of the Titanic and the suspected position of the Californian and on that basis argued that the ship must have seen the distress signals. Furthermore, it is reported that the Californian stopped moving at approximately 10:20pm at which point Captain Lord sent out an ice warning. The ship did not move again until approximately 5:15am in the morning. Captain Lord vehemently denies being near the sinking Titanic and ignoring distress calls. In his defense, there are other reports of the location of his ship (and disturbing information about how Titanic rockets were fired). To this day whether or not the Californian ignored Titanic's distress calls is the most contested part of Titanic history. The Californian's scrap log disappeared and is not a part of the historical paper trail. While most of the Titanic authors I have read seem to believe the story about the Californian, some do not. Furthermore, some of the reasons given for why Lord would intentionally ignore distress calls do not seem feasible. For example, some have posited that Lord may have mistaken Titanic for a German ship and thus decided not to assist out of competition. This is not possible. All shipping companies had a particular kind of distress rocket (that differed by color). Each ship had a guide detailing what color denotes which company's signal. Thus had Captain Lord seen the signal, we know at minimum that he would have known it was a White Star Line ship (White Star used two green lights simultaneously). This brings us to the firing of rockets during the Titanic incident.

The Titanic Historical Society notes the firing of rockets as integral to understanding the supposed Californian incident. Regardless of this claim, reviewing the handling of the rockets is at minimum critical to understanding how disorganized the Titanic crew was, during an emergency. First, it may be assumed that all rockets are the same but actually company signals differed from distress signals. Therefore, the firing of rockets itself would not have denoted a call for help to a nearby ship. Furthermore, there were clear and specific regulations as to how distress was to be conveyed. The Merchant Shipping Act of 1894 reviews the procedures a ship should follow when in need of assistance. In Article 27 (later called Article 31) it reviews nighttime procedures for signaling distress. In a nutshell, there are three steps: a gun fired at one minute intervals, flames on the ship signaling distress, and rockets fired one at a time in short intervals of approximately one minute apart. There were tremendous discrepancies between testifying Titanic crewmembers as to the firing of rockets. Surviving witnesses (in the lifeboats) reported that it took over one hour for eight rockets to be fired, and that they were fired at inconsistent intervals of four to six minutes apart. Most important is that while Titanic had a stock of thirty-six rockets only eight were fired in total. In addition to the disorganization surrounding signaling distress, the lifeboats were not filled to capacity.

The disorganization surrounding the firing of distress signals pales only in comparison with the disorganization surrounding the filling of the lifeboats. Several issues are worthy of attention: the under-filling of lifeboats, the flow of information to passengers, and the impact of social class, gender and age on one's likelihood of receiving a seat in a lifeboat (all of which were no doubt interlinked in the lived experience of the event).

The Titanic crew had not been properly trained in lifesaving drills and as a result, the lifeboats left Titanic under capacity, causing the deaths of hundreds of people who could have been saved. For example, one lifeboat had the capacity for sixty-five human beings, yet it carried only twenty-eight. Another lifeboat had the capacity for forty people but carried only twelve, seven of whom were Titanic crew. The Titanic Historical Society maintains that Captain Smith is ultimately to blame for allowing lifeboats to leave the ship under capacity. Furthermore, it is argued that Smith did not take proper control of the proceedings from the point of collision through the sinking, which was his responsibility. Adding to the disorder, many of the first-class women offered places in the boats, initially chose not to enter the boats because they had not been told of the severity of the situation. This lack of open communication, which was clearly gender-related, undoubtedly impacted some people's behavior.

Bruce Ismay escaped on a boat carrying thirty-nine people. Whether he did so in secret or crewmembers led him to safety over others remains disputed. Furthermore, while we see in the following chapters that Ismay was narrated as a Titanic villain in the American press and later commercial films, the Titanic Historical Society argues that Ismay has only been written as a villain because he survived. They add that he escaped on the last boat when no other passengers were around and that had he not jumped into a boat it would have simply resulted in one more death. The manner of the survival of Ismay remains highly contested and based on what I have read, it seems impossible to reconcile at this point in time. Captain Smith and Thomas Andrews made no attempt to save themselves. The ship's band played to the end, it is assumed as a comfort to the passengers. None of the band members survived.

Of those who were saved, the majority were women and children and it has been written time and time again that the crew strictly enforced the "rule of the sea." However, social class also played a critical role in the Titanic event. The crew locked the gates of the steerage section so that many third-class passengers did not have a chance to make it to the boats. While this report was highly contested by crew and upper class survivors in 1912, and continues to be written as fictionalized and exaggerated, on March 30th 1998 it was publicly announced that an exploration of Titanic's remains confirmed the locking of steerage gates. The expedition showed that the gates remain locked as Titanic sits on the Atlantic floor. Eighty-six years later, this part of the Titanic mystery was finally put to rest. It has been speculated that some third class passengers who freed themselves, were threatened with a revolver and even shot, though this too remains highly contested. Most of the boats were already gone and less than one quarter of the third class passengers were saved. Survivors have described rowing to safety knowing they would live while watching Titanic sink amid a chorus of people in the water crying out, begging for help. While passengers were provided with life-vests, due to the freezing temperatures, those in the water froze to death. Eventually when one lifeboat returned, there were only three people still living (one of whom died later). Despite lifeboat capacity for over 1,100 people, 1,503 people died while only 705 were rescued. Two first-class dogs were also saved. In order to understand the role of gender and social class in the event, the following chart, adapted from Butler, is helpful:[26]

Saved	Men	Women	Children
First-Class	57	139	5
Second-Class	14	79	23
Third-Class	75	76	26

What this chart reveals is that while gender was clearly a factor in the upper-classes, gender had no role in the saving of third-class passengers. Men and women of the third-class were saved in equal proportions indicating that "the rule of the sea" was in fact *classed*. This also becomes painfully clear when looking at the deaths of children, who were purportedly "protected" under "the rule of the sea." While only one child in the upper-classes died, 53 children staying in third-class died. This again indicates that, in actuality, the myth of "women and children first" was regulated by social class.

The frozen corpses of those who died were found as late as June of that year. Titanic was not discovered until 1985. Experts estimate that Titanic will completely disintegrate within the next twenty years.

The Columbine High School Shootings[27]

As you may recall, on April 20th 1999, the day of the Columbine school shootings in Littleton Colorado, the nation seemed glued to the television as the normal flow of news was interrupted to make way for saturation coverage of the event and its aftermath. Indeed, in the United States it appeared as though nothing else was happening that day. The Columbine shootings were thrust into the public and/or captured the public's imagination from the moment live coverage began. Columbine quickly became a site of moral panic and the writing of many cultural and political narratives. The following is a brief timeline of how the event itself unfolded, according to the best sources of information available.

At 11:10am On April 20, 1999 Dylan Klebold and Eric Harris each arrived at Columbine High School in Littleton Colorado, where they both attended school. They each parked their vehicles and exited to the lower level of the school near the Cafeteria where a survivor reported they told him to leave because they "liked" him. Between 11:14am and 11:22am Harris and Klebold brought two duffel bags of explosives into the school and left them next to two lunch tables in the Cafeteria just before the first lunch was to begin. The timers were set to go off at 11:17am, a time that, reportedly, was when the maximum number of students would be localized there. Harris and Klebold returned to their cars and waited for the explosions which did not go off as planned.

At 11:19am a local caller reported an explosion to the Jefferson County Dispatch office. This explosion was later determined to be a diversion (though with Harris and Klebold dead this can not be certain). The sheriff and fire department were, at that point, called to action.

Between 11:19am and 11:23am Harris and Klebold reportedly began their assault on the school from the top of a west side staircase, the highest point on the school grounds. Harris and Klebold began shooting, killing one student and wounding another. At 11:23am the first 911 call was made from Columbine. The gunfire continued as Harris and Klebold shot students at both close range and from a distance, while also throwing explosive devices up onto the roof. Harris and Klebold entered the school on the west side and shot at a student and a teacher, both of whom ultimately survived. One police officer arrived at Columbine at 11:24am and exchanged gunfire with Harris, who was not hit or detained. At 11:26am Harris and Klebold continued shooting students in the hallways and then entered the library hallway. They were also throwing pipe bombs. Between 11:29am and 11:36am Harris and Klebold entered the library and began to shoot students. They asked one student, Cassie, if she believed in God. When she reportedly replied "yes" they shot her fatally. In their racialized attack, one African-American male student was reportedly called "nigger" and shot dead. During this time, 10 people were killed and 12 were wounded.

Between 11:36am and 11:44am, Harris and Klebold returned to the hall and began to move toward the science hallway. They again placed pipe bombs around the halls. The pair then went down to the cafeteria at 11:44am. While in the cafeteria, the two attempted to explode the bombs they had placed there earlier, but were unsuccessful. After two minutes, they moved and some of the bombs partially detonated.

At 11:47am Denver's KMGH-TV Channel 7 announced that there had been gunshots reported at Columbine High School. Soon after, a barrage of news cameras and reporters traveled to the school to capture the event (and its aftermath). It wasn't until sometime after 11:59am that Harris and Klebold eventually turned the guns on themselves and thus, there were live news feeds of students and staff fleeing the school. In total, fifteen people were killed (including the two gunmen) and twenty-three wounded.[28] Reportedly, their diaries later confirmed that the attack was intentionally planned for the anniversary of Adolph Hitler's birthday in order to pay homage to Hitler.

The Attacks of Pearl Harbor and September 11th: An Abridged Timeline of Events

I am grouping Pearl Harbor and September 11th together as they have commonly been viewed in the United States as "surprise" attacks on American soil, and both resulted in significant losses of life as well as material destruction. While there are significant differences between these events, (and I find the use of Pearl Harbor as a metaphor through which to interpret September 11th highly problematic), as it pertains to this project, the attacks can be considered as belonging to the same broad category of event. Any meaningful historical analysis of Pearl Harbor or September 11th would need to look at the events in the context of the larger wars of which they were a part. In other words, Pearl Harbor can only be properly understood in the context of World War II and many other related issues. With this said, and for the purpose of examining how these events became iconic within different spheres of American culture, I examine them in a contained way. So, in the following timeline of each event, I look only at the specific event as beginning and ending within a period of hours (providing only information about warnings immediate to the event). This is not to disregard the political climate in which these events took place, but rather to help pinpoint the event itself, that although part of a larger political and social upheaval, has taken on great social significance.

Two further points before I present the timelines: The first is a question one might fairly ask: Why provide a simplistic historical overview of events that Americans are already quite familiar with? This is particularly valid given how rough and contained these sketches are. The answer is that, in order to have a better appreciation of later representations of the events in newspapers, books and films, as well as the process whereby these events took on various politicized dimensions, it is important that some basics (who, what, where, when) are laid out. The second and related point to address is the accuracy of these accounts. In this vein, even information that seems like it should be well known, such as exact times and exact losses of life, are often contradicted in different texts making it more difficult to lay claim to. However, I have checked multiple sources, noted inconsistencies when appropriate, and the timelines that follow are only meant to provide a sketch of the events. In fact, minor qualms regarding particulars are not relevant because the goal of this book is not to rewrite the history of these events, but rather to understand the social process by which they have come to take on different kinds of significance in American culture. In terms of the accuracy of these accounts it is also important to disclose that I am using American sources as I am ultimately interested in the role of these events within American culture. No doubt a Japanese history of Pearl Harbor or an Afghan history of September 11th might appear quite different.

December 7th 1941[29]

In July of 1941, Japan, which relied on oil imports, made a deal to access natural resources in Southeast Asia. President Roosevelt responded with an embargo on the shipment of oil to Japan. The government of the Dutch East Indies followed out of need for American support. At this point, Japan was planning a "surprise" attack on America, led by Admiral Isoroku Yamamoto the commander-in-chief of the Japanese fleet. After many communications between Japan and the United States, on Saturday December 6th 1941 U.S. President Franklin Roosevelt re-

portedly appealed to the Emperor of Japan for peace. President Roosevelt did
not receive a reply and the U.S. code-breaking service began to decipher a four-
teen-part message from the Japanese. The first thirteen parts were deciphered
and presented to the President and Secretary of State, and the U.S. government,
at that point, believed that an attack was imminent but did not know precisely
where and when the attack would occur.

On Sunday December 7th 1941 the Japanese military led a two-wave attack
of the US Pacific Fleet at Pearl Harbor, located in Hawaii near Oahu. The Japanese military were led by Admiral Nagumo and had six carriers loaded with 423
planes. The Japanese intended the attack to be a surprise (and the element of
surprise has been historicized as the greatest weapon that the Japanese had
available, for this attack). In addition to achieving surprise, the Japanese military
secretly created "The Zero"—(a fighter plane, that could outperform all other
fighter planes at the time), especially for this mission. Its light weight (reduced
even further through the release of fuel) allowed it to fly higher and faster than
other fighter planes. The silver Zeros were marked only with red circles, the
symbol of Japan. The Japanese put the same effort into developing effective
torpedoes and specifically designed ones that were housed in wood boxes so
that, when dropped from the planes into the Pacific the boxes would break off
and the torpedoes would travel at high speed in the shallow harbor water towards their target.

Pearl Harbor was not on a high alert because it had been concluded by officials that there was no imminent threat. This is important because the aircraft
were parked wingtip to wingtip on the airfields, the aircraft guns were not
manned, and supplies of ammunition were locked up (in compliance with peace-
time regulations). To make matters worse, the ships were moored close together,
and there weren't any torpedo nets protecting the fleet anchorage. Furthermore,
the attack occurred early on a Sunday morning when many officers and crew
were sleeping in their bunks.

Unbeknownst to those stationed at Pearl Harbor, at 6:00am 183 planes took
off from carriers located 230 miles from Oahu and headed towards Pearl Harbor.
One plane was lost on takeoff and another had engine trouble, but the remaining
took off without a hitch. In total, at this point, 49 bombers, 51 dive-bombers, 40
torpedo-planes, and 41 zero fighters were heading to Pearl Harbor. This was the
first wave of the attack. At 7:00am Japanese Commander Fuchida, the flight
leader, picked up music from a Hawaiian radio station, and stayed on the station
which alerted him that the Americans did not know that the attack was coming.
At 7:02am two Army operators at the Oahu Northern radar station, detected a
group of more than fifty planes approaching. The operators passed the information along to a junior office who disregarded the report because he thought the
approaching planes were the American B-17 planes that were due to arrive that

day.[30] Also unbeknown to those stationed at Pearl Harbor, at 7:15am 167 Japanese planes took off from carriers and headed towards Pearl Harbor, constituting the second wave of the attack.

At 7:53am Commander Fuchida sent the now famous radio message, the battle cry: "Tora, Tora, Tora" which translates to "Tiger, Tiger, Tiger" and indicated that the first wave of the attack took the Americans by complete surprise. In fact, when the first bomb dropped on Pearl Harbor most of the Americans stationed there, thought it was dropped by one of their own planes, mistakenly. Moments later, when a dive-bomber blew up a hanger at the Command Center, American Commander Ramsey realized Pearl Harbor was under attack and radioed this message: "Air raid, Pearl Harbor. This is no drill." It was 7:55am and Pearl Harbor, whose crew had been awake for less than two minutes, was under a full force attack.

The first wave targeted airfields and battleships. The second focused on other ships and shipyard facilities. At approximately 9:00am Ambassador Nomura and Special Envoy Kurusu went to the State Department to deliver Secretary of State Hull a message from Tokyo. They had been ordered to deliver it an hour earlier but had to postpone the delivery because of difficulty deciphering the fourteenth part of the message. The message said, in part, that "the peace of the Pacific through cooperation has finally been lost" and that it was now "impossible to reach an agreement through further negotiations." Secretary of State Hull had already seen reports coming in from Pearl Harbor and knew it was a bloody attack. He responded by saying he had never known a government to engage in such "infamous falsehoods and distortions." As he spoke, the second wave was attacking Pearl Harbor. The complete attack lasted until 9:45am.

The damage at Pearl Harbor, on the American side, included eight damaged battle ships with five sunk. The Arizona, which was lost, was also the site of the greatest loss of life (most of the crew was killed when a 1,760-pound air bomb penetrated it, causing a massive explosion). While other battle ships were being repaired and returned to service, the Oklahoma was also lost. In addition to other damage, three light cruisers, three destroyers, and three smaller vessels were also lost. One hundred sixty-two aircraft were destroyed and another 150 were damaged. Despite the great material loss, there were some prime targets that were spared. Three aircraft carriers were not in the port and the base fuel tanks were not hit. In total 2,403 and Americans were killed. Of the dead, 2,335 were in the service and 68 were civilians. The greatest single loss happened on the battleship USS Arizona when 1,104 men were killed. In addition to the dead, 1,178 Americans were wounded. The following charts, adapted from Michael Slackman, detail the human losses.[31]

United States Personnel

Service	Dead	Wounded
Navy	2,008	710
Marine	109	69
Army	218	364
Civilian	68	35
Total	2,403	1,178

Japan Personnel (reliable numbers of Japanese wounded are not available)

Service	Dead	Prisoner
Airmen	55	0
I-70 (approx)	65	0
Midget Sub. Crewmen	9	1
Total	129	1

Later that day, radio news of the attack was broadcast to the American public. Some of these bulletins interrupted popular Sunday entertainment programs.

On December 8th 1941 President Roosevelt delivered a speech in which he referred to December 7th as "a date which will live in infamy." He also said "Very many American lives have been lost." When speaking to Congress, Roosevelt listed the numerous non-US sites attacked by the Japanese on the same day. He then said "I ask that Congress declare that since the unprovoked and dastardly attack by Japan on Sunday, December 7th, a state of war has existed between the United States and the Japanese Empire." The resolution was passed by the Senate 82 to 0 and passed by the House of Representatives 388 to 1. At 4:10pm on December 8th President Roosevelt signed the declaration of war. That same day Britain also declared war on Japan.

September 11th 2001[32]

On September 11th, 2001 four American commercial flights were hijacked. All of the people on board died, as well as many more at the sites the planes crashed. A review of many published timelines of that morning contain vital discrepancies regarding the precise take-off time of some of the flights as well as the extent to which the American government was or was not "on the job" and so this, as all 9-11 timelines, is highly contested. Nonetheless, what follows is the official and most widely circulated outline of events which is not to reify or endorse this version, but merely present it.

At 7:59am American Airlines Flight 11, a Boeing 767 with 92 people on board, departed from Boston's Logan International Airport. At 8:14am (this time is contested) United Airlines Flight 175, a Boeing 767 with 65 people on board, also departed from Boston's Logan International Airport. Both flights were bound for Los Angeles. At 8:20am American Airlines Flight 77, a Boeing 757 with 64 people on board, departed Washington Dulles International Airport also heading for Los Angeles. At 8:40am The FAA notified NORAD's Northeast Air Defense Sector that there was a possible hijacking on American Airlines Flight 11. The fourth hijacked flight was delayed on the ground at Newark International Airport. As a result the flight left at least 45 minutes after it was scheduled to depart. The time this flight departed is highly contested. Official accounts put the departure at 8:42am; however, resistive accounts put the departure as much as ten minutes later (which is significant as that meant the flight departed after the first trade center tower was hit). In any event, sometime after 8:42am United Airlines Flight 93 a Boeing 757 with 44 people on board, departed from Newark on route to San Francisco International Airport. At 8:43am the FAA notified NORAD's Northeast Air Defense Sector of the suspected hijacking of United Airlines Flight 175. At 8:45am-American Airlines Flight 11 crashed into the north World Trade Center tower (Tower 1) in New York City. At 9:03am, as the first crash site was being broadcast on American television, United Airlines Flight 175 crashed into the south World Trade Center tower (2 Tower). Five minutes later the FAA banned flights taking off that were intended to go through New York airspace. At 9:17am all New York City airports were shutdown and four minutes later bridges and tunnels were closed. At 9:24am the FAA informed NORAD's Northeast Air Defense Sector of the suspected hijacking of American Airlines Flight 77. At 9:25am all American airports and airspace was shutdown.

At 9:31am President George W. Bush addressed the public from an Elementary School in Sarasota, Florida where he had been visiting. He referred to the crashes as an "apparent terrorist attack."

At 9:40am American Airlines Flight 77 crashed into the west side of the Pentagon. Five minutes later a telephone operator received a cell phone call from a passenger on United Airlines Flight 93, who reported that the flight had been hijacked and that the passengers were planning to try and regain control of the airplane. At 10:05am the south World Trade Center tower (Tower 2) collapsed, on live television. At 10:10am (this time is also contested) United Airlines Flight 93 crashed in a field near Shanksville, Pennsylvania. At 10:10am a part of The Pentagon collapsed. At 10:29am the north World Trade Center tower (Tower 1) collapsed, on live television.

At 12:36pm President Bush made a brief statement from Barksdale Air Force Base near Shreveport, Louisiana. The speech began "Freedom itself was

attacked this morning by a faceless coward and freedom will be defended."
Later in the statement he said "The United States will hunt down and punish
those responsible for this cowardly act." He concluded "The resolve of our great
nation is being tested. But make no mistake: we will show the world that we will
pass this test. God bless."

At 5:25pm World Trade Center 7 collapsed.

At 8:30pm President Bush gave a television address from the Oval Office.
The speech began "Good evening. Today, our fellow citizens, our way of life,
our very freedom came under attack in a series of deliberate and deadly terrorist
attacks." In the address Bush several times employed the word "evil" and pro-
posed "America was targeted for the attack because we're the brightest beacon
for freedom and opportunity in the world." Bush also declared that the "search"
was underway for those responsible, adding, "We will make no distinction between the terrorists who committed these acts and those who harbor them." Referring to "our allies" Bush said "we stand together to win the war against terrorism." He ended the speech with a combination of religious discourse, marking
the event with historicity, focusing on going after the perpetrators, and reaffirming his interpretation of the event as an assault on "freedom." The speech concluded, "I ask for your prayers for all those who grieve, for the children whose
worlds have been shattered . . . And I pray they will be comforted by a power
greater than any of us, spoken through the ages in Psalm 23: "Even though I
walk through the valley of the shadow of death, I fear no evil, for you are with
me." This is a day when all Americans from every walk of life unite in our resolve for justice and peace. America has stood down enemies before, and we
will do so this time. None of us will ever forget this day. Yet, we go forward to
defend freedom and all that is good and just in our world. Thank you. Good
night, and God bless America."

On September 15th, 2001 President Bush declared "We're at war" and
named Osama Bin Laden as the "prime suspect" who orchestrated the 9-11 hijackings. The hijackers were said to be members of Al Qaeda.

On October 7th, 2001 the U.S. military began their assault against Afghanistan, using cruise missiles.

On January 29th, 2002 President Bush delivered his State of the Union address in which he characterized countries that harbor or otherwise support "terrorists" as constituting an "axis of evil." Iraq was among the countries named.

An estimated 2,792 people died in the September 11th attacks.

The Shirtwaist "Triangle" Factory Fire[33]

Many Americans have not heard of the Triangle Shirtwaist Factory Fire of 1911 which resulted in the greatest number of deaths in the workplace in the United States until September 11th, ninety years later. What follows is a very brief history of the factory, fire, and its aftermath.

In 1906 The Triangle Shirtwaist Company opened a factory in the Asch building at Greene Street and Washington Place in New York City. The Triangle Shirtwaist factory occupied the top three floors of the ten-story building which was designed in 1900 and completely constructed on January 15, 1901. The factory employees were primarily young females, most in their teens or twenties and most were immigrants, many of whom spoke very little English. In June of 1909 a fire prevention specialist sent the factory management a letter suggesting improved safety measures but no changes were implemented and the next year the factory passed a routine fire inspection. When considering the Triangle Factory's compliance with building and safety laws at the time, it is clear that some standards were surprisingly low, allowing the factory to avoid violations. In some instances, whether or not the factory violated policy was questionable, and there were some outright violations of relevant policy, though the factory had not been written up for them. In terms of compliance with what would now be viewed as weak laws, the factory did not have any sprinklers; however, none were legally required. Buildings that were 150 feet or higher, had to comply with requirements regarding the prevalence of non-wood surfaces (that did not burn as quickly as wood); however the factory was 135 feet (one story shy of the law) and thus did not face any restrictions on wood surfaces. Furthermore, the company never ran any fire drills which were not required by law.

It is in the area of door construction that the factory owners skirted the law, either through loopholes or directly breaking the law, depending on how one now interprets this bit of history. There are two major issues both linked to the same piece of law. New York State Labor Law Article 6, Section 80 read in part: "All doors leading in or to any such factory shall be constructed as to open outwardly, where practicable, and shall not be locked, bolted, or fastened during working hours." The 9th floor door at the factory did not open outwardly; however, this was not recorded as a violation because only the width of a stair separated the door from the staircase making it not "practicable" for the door to open outwardly (it was on the 9th floor that 145 out of the 146 victims were working). Whether or not the door had been locked, was a key issue, later at trial (and if this was the case, whether the owners were aware of it). Many survivors testified to the fact that the door was kept locked to prevent theft and unauthorized breaks.

As for outright failure to comply with safety standards, the issue of fire escapes emerges. There weren't any uniform policies regarding fire escapes in general, but in the case of each building the matter was left to the discretion of the building inspector. While still in the planning stages, the inspector for the Asch building was adamant that the fire escape had to lead to something more "substantial" than a skylight (which was pictured in the plans). Despite the architect's promise to comply, once the building was completed, the fire escape still ended at a second floor skylight. During the fire this fire escape collapsed.

Though the factory did pass its final inspection before the 1911 fire, there were related things happening, that both indicate the failure of Shirtwaist management to upgrade their safety procedures, and also the larger context within which this kind of neglect may have been routine. For example, on November 25, 1910 there was a factory fire in Newark that caused 25 fatalities. This brought fire prevention into the public domain. A report published on March 16, (just days before the deadly fire), claimed that many buildings in New York City lacked "even the most indispensable precautions necessary" indicating that the problem was widespread. As for Shirtwaist, in addition to skirting the scant existing building safety law, January 15, 1911 was the last time cutaways (over a ton's worth) had been picked up from the factory. This is important as the gigantic accumulation of these materials helped fuel the March fire (cotton material in the cutters bin was more flammable than paper. Explosively so).

Much like how one might analyze the Challenger explosion or sinking of Titanic, these policy failures, normalized deviance, as well as other economic and social issues, all contributed to the tragic events of March 25th, 1911.

The Fire and Aftermath
At 4:40pm on March 25th, 1911 an eighth floor worker screamed, "Fire!" New York City firefighters arrived at the scene six minutes later. At that time the fire was spreading upwards, so many eighth floor employees headed downstairs, some from the tenth floor headed to the roof, while many on the ninth floor were trapped. Several ninth floor employees jumped out of the building, the last body falling to the sidewalk at 4:57pm New York University Law School Professor Frank Sommer was teaching a class fifteen feet above the Asch building roof when he saw Shirtwaist workers making their way to the roof. Professor Sommer and several of his students found old painting ladders and placed them across the buildings so that employees could make their way to the university roof. The quick blaze was brought under control by 5:05pm and practically over by 5:15pm.

In total 146 workers were killed, 145 from the ninth floor and one from the tenth. Several jumpers survived the fall but died within days. The youngest victim was eleven years old. Some of the dead were relatives. For example, Catherine Maltese, who died, was the mother of two girls who also died in the fire, Lucia age 20 and Rosalie age 14. The girls' brother identified all three bodies. The corpses were taken to a temporary morgue located at a covered pier on East 26th Street.

Blanck and Harris were indicted on manslaughter charges in the case of Margaret Schwartz, one of the victims who reportedly died as a direct result of the exit door being locked. The trial began on December 4th, 1911. Over a dozen witnesses testified for the prosecution, that the doors had been locked, ultimately causing the death of Margaret Schwartz. A co-worker Kate Alerman testified:

> . . . I noticed someone, a whole crowd around the door and I saw Bernstein, the manager's brother trying to open the door, and there was Margaret near him. Bernstein tried the door, he couldn't open it and then Margaret began to open the door. I take her on one side I pushed her on the side and I said, "Wait, I will open that door." I tried, pulled the handle in and out, all ways—and I couldn't open it. She pushed me on the other side, got hold of the handle and then she tried. And then I saw her bending down on her knees, and her hair was loose, and the trail of her dress was a little far from her, and then a big smoke came and I couldn't see. I just know it was Margaret, and I said, "Margaret" and she didn't reply. I left Margaret, I turned my head on the side, and I noticed the trail of her dress and the ends of her hair begin to burn.[34]

The defense called fifty-two witnesses to counter. The judge told the jury that in order to deliver a guilty verdict they had to find that Harris and Blanck knew or should have known that the door was locked and that this locked door had caused the death of Margaret Schwartz. In less than two hours the jury delivered a verdict of not guilty. One juror said he had believed the doors were locked but could not conclude beyond a reasonable doubt that the owners knew that the door was locked. There was an attempt to prosecute the defendants for other fire deaths but rules of double jeopardy ultimately prevailed (which prevent a person from being tried more than once for a single crime). Three years later, on March 11th, 1914 twenty-three civil suits against the Asch building were settled, with an average payout of $75 per death. On February 22nd, 2001 Rose Freedman, the only remaining fire survivor, died at the age of 107. Freedman devoted much of her life to worker safety issues.

While the Shirtwaist Fire impacted building safety and fire codes, and continues to serve as a benchmark case in worker health and safety literature, it ultimately failed to achieve mythic status within American culture.

The Inherent Dilemma in Historical Representation

The information presented in this chapter, like all historical analyses, is compressed, and, no doubt, contested. This is the nature of, and central contradiction within, the practice of historiography Historical representation always undergoes a process of reduction,[35] displacement, and signification.[36] Rosenstone explains that people who work with historical evidence must "make personal judgments" as they gather different pieces of information and form them into an interpretation of the past.[37] The historical sketches presented in this chapter are not perfect reflections of the past, but rather interpretations based on an assessment of other historical representations, including primary sources. These sketches are not intended to serve as "the truth" against which other groups' interpretations are then judged, but instead serve as a general baseline from which to explore how these iconic events have been represented in different venues: journalism, politics, and popular culture.

Notes

1. Stephanie Barczezewski, *Titanic: A Night Remembered* (New York: Hambledon and London, 2004).

2. Butler's statement is ironic considering that years before the Titanic sinking a published work of fiction titled *The Titan* chronicled an eerily similar event.

3. Daniel Allen Butler, *UNSINKABLE: The Full Story of the RMS Titanic* (Mechanicsburg, Pa.: Stackpole Books, 1998) ix.

4. Butler, *UNSINKABLE*, xii.

5. The next two sections rely on the following sources:

Stephanie Barczezewski, *Titanic: A Night Remembered* (New York: Hambledon and London, 2004).

Donald Lynch, *Titanic: An Illustrated History* (New York: Hyperion, 1992).

Daniel Allen Butler, *UNSINKABLE: The Full Story of the RMS Titanic* (Mechanicsburg, Pa.: Stackpole Books, 1998).

Wyn Craig Wade, *The Titanic: End of a Dream* (New York: Penguin Books, 1979).

Michael Davie, *Titanic: The Death and Life of a Legend* (New York: Henry Holt and Company, 1988).

Archibald Gracie, *Titanic: A Survivor's Story* (Chicago: Academy Chicago Publishers, 1996).

Jack Winocour ed., *The Story of the Titanic as Told by its Survivors* (New York: Dover Publications, Inc., 1960).

Charles Pellegrino, *Ghosts of the Titanic* (New York: HarperCollins Publishers, Inc., 2000).

"Titanic Myths." *The Titanic Historical Society.*
http://www.titanichistoricalsociety.org/articles/titanicmyths.asp (January 20, 2006).

Louise Laroche. "A Haitian French Family Which Traveled in Second Class Aboard Titanic." *Titanic Historical Society.*
http://www.titanichisttoricalsociety.org/people/louise-laroche.asp (January 20, 2006).

William B. Saphire. "The White Star Line and The International Mercantile Marine Company." *Titanic Historical Society.*
http://www.titanichistoricalsociety.org/articles/mercantile.asp (January 20, 2006).

Edward S. Kamuda. "Titanic Past and Present." *Titanic Historical Society.*
http://www.titanichistoricalsociety.org/articles/titanicpastandpresent1.asp

6. Michael Davie, *Titanic: The Death and Life of a Legend* (New York: Henry Holt and Company, 1988), 9.

7. Pirrie did not make the maiden voyage or the Titanic Inquiry due to prostate problems and was thus largely written out of Titanic history, or at least mainstream collective memory. Despite his absence from Titanic memory Pirrie's business exploded after Titanic as he gained the reconstruction jobs that emerged due to new ship regulations. He died at sea in 1924 as a result of pneumonia.

8. The date of the Challenger launch was similarly changed, impacting the weather conditions that became integral to the explosion.

9. Despite its early problem Olympic eventually transported more troops than any other ship during World War I. The third ship, Britannic was sunk by German mine in 1916; Butler, *UNSINKABLE*, 4.

10. Donald Lynch, *Titanic: An Illustrated History* (New York: Hyperion, 1992), 20.

11. Lynch, *Illustrated History*, 20-2.

12. Wyn Craig Wade, *The Titanic: End of a Dream* (New York: Penguin Books, 1979), 7.

13. *White Star Line, Royal & United States Mail Steamers Olympic and Titanic 45,000 Tons Each the Largest Vessels in the World* (Liverpool, U.K.: Liverpool Stationery Company, 1911) 3–5. (Bold Emphasis Added)

14. *White Star Line*, 72. (Bold Emphasis Added)

15. Barczewski, *Night Remembered*.

16. To this day the numbers of passengers are not universally agreed on. While the number of survivors is widely accepted reported numbers of those who died vary slightly. The numbers I am reporting seem to be the most widely cited numbers; however, this does not mean they are the most accurate.

17. Barczewski, *Night Remembered*, 13.

18. Lynch, *Illustrated History*, 72.

19. Lynch, *Illustrated History*, 72.

20. Lynch, *Illustrated History*.

21. Sociologist Diane Vaughan (1997) discusses how the same processes of ritualized deviance occurred with the decision to launch the Challenger. Vaughan analyzes the ritualized culture of deviance at NASA by unraveling in-house procedures of risk as-

sessment influenced by external pressures. This framing is equally applicable to the treatment of ice warnings on Titanic. In both the case of Challenger and Titanic the air temperature would have been a danger indicator alone had outcome-driven ritualized deviance not superseded critical pause.

22. Lynch, *Illustrated History*, 41.

23. Lynch, *Illustrated History*, 77.

24. Ironically, after dinner that evening approximately 100 passengers in second-class met in the dining saloon to sing hymns many of which warned of the dangers at sea; Butler, *UNSINKABLE*, 77.

25. Lynch, *Illustrated History*, 79.

26. Butler , *UNSINKABLE*.

27. This section relies on the following sources:

"Charting School Violence," *Columbine Angels* April 28, 2006, *http://www.columbine-angels.com/Violence_Chart.htm* (March 20, 2006).

"Columbine Memorial." *Columbine Memorial.* *http://www.columbinememorial.org* (April 19, 2006).

Associated Press, "Timeline of Columbine Attack," *BC cycle*, 16 April 2004, State and Regional.

"Columbine Killing Took 16 Minutes." *BBC News.* *http://news.bbc.co.uk/2/hi/americas/749966.stm* (May 15, 2006).

"US Moms Protest Against Guns." *BBC News.* *http://news.bbc.co.uk/2/hi/americas/747619.stm* (May 15, 2006).

"Analysis: What is the NRA." *BBC News.* *http://news.bbc.co.uk/2/hi/americas/332555.stm* (May 15, 2006).

Mary Leonard. "Million Mom March' Against Guns on Mothers Day, May 14." *Common Dreams.org. http://www.commondreams.org/headlines/032900-01.htm* (May 15, 2006).

"Some Mothers See Million Mom March For Gun Control as Personal Memorial." *CNN.com Transcripts.* *http://transcripts.cnn.com/TRANSCRIPTS/0005/14/sm.07.html* (May 15, 2006).

"Million Mom March Concludes on National Mall." *CNN.com Transcripts.* *http://transcripts.cnn.com/TRANSCRIPTS/0005/14/sun.02.html* (May 15, 2006).

28. "Charting School Violence," *Columbine Angels* April 28, 2006, *http://www.columbine-angels.com/Violence_Chart.htm* (March 20, 2006).

29. This section relies on the following sources:

Michael Slackman, *Target: Pearl Harbor* (Honolulu: University of Hawaii Press: Arizona Memorial Museum Association, 1990).

John Toland, *Infamy: Pearl Harbor and its Aftermath* (Green City: N.Y.: Doubleday, 1982).

Gordon W. Prance; Donald M. Goldstein and Katherine V. Dillon, *Dec. 7 1941: The Day the Japanese Attacked Pearl Harbor* (New York: McGraw–Hill, 1988).

"8 December 1941: A Day Which Will Live in Infamy." *Osprey Essential Pearl Harbor. http://216.168.37.48/FMPro?-DB=osehph.FP3&-*

FORMAT=/scribe/osehph/osehphfmtday.html&ReferenceNumber=OSEHPH344&-Max=1&-Find (January 20, 2006).

"7 December 1941: Tora, Tora, Tora!." *Osprey Essential Pearl Harbor. http://216.168.37.48/FMPro?-DB=osehph.FP3&-FORMAT=/scribe/osehph/osehphfmtday.html&ReferenceNumber=OSEHPH343&-Max=1&-Find* (January 20, 2006).

"Pearl Harbor Timeline." *Osprey Essential Pearl Harbor. http://www.essentialpearlharbor.com/osehphtime.html* (January 20, 2006).

"The Morning of December 7, 1941 at Pearl Harbor, Oahu, Hawaii." *Pearl Harbor. http://projects.pisd.edu/webmastering/vines/pearl_harbor/contents3.html* (January 20, 2006).

"The Pacific War: A World War II Special Feature." *War Times Journal. http://www.wtj.com/articles/pacific_war/articles/pearl_harbor.htm* (January 20, 2006).

"Pearl Harbor, Hawaii, Sunday December 7, 1941." *The History Place. http://www.historyplace.com/worldwar2/timeline/pearl.htm* (January 20, 2006).

30. The ritualized deviance of the disregarded report bares similarities with disregarded Titanic ice warnings both indicating how tragic events could, perhaps, be avoided or altered if warning systems and regulations in both industry and the military were, at the time, carefully followed.

31. Michael Slackman, *Target: Pearl Harbor* (Honolulu: University of Hawaii Press: Arizona Memorial Museum Association, 1990).

32. This section relies on the following sources:

"September 11, 2001 attacks timeline for the day of the attacks." *Wikipedia, the Free Encyclopedia.* May 31, 2006. *http://en.wikipedia.org/wiki/September_11%2C_2001_attacks_timeline_for_the_day_of_the_attacks* (March 23, 2006).

"Timelines, Images, and Graphics from the September 11, 2001 Attacks on the World Trade Center in NYC and the Pentagon in Washington." *September 11th News.com.* 2001–03. *http://www.september11news.com/AttackImages.htm* (March 23, 2006).

"Timeline of Events: September 11–18, 2001." *Teachervision.com.* 2005–06. *http://www.teachervision.fen.com/war/unitedstates/6825.htmlhttp://www.teachervision.fen.com/war/united-states/6825.html* (March 23, 2006).

Cummings, Scott. "September 11, 2001 Timeline" *The Patriot Resource History: September 11, 2001.* 2001–05. *http://www.patriotsource.com/wtc/timeline/sept11c.html* (March 23, 2006).

Yvonna S. Lincoln and Norman K. Denzin. *9/11 in American Culture.* (Alta Mira Press, 2003).

David Ray Griffin, *The New Pearl Harbor: Disturbing Questions about the Bush Administration and 9-11.* (Northampton, Mass: Olive Branch Press, 2004).

33. This section relies on the following sources:

"Excerpts From Trial Testimony in the Triangle Shirtwaist Fire Trial." *University of Missouri–Kansas City School of Law.*

http://www.law.umkc.edu/faculty/projects/trials/triangle/triangletest1.html (April 12, 2006).

"Stories of Survivors and Witnesses and Rescuers Outside Tell What They Saw," *New York Times, 26 March 1911*, 4.

"Three Blame Shifted On All Dies For Fire Horror," *New York Times*, 28 March 1911, 1.

"Triangle Waist Men Put on Trial," *New York Times*, 5 December 1911, 16.

"Girls Fought Vainly at Triangle Doors," *New York Times*, 12 December 1911, 4.

"Say Triangle Doors Were Never Locked," *New York Times*, 21 December 1911, 20.

"Triangle Case to the Jury Today," *New York Times*, 27 December 1911, 6.

"Triangle Owners Acquitted by Jury," *New York Times*, 28 December 1911, 1.

David Von Drehle, *Triangle: The Fire That Changed America* (New York: Atlantic Monthly Press, 2003).

34. "Excerpts From Trial Testimony in the Triangle Shirtwaist Fire Trial." *University of Missouri–Kansas City School of Law.* *http://www.law.umkc.edu/faculty/projects/trials/triangle/triangletest1.html* (April 12, 2006).

35. Kenneth Cameron, "America on Film: Hollywood and American History," (New York: Continuum, 1997), 238.

36. Hayden White, *Metahistory: The Historical Imagination in Nineteenth Century Europe* (Baltimore, Md.: Johns Hopkins University Press, 1973),11.

37. Robert A. Rosenstone, "Revisioning History: Film and the Construction of a New Past," (Princeton, N.J.: Princeton University Press, 1995), 7.

Chapter Three

The Represented Event: Journalism's Initial Spin

The story cannot be told without form, and the form carries the meaning. History cannot, apparently be separated from its own retellings,[1] nor can journalism escape this truth.[2]

Journalism plays a central role in the construction of collective memory. It is through the press that citizens come to find out about a range of social and political issues, and it is through the press that we learn about major events that we were not personally involved in. The press, the umbrella term for organizations that produce the news, make daily decisions about what will be presented as "news." Common wisdom dictates that the role of the press is to communicate to the citizenry, issues of public interest and importance. Some scholars also argue that journalism is meant to inform citizens in the service of democracy and thus by extension, it should play a vital role in the execution of democracy.[3] Regardless of whether or not one is "optimistic" or "pessimistic" about the news as being central to the democratic process (and if optimistic, one might then consider caveats that separate political and economic news from entertainment or sports news), it is clear that the press also decides what is of public interest or importance. Once an issue or event has been signaled as important, journalists need to help people make sense of it. Like any other business, journalists operate under a range of commercial imperatives. Furthermore, as any other profession, journalism carries with it a set of institutional practices, endemic to the field. More specifically, journalists are an interpretive community[4] with a commercial system backing them.[5]

In order to get a real picture of the kind of work journalists do it is necessary to consider both the institutional practices common to their field as well as the cultural practices of storytelling that they employ. Of course, with technological and other social changes, these practices vary over time. In the United States one journalistic practice is the professional conception of objectivity.

Modern American journalism cannot be understood without considering its reliance on an ideal or ideology, as Michael Schudson[6] would say, of objectivity. Though some newspapers like *The New York Times* had already followed an "information model" for decades, it wasn't until the 1930s that the journalistic ideal of objectivity developed as a response to the public's perception of bias. By the 1960s, citizens were seriously questioning and challenging powerful institutions (first and foremost—the government), and objectivity became viewed as central to the practice and making of journalism; becoming increasingly appreciated as a *distinct* source of information. Journalism's notion of objectivity is linked to a view of the news as a flow of information and journalists, as conduits of this flow, (presumably with special professional training that makes them well-suited for the task of presenting "objective news.") Popularly, the term objectivity has been conflated with ideas about "truth" and "fact" and thus, by presenting the news as objective it is implied that it is factual in so far as there is a true and knowable version of some reality, this being the version that journalists present. However, even if one believes that there are true and knowable realities to be reported on, this is not how the practice of objectivity operates within commercial journalism. In the confines of journalism, a newsmaker can make all sorts of claims if they are validated by expert or eye-witness sources. In other words, claims can be made when they are legitimated through the particular channels journalists have set up to maintain a system of checks and balances. Furthermore, the notion of one true and "objective" reality simply doesn't hold up and what we are left with is the realization that the one thing journalists can't escape is their own subjectivity. Many scholars of journalism argue that objectivity is the biggest myth and distorter of all.[7]

For this project, claims of objectivity are just as important as they would be, for any analysis of journalistic representation, but also raise additional questions. Are journalists able to maintain an image of objectivity during the reporting of tragic events? How does this differ from print to media culture? Michael Schudson[8] has insightfully argued that during national tragedies, journalists openly abandon claims to neutrality that normally help define their profession and their professional authority. Similarly, Daniel Dayan and Elihu Katz[9] argue that "media events" provide television journalists an opportunity to abandon neutrality. The case is easily made when considering September 11th and moments such as

CBS anchor Dan Rather telling late night host David Letterman that he is not a reporter, he is an American (in the midst of his ongoing coverage of the event and its aftermath). In his final television appearance before his death television news anchor Peter Jennings, dying of lung cancer, admitted to being "weak" after September 11th and smoking cigarettes again. This was the last message Jennings offered the American public. Despite examples of journalists disclosing their own subjectivity, only a detailed analysis of press coverage of multiple major events can really show us how and when this occurs, and the extent to which it is normative.

In addition to professional notions of objectivity, journalists use particular kinds of frameworks for telling their stories. These practices reflect several interrelated realities: the cultural context in which journalists operate (which provides a shared context full of previous narratives, images, stereotypes, and so forth), the commercial context of journalism (requiring that journalists create compelling narratives for public consumption), as well as the institutional or structural context of news making (decisions are not made in a vacuum but rather, are a collaboration between reporters, editors, publishers, and to varying degrees—advertisers).

In order to meet commercial demands and to legitimize themselves as the major information-bearing community within society, individual reporters share in the decision-making process within news organizations. They are influenced by a range of factors including industry standards as judged by editors and publishers, formal and/or informal pressure from advertisers, as well as the medium within which they work. As media scholar Barbie Zelizer[10] articulates, enmeshed within all of this is the fact that the profession as a whole reinvents its own place of prominence within the culture, not through day-to-day reporting, but through the canonization of major events which greatly increase their audience size and perceived importance. The circulation of daily newspapers always increases during important events.[11] Furthermore, individual journalists, themselves engaged in their own career-building can also use events in order to develop authority and gain a sense of value often missing from the day-to-day work of journalism, most of which occurs outside of old-school romantic notions of investigative reporting (which constitutes a very small percentage of what journalists actually do). A central part of the process by which journalists ultimately help construct iconic events, are the frameworks and techniques used for reporting. This speaks to the cultural dimension of news making.

First, when the press defines an event as having considerable social significance they may alert the public to the historic quality of the event in different ways. These techniques include extensive representation in newspapers or a non-stop looping on television, using language in ways that point to the historic qualities of the event, and providing context, situating it in relation to other events. Sociologist Iwona Irwin-Zarecka[12] refers to these initial representations as "instant memory." First impressions can be lasting and so these early interpretations are important in that they may subsequently appear as a naturally occurring chronological record.

In addition to marking the event with relevance, the press immediately provides a basic understanding of the facts, which as seen later in this chapter, are often changed as additional information becomes available. This factual baseline of "who, what, where and when" is linked to the manner in which journalists typically present stories. Print news traditionally follows an inverted-pyramid structure where a story begins with a lead, then addresses the "who, what, where, when" (and sometimes why), and then goes through key features of the story topically and by order of importance.[13] Television journalists have an additional fear to contend with, namely—the remote control. Television news has to be catchy and flashy to keep a viewer with a presumed limited attention span from switching stations. This is part of the reason that television news follows a thematic structure. Journalists employ other conventions in their reporting as well.

Even if we are to assume best faith efforts at objectivity and "factual" reporting, there is no escaping the fact that journalists serve as social interpreters, the "why" being open to subjective reasoning—a license for the journalist to offer an opinion within the guise of "objective" reporting. Furthermore, they are communicators, and their primary mode of communication is narrative or storytelling. For example, the use of present tense in leads to create immediacy (also giving the impression of being a trusted "inside" source), the enlarging of print, photographs, human-interest writing, and the general narrative frames through which journalists ultimately tell stories (complete with central characters). All of these facets of American journalism are best understood, not just conceptually, but rather by looking empirically at coverage of events that later became iconic. By using empirical data, the nuances of how the press presents current events and the nature of their role in capturing the public's imagination reveals itself.

The question guiding this chapter is: what stories do the American press spin for the culture as they report in the days and weeks following an event they have deemed important? How are events that later become mythic within the culture, initially represented to the public? The repository of print or multimedia representations that the press creates, comes to comprise "the represented event" which is *the initial mass-mediated version of the event constructed in the news*. This version carries historical significance because it is how citizens first come to think about a given national or international event. Moreover, the accumulation of representations created during this time serve as the baseline public memory of the event, and therefore, the backdrop against which all future representations are measured. With this in mind, what kinds of narratives did the mainstream press spin for society when Titanic sank?

On April 14th, 1912 RMS Titanic, popularly referred to as "the Ship of Dreams" hit an iceberg at 11:40pm and sank in under three hours. The ship carried lifeboats for over half of the passengers yet only 705 were rescued while 1,503 people, disproportionately third-class passengers, died in the freezing waters of the Atlantic. How did American newspaper journalists initially interpret this event and communicate ideas about it?

A Near Miss: April 15th 1912 Day One Titanic Newspaper Coverage

On April 15th 1912 the Titanic collision was front page news across the U.S. White Star officials reported they were "not worried about [the] liner." The Vice President of White Star Line, Mr. Franklin, was quoted saying that he was confident the ship was in good condition and that his long-time friend Captain Smith would have known what to do. White Star reports praised Smith. Representatives from the construction company that built Titanic were also quoted saying that the ship was "surely safe." They explained that the ship would not have sunk because two of the watertight compartments could completely flood and the ship would remain afloat. *The press went with this story.*

Having been given misinformation and without waiting for further corroboration, newspapers reported that there had been a major collision but that, ultimately, the ship and its passengers had survived.[14] While Titanic was not represented as a national tragedy until the next day, this first day of reporting reveals hints about how the event would later be interpreted. On the 15th the *Denver Post*[15] lead headline read: "Largest Steamer in World Hits an Iceberg; 1,500 Passengers in Peril for Many Hours" which was followed up with "Carpathia, Answering Signals by Wireless, Rescues All Aboard Disabled Ship."[16] Despite the initial mistake in claiming all had survived, which severely downgraded the seriousness of the event, recurring themes still emerged. On this first day two major issues developed. First, detailed information was distributed as factual. The techniques by which this occurred, revealed current shortcomings of American journalism, as within a day, much of this early reporting would be discounted. Second, in spite of erroneous reporting, the initial reports contained themes that would become a part of many future Titanic representations, including social class (specifically the wealthy), technology in the incident (specifically radio), and the evocation of religious imagery. What follows is a brief review of the misinformation presented as the "who, what, where and when."

In addition to reporting that the ship Carpathia "presumably" rescued all of the passengers, journalists reported that other ships also hurried to the scene and though damaged, Titanic was able to travel under its own steam to Halifax.

Newspapers reported the time of the collision as being 10:25pm though all future reports would put the collision at around 11:40pm. The weather was reported to be clear at the time of the collision, information which supposedly came directly from the ship's wireless operator. Other eyewitness claims were made, though they would all later prove to be totally wrong. For example, evoking images of God, several articles described passengers praying that other ships had picked up their wireless signals. Descriptive language was used to paint a picture. In this vein the *Denver Post* reported that passengers prayed that their ship would not become "a living tomb." Additionally, wireless technology was reported as being the hero of the near disaster. The use of specifics such as numbers of those in peril, names, time, weather reports and eyewitness accounts—the markers of *authentic* temporally ordered history within print culture—shaped the reports so that they appeared to be documentary, as if the press were simply reporting a "truth" versus piecing together a story about unfolding events. This connects to the major themes during that first day of reporting.

As noted, wireless technology received considerable coverage. Many reporters wrote that the collision of Titanic was the most shocking news from the sea since "wireless telegraphy."[17] One article, similar to many across the nation, showed a picture of Titanic that took almost the entire top half of the newspaper page. The caption underneath read: " . . .The picture shows a decided innovation in the absence of all masts save one, to be used for the crow's nest for the lookouts, as a signal mast and for the suspension of the aerials of the wireless telegraph . . ."[18] On this day, the press took the hopeful, poetic position that the modern technological progress materialized in Titanic, was also its ultimate rescuer.

The last theme to emerge, centered on the mystique of Titanic as a luxury liner. Newspapers all ran major stories about the "many notables" aboard. Many articles also offered detailed accounts about the wealthy who were saved. John Jacob Astor was uniformly the first to be listed as saved by the Carpathia. The immediate listing of names, only of the first and second class passengers of note, created a foundation for who would be written about as the stars of the Titanic story. The next day, the public learned that Mr. Astor was one of the 1,503 who died after refusing to accept a place in a lifeboat.

Given what actually happened, it is interesting that there was barely any mention of the near collision that Titanic almost had during departure, even though officials knew about the near miss. In the *Denver Post* there was one small article placed further back in the newspaper than any other Titanic story and amid an array of national interest pieces. The article failed to state Titanic's inability to maneuver, as the cause of the near miss but rather, referred to the suction created by the large liner in relation to the smaller cruiser New York.

White Star funneled the most positive, perhaps hopeful, version of events to the press and that was the story they ran with, while simultaneously setting up who and what would become memorable in later reporting. After reading the first-day newspaper accounts, one would likely be left thinking this: on its maiden voyage the "unsinkable" Titanic, which carried wealthy Americans including John Jacob Astor, had an accident but due to technological prowess, the ship and its passengers were saved.

Journalism's Treatment of the Titanic Event

On April 16th 1912 newspapers informed Americans that Titanic had sank and over half the ship's passengers had died; however, this number was misreported and headlines read that 866 had been rescued when only 705 were actually rescued[19]. Newspapers from this day and consistently for weeks thereafter, did several things: First, journalists marked the event with major social significance, next they spun ideas about gender and social class through their coverage, and lastly they determined who were to be the central historic figures of this narrative—including heroes and villains.

The press immediately marked the event with social significance. This primarily occurred in three ways. First, the event received saturation coverage, filling newspaper pages from cover to cover for weeks. The sheer extent of reporting alone imbues an event with meaning. Second, journalists wrote extensively about the uniqueness of the ship itself, particularly its size and technological advances. While *The New York Times* used a photograph of Titanic in Belfast Harbor, most American newspapers selected pictures that made the size of Titanic stand out. For example, the *Denver Post* used an illustration comparing Titanic to Denver's business district. Many regional newspapers used this technique and presented illustrations comparing Titanic to local city streets or landmarks in order to denote a sense of the ship's mammoth size. Third, the Titanic disaster was uniformly presented as a great loss of important capitalists. This is fleshed out when discussing the themes of journalistic interpretations, but for now, it is sufficient to note that emphasizing human loss imbued the event with historic meaning.

Journalists developed two major themes: the great loss of wealthy men, and that women and children were saved first. Furthermore, the way in which these stories were written and placed in newspapers, painted a picture that the loss of great men was linked to the saving of women and children. This resulted from the disproportionate coverage and the frequency with which these themes appeared on front pages and in headlines as well as the juxtaposing of stories in relation to each other. The content and form consistently employed by journalists, served these two interrelated themes. In terms of form, Titanic stories primarily followed conventions of plot-driven storytelling written through simplistic characters of exceptionally good or bad character helping to lend the story a stereotypical, easy to understand thread. Throughout all Titanic reporting, the content of most stories focused on these two themes.

The Construction of Male Heroism

The association of Titanic with the loss of wealthy men was swift and uniform. On the 16th *The New York Times* reported "Noted Names Missing"[20] and mentioned that Bruce Ismay and Mrs. Astor were probably safe. The sub-headings reported that Colonel Astor, Isador Straus and Major Butt were aboard and that the "Rule of Sea"[21] was followed. An additional sub-heading read: "Women and Children First."[22] *The New York Times*, as did many other papers, also printed a partial list of survivors including only upper class passengers. Next to some first class names it read "and maid." the *Denver Post* similarly reported "Kings of Finance, Captains of Industry; World-Famed Men Who Went Down in Titanic."[23] The list that followed was not alphabetical but rather, hierarchical with men being listed by wealth, beginning with John Jacob Astor. In many newspapers throughout April only the first and second-class passengers were listed among the dead. Other article headlines included: "List of Dead Includes Notable Men of Affairs"[24], "Bravery Shown by Men Passengers"[25], "585 Women and Children Aboard."[26] The paper also contained two human interest pieces about John Jacob Astor and his wife as well as Molly Brown and other "Rich Denverites." *The New York Times* included photographs of some of the "notable passengers." The article, like many that would follow, included Astor, Guggenheim and Widener; however, three out of the twelve photographs were of women. The women portrayed were the wives of those three men and were referred to exclusively as their wives. Titanic articles consistently included photographs of the dead which serves two main functions in journalistic storytelling. First, it matches faces to a major developing news story. This is a staple practice in the building of event collective memory. Giving a story a "human face" creates an emotional connection between the consumer and the event.[27] Second, this technique informs citizens as to who the key players in an event are. Journalists routinely wrote about wealthy, white, male passengers using the terms heroism, courage, bravery, chivalry, and gallantry. According to media scholar John Storey "powerful elites" are most frequently the subject of hero transformation within dominant mediums.[28] The press of 1912 ultimately constructed Astor, Guggenheim, Widener, Mr. and Mrs. Straus and Captain Smith as heroes. In contrast, the American media crucified Bruce Ismay and immediately characterized him as a coward for having taken a place in a lifeboat. In cartoon illustrations he was often imaged as sneaking into a lifeboat wearing a woman's shawl. (The Titanic Historical Society continues to validate Ismay's saving of himself and charges the press with failing to hold Captain Smith responsible for the disaster).

At this point, two things are clear. First and most specifically, journalists spun Titanic as a story about the wealthy, reinforcing the myth that the ship was solely a luxury liner and suppressing investigative journalism into the larger role that social class and ethnicity played in the Titanic event. In this vein, several of the wealthy male passengers started to become the central figures that Titanic narratives would forever rely. Second, and more generally, something larger about the role of culture on the practice of journalism at that time, is revealed. Namely, the social climate in which journalists were operating clearly impacted their reporting of the event. Can one imagine newspapers after 9-11, listing the missing or dead by social class, and wholly eliminating contingents of the dead, solely based on their social class? In fact, as seen later, journalists took a very different route in this regard after 9-11, focusing on the mundane and ordinary qualities of the victims as evidenced by *The New York Times* "Portraits of Grief"[29] which listed victims' unexceptional qualities and bonded 9-11 victims as "Americans" and *not* individuals. This is not at all to imply that journalists in 2001 were less influenced by cultural factors than their 1912 counterparts, but rather to offer one example of the role cultural bias plays in journalistic practice.

Newspaper reporters were quick to run with the story of "Women and Children First." One representative headline from the *Denver Post* read: "Wives Dragged From Husbands to Safety"[30] and was followed up with "Scantily-Clad Women and Children float to safety as they watch their loved ones perish."[31] The story underneath read: "Bravery of Those Facing Certain Death Makes Chapter in History."[32] The linking of stories about women being forcibly saved, to male heroism was routine, creating the connotation that bravery was gendered and classed: the wealthy men listed are the ones that exhibited "historic" bravery. Another example of this is a set of photographs of "Famous Men" who drowned in one newspaper column, four photographs with the headline "Two Prominent Women Saved and Two Men Who Were Drowned"[33] on the other column. The use of photographs also reinforced for future narratives, who the key players were, perhaps more generally.

Newspapers circulated stereotypes about gender as they constructed heroes out of upper-class male passengers and vilified the poor. A recurring dominant theme was that "the rule of the sea" was followed. This meant that men had saved women and children before themselves. Journalists developed this myth in several ways all of which allowed them to use a hero-villain plot line that was already resonant in the culture. First, there were many stories of male bravery positing that men ensured women were saved by gallantly "following the rule of sea" which was at times accomplished by actually dragging them from their husbands. This kind of narrative spun two ideas: First, men were chivalrous and this benefited women who were saved in greater numbers than men. Chivalry was often used as the marker of heroism, thus gendering heroism. Second, women of the upper-class behaved badly, and some delayed rescue attempts by refusing entry into boats. In fact, many journalists crucified women of the upper-class for this reason without exploring whether or not they had been informed about the impending sinking. The other major and contradictory gendered theme that the press created was a "survival of the fittest" narrative that questioned the rule of the sea, not as indicative of gender discrimination towards women, but rather as having caused the loss of great and reportedly heroic men. Journalists further created heroic figures out of the wealthy by comparing them to the third-class passengers in highly raced and classed ways. The following is an example of how gender, race, and class were written about with regards to the popular "rule of the sea" and survival of the fittest narratives.

The following is an excerpt from an article titled "Men of Brains and Millions Sacrificed for Lowly Women: By the Inexorable Law of the Sea, Which Demands Salvation of Women First, Nation Suffers Untold Loss" that appeared in the *Denver Post*. This article is representative of the ways in which gender, race, and class were routinely written about in newspapers.

> When men go down to sea in ships, chivalry flowers like the rod of Aaron. The wreck of Titanic serves notice to the civilized world that men are as brave and unselfish today as when poets wrote their lives and proclaimed their deeds, and by this latest ocean horror does the question arise concerning the truth or fallacy of the survival of the fittest law. There is a law of the sea- unwritten and inelastic- which decrees that, in times of peril, men must give way while women and children are passed to safety. It is a law which levels all social and race distinctions; a law out of which springs much injustice; if the good of society is to be balanced against individual worth. But it is a law that now and again makes creatures made in the image of God worthy of the model . . . The steerage, new and shining, was filled with creatures wearing of the dragging, dreary days of the old world- bound for what they considered liberty and the great chance . . . Huddling together, the chattering women envied the lovely ladies who came to look at them, wrapped warm in rich furs; the men, lifting their eyes, vowed to someday be as the elegant gentlemen, and the filmy-eyed children of peasants were quite willing to play with the little ones in smart sea togs, who, with their parents or nurses, were brought to look at them. . . There were men whose services to humanity cannot be computed . . . There were beautiful women whose aim was pleasure- only . . . And here steps in the law of the sea. The women and children go first- after them, if there be room, the men may have place in the life boats. The law is inexorable. John Jacob Astor owns two hundred million dollars worth of property; he is newly married to a fair young woman and to them is soon to be born an heir. Chattering near by is a peasant woman, holding fast to a low-browed man who clasps in his arms a child marked with the blight of Europe- a child that will be denied entrance to

the United States . . . John Jacob Astor would give all he possesses for the place of that woman and child in the lifeboat. He is a citizen of the country toward which they are drifting; in a way, he has been among the builders, and has proved himself loyal in the time of the country's need. Why can't he now buy what he wants? Because of the law that based on a sentimental ideal of manly courage and chivalry which bids men hold back, or be forever branded as cowards and bullies! . . . So Major Archibald Butt bows to the Law of the Sea and beholds a hallow-chested, bleary-eyed woman, gibbering strange sounds, assigned a place in the boats while the cold waters of Death creep nearer and nearer to him and his friends . . . The disease-bitten child, whose life at the best is worthless, and whose value as a prospective citizen of the United States is less than worthless, goes to safety with the rest of the steerage riff-raff, while the handler of great affairs, the men who direct the destinies of hundreds of thousands of workers, the learned men whose talents are dedicated to the cure of physical afflictions; writers whose words are as burning lamps in troubled darkness, and whose energies have uplifted humanity, stand unprotestingly aside. This acknowledgement of the Law of the Sea is the grandest exhibition that exists of the working of the code which protects the weaker element in the face of certain death, without taking note of their worthiness . . . It leaves women helpless in their widowhood, and thrusts them on the cold charity of a society which is resentful against them for taking room that might have been given to someone who makes the world better and stronger by his presence . . . The despair in the heart of the coughing peasant woman faded, perhaps, as she found that for her there was a place in the rocking boat by the side of the white-faced lady of the splendid furs. By every law of common sense and reasoning, the passenger list of Titanic should have been combed . . . The Law of the Sea is chiseled on the tablets of Time, and it cannot be changed. On its endurance depends, to a great extent, the continuance of genuine manliness... John Jacob Astor going to a sea burial is a far more important figure than John Jacob Astor ever could be by owning unusual quantities of money. Probably he stood shoulder to shoulder with a hulk of flesh from Austria or Italy and embraced his brother with a cheering word as the cold waters flowed over them . . .[34]

It would not be until 1998 that the press would report Astor probably did not offer a kind word to his "Ethnic brother" because the third-class gates were locked.

This article and the countless others like it, communicated several messages to the public. The press relied extensively on gendered stereotypes as well as interrelated stereotypes pertaining to social class and ethnicity. In this way the press interpreted Titanic via prejudices particular to the time, that were not simply about gender or class but rather interconnections *between* gender and class. As a result women of the upper-class were trivialized and portrayed as shallow and helpless, women of the third class were characterized as pathetic, men of the third class were portrayed in animalistic and violent terms, and selected men of the upper class were represented as heroes. Religious imagery was repeatedly used to construct male heroes, for example comparing male chivalry to "the rod of Aaron." In this way the press connected ideals of Christian virtue with male heroism further reinforcing their biblical tale of good and evil.

By creating narratives asserting that the rule of the sea saved women and also cost the lives of great American men, and simultaneously questioning why important men had to die so that stereotypically feminine women might be saved, women were in fact represented as weak on two counts. Women needed male protection because of physical inferiority and likewise, women were weak in character, morality, and intellect because they "allowed" men to be sacrificed so that they might be saved. Moreover, the reporting is explicitly racist.

Isolating a particular element of Chinese politics, newspapers across the country brought "Chinamen" into Titanic reporting by claiming that if Titanic had been a Chinese vessel, men would have been saved first, then children and last women. *The Denver Post* reported this on April 17th and *The New York Times* on April 18th. Journalists asserted that men are saved first in China because it is culturally recognized that they are the most valuable citizens. Furthermore, children can always be adopted but women without husbands become useless and destitute. These articles signal the tensions within the gendered narratives that dominated newspapers in April 1912. The "Chinamen" pieces were placed near articles claiming that, *by law*, women must be saved first. In this context the racialized language through which Chinese policy is expressed seems natural. Chinese men were cowards, just as Bruce Ismay.[35] However, the same newspapers circulated many articles that attacked the rule of the sea, and the women, whom purportedly benefited from it. In this way the article about Chinese policy was used as a vehicle for opening a space to discuss abolishing the rule of the sea, though ironically on the basis of gender inequality for men, not for women.

Of note is also the press' extensive but highly limited consideration of class in the Titanic experience. This is important because it helps explain why, almost a century later, "women and children first" continues to be a prominent theme in Titanic interpretations even though the implementation of that policy was explicitly linked to social class. Moreover, while journalists focused a great deal on the disproportionate saving of women as compared with men, they did not report the disproportionate saving of the wealthy as compared with third-class passengers. In fact, a content analysis of newspapers articles reveals that class and race narratives were almost entirely written through the lens of gender, and the gendered hero narrative, thereby making gender the primary issue to come out of early interpretations.

Linked to the use of extreme stereotypes, the press also wrote stories that appear, in retrospect, to have been completely fictitious and derived solely from stringing together dominant stereotypes, prevalent at the time. For example, the press reported conversations between Astor, Butt, and third-class women and children that never occurred, nor did they offer *any* evidence that such interactions had occurred. In these instances journalists constructed entirely fictive narratives out of stereotypes, creating mini-plots based on these fallacies. These narratives were presented as informational and appeared amongst reports about "factual" aspects of the event—all of which had the combined effect of masking any journalist subjectivity. Additionally, many articles contained eye-witness accounts and survivor quotes that served similar myths about how gender and social class played out in the tragedy. Generally speaking, survivor accounts are very persuasive, as they come from the only people who directly experienced the event. In the case of traumatic events, it is certainly difficult (if not impossible) to challenge the recollection of a survivor. With this said, the survivors quoted in early Titanic stories, were all in the upper class. Crew members were interviewed as well, and again, their personal motivations for recalling the events in particular ways, were never questioned.

Visual imagery, beyond photographs, is also a tool that journalists may employ as they narrate current events. Cartoon illustrations were an important component in the construction of Titanic collective memory[36] and were frequently used to represent Captain Smith's noble death, Astor and Guggenheim's bravery in the face of death, and Mr. and Mrs. Strauss' emotional death scene. The *Denver Post* produced a number of illustrations portraying crewmen with revolvers holding back poverty stricken and unruly male steerage passengers that were depicted attempting to "illegally" enter the lifeboats before women. While these powerful images explicitly pertain to race and class, they also represent gender-specific male actions.

These cartoon images reinforced the hero-villain narratives circulating in the press and matched powerful visual images to the gendered and classed stories that the press were writing. First, the cartoons portrayed the crewmen as brave. These images began after April 19th (when the United States Senate begin its official inquiry into the incident) and are important because they presented the public a visual image of the crew "following the law of the sea" which counteracted reports (under-reported in newspapers) from passengers, that the crew unnecessarily used guns to thwart the attempts of immigrants to save themselves (only a few of those who had been positioned to witness the actions lived to tell). These images also fostered cultural beliefs that the lower-class passengers were cowardly, which was then juxtaposed with the white faces of brave men such as Astor who died "calmly." Furthermore, many illustrations reinforced gendered narratives including the saving of women, the idleness of upper-class women, and third-class women portrayed as peasants.

The Press Narrative about Titanic

A review of early Titanic reporting reveals several phenomena. First, the event was immediately marked with social significance through compelling language, print size, graphics, and the several week-long monopolization of newspaper space. A great many of the stories were "human interest" pieces that focused on passengers, their stories being framed as hero-villain narratives.

Extreme stereotypes about social class and gender circulated through Titanic coverage, creating the idea that wealthy men were the heroes of the event, women were saved regardless of status, and third-class male passengers acted in animalistic ways. The use of lists and photographs, which focused entirely on the wealthy passengers, reinforced who the key players of the story were while excluding others. Initial journalistic interpretations also resulted in time-tested myths of "women and children first" and the mythical concepts of heroism and cowardice which were then available for transfer into other stories.

The next section provides an analysis of how the American press presented Columbine, Pearl Harbor, and September 11th to the public. Patterns in journalistic practice with regards to significant current events begin to emerge when compared across genre, considering scope and historical time period.

The Press Narrates the Columbine Shootings Creating a Site of Moral Panic

The 1999 shooting spree at Columbine High School is the largest incident of school violence in U.S. history and was unquestionably a tragic event. The initial attention it was paid in the press, as with all the events in this book, therefore makes sense. Having said this, the volume of that initial reporting (round-the-clock television coverage and newspapers filled with Columbine narratives) does not seem proportionate to the significance of the event. Columbine was tragic but it was not an event that changed the course of human history or that even temporarily impacted the world on a global level. Furthermore, only fifteen people died in Columbine (two by suicide). At best, Columbine can be categorized as a middle-range event (arguably on the lower end of this category). What makes the apparent over-reporting of Columbine more curious is that it occurred during the "conflict" in Kosovo which received considerably less coverage. In fact, a major bombing occurred in Kosovo on the day of Columbine. Therefore, it is important to examine the volume of Columbine reporting in its multi-media forms as well as the substantive content of that reporting. How did the press initially mark this event and proceed to make sense of it? What stories about good and evil and the nation's "youth" did journalists produce for the culture?

What ideas about race and gender circulated via early Columbine reports? How did Columbine stories bump up against Kosovo reports?

The press immediately marked the Columbine shootings with historic significance thereby setting the stage for Columbine to acquire iconic status within the culture. This occurred primarily, in two ways. First, as pointed out, the amount of coverage that the event received was itself historic. Second, the language and categories of interpretation used by journalists marked it with significance.

At 11:47am on April 20, 1999, the first news-station learned of the events unfolding at Columbine High School in Littleton, Colorado. Soon after, a barrage of news cameras and reporters traveled to the school to capture the event. From that point and continuing for more than a week, Columbine became the subject of saturation coverage, appearing on television news in a 24-hour cycle while comprising a great deal of space in newspapers, magazines, and Internet news. For example, *The New York Times* ran eight front page stories in the first four days following the event while the *Denver Post* was filled, cover to cover, with Columbine stories. The coverage included the extreme repetition of two images, selected from extensive video coverage, one of which showed students running outside of the building with their hands on their heads and a second an image of a bloody boy dangling from a broken window as he was being rescued. What these two images have in common is that they both portray the extreme fear experienced by innocent young people. Through their widespread repetition these two images became iconic and came to represent not only Columbine, but school violence in the United States, as Columbine became used as the signifier of such violence.

It is important to note that because the press represented Columbine on a 24-hour loop, indicating that it was the only happening of import, other news stories were pushed to the peripheries. The situation in Kosovo, which the press and state uniformly referred to as a "conflict," was relegated to an occasional mention in the runner at the bottom of the television screen. This configuration, which continued for weeks, normalized the narrative of Columbine as a bloodbath and Kosovo as marginal.

Returning to initial Columbine reporting, in addition to the monopoly afforded Columbine on the cultural landscape, journalists also framed Columbine in very particular ways. The event was instantly labeled a "massacre" on most networks with headlines like "Massacre at Columbine" while the second most evoked word was "terror" as illustrated in headlines such as "Terror in the Rockies."[37] The mediated version of the event always classified Columbine as a massacre. There was never an interpretive frame of the event that was free from the categories "massacre" and "terror" and so the public consumed it as such. The use of superlatives helped to mark the event with a historic quality. The two iconic images mentioned earlier, both clearly disturbing, were often used in conjunction with the words "massacre" and "terror" thus illustrating and legitimizing these interpretive categories. There is no doubt that for those directly involved in the event, it was a day of terror. This does not diminish the need to question the press classification of the event through the lens of "terror" (which perhaps becomes clearer when thinking about how 9-11 was also labeled in this way. Clearly these two events are not equivalent in terms of loss of life, material destruction or long-range global impact.)

In addition to breadth of coverage and the massacre/terror frame used, the press quickly developed several themes in their Columbine stories and also employed a standard script for narrating the event to the American public. The press immediately created characters for their narrative, thus determining which of the victims would receive prominence in the Columbine story and who would be relegated to the margins. Furthermore, the press constructed their narrative using several techniques (that are difficult to challenge) including interviews with survivors and the bereaved, live images, lists of the dead with photos, and a range of human interest stories including individual commemorations. Finally, the press engaged in some unusual practices to further mark the event with significance, including the live broadcast of funerals.

Newspaper Coverage of Columbine

From April 21st through May 4th, the two-week period following the event, Columbine was the main story in both *The New York Times* and the *Denver Post*. The *Denver Post*, given the local significance, covered the story almost exclusively during those weeks while each day, *The New York Times* featured multiple Columbine stories, prominently. Journalists at both newspapers referred to the event with the same kind of language already embedded in the public's consciousness. The *Denver Post* showed the picture of students fleeing with their hands on their heads and headlines that read:

"High School Massacre"[38]
"Columbine Bloodbath"

The New York Times front-page headline used the words "Siege" and "Terror." All of the language and imagery used, reinforced the singularity of the event, in the fear-driven way that developed in the preceding twenty-four hours.

The most interesting dimension of front-page representation emerges when looking at the mapping of the *entire* front page. On April 21st, 22nd, and 30th, *The New York Times* front page consisted of three side-by-side stories, with Columbine favored. Referred to in "terror" language, Columbine was placed alongside a Kosovo story and a story about racial profiling (at the time there was a widely publicized case involving New Jersey police officers). On April 22nd the editorials page was also configured in this way, again privileging the Columbine story.

"The Colorado School Slayings"[39]
"Racial Profiling in New Jersey"[40]
"Keeping Ethnic Tensions From Turning Violent"[41]

Despite this layout, the recurring theme of racism on local and global levels prevalent in all three stories, was *never* explored. This illustrates the press reporting stories that all have clear and direct connections to larger issues about racism, yet the three contained stories, placed next to each other, were reported in complete isolation from each other, as if each "reality" existed in its own vacuum. This did not occur once, but *four times* in *The New York Times*, three of which were on the front page. The press, thus had an opportunity to create a complex discourse about race, but did not take advantage of this and arguably went well out of their way to ignore the possible interconnectivity. The privileging of Columbine as the center story, given the widespread consequences of Kosovo and racial profiling in the United States, marginalized what might otherwise have been presented as the more serious events. A story's placement is therefore an important way in which a hierarchy of significance is created, seeming to appear natural. This is reminiscent of the initial reporting of Titanic, to the exclusion of reporting the lynching of an African-American man on the same day, the latter of which, was at the time, a national problem.[42]

The press immediately and uniformly constructed a simplistic meta-narrative about Columbine presenting it through a standard dualistic, good versus evil script, similar to the Titanic meta-narrative and dependent on the repetition of the villain, hero, and martyr concepts. This script reinforced the labeling of the event as an act of "terror" and also allowed for the continued writing of human interest pieces in which players in the event were repeatedly characterized as heroes, villains or martyrs. This kind of writing, focusing on individuals, created an emotional connection between the event and the public which then allowed for the disproportionate coverage of the event which in turn served press mandates of commercial success, and legitimized journalistic authority over an event of (purported) import.

The press narrative went like this: two atypical troubled "youth" committed a heinous violent act against innocent and brave "god-loving" heroes. Press stories consistently juxtaposed the villain and hero or villain and martyr concepts so that stories about the killers were always contrasted with stories about the

courageous, peaceful and often god-loving victims who were immediately classified as heroes and martyrs. Just as in the case of Titanic, photographs of the
victims often accompanied the articles, putting a human face to the tragedy. The
following are some of the headlines derived from the "good versus evil" dualism.

"True Courage in Time of Terror"[43]
"Carnage and Courage at Columbine High School"
"In The Face of Evil, Human Decency Triumphs"[44]
"Courage in the Face of Evil"[45]

Columbine was written as a story about individuals who possess exceptionally
negative or positive qualities.

The villain part of the press narrative focused on labeling the gunmen as
outcasts. In each instance in which the "outcast" story was reported, two sub-
narratives circulated: the "Trenchcoat Mafia" and "goth youths." The self-
proclaimed trenchcoat mafia was a clique of students who self-identified as outsiders within the school social system. Klebold and Harris were marginally involved with this group though initial media reports linked the killings to mem-
bership in this group—whose defining characteristic was that they dressed in
dark clothes. The stories referring to the trench coat mafia and goth culture
(identified in the media by particular styles of music and dress) were generally
presented with a photograph of that group. Most articles on these subjects had
headlines that began with a horror-filled word, most frequently "carnage."

"Carnage Puts Spotlight on Trench Coat Mafia"[46]

The content of these stories focused almost exclusively on teenage isolation,
disconnection, and the alienation of outcasts who, beyond their desperate mar-
ginalization, shared an interest in dark clothing and gothic music (which was
narrowly defined by repeated reference to Marilyn Manson and messages of
"apocalyptic rage"). Through the style, layout, repetition and substantive content
of these initial narratives, clear connotations were created. Headlines with
bolded words like carnage naturalized this as a highly dangerous association.
Chapter four explores the social and political relevance of this press narrative.

Simultaneous to the construction of the two gunmen as villains, several of
the victims were quickly branded as heroes and martyrs. In particular, the coach
(the only adult to be killed) who had reportedly stayed behind to help others
escape was quickly transformed into a hero. The press routinely circulated the
story of Cassie, a blond Caucasian student who reportedly was asked at gunpoint
"Do you believe in God?" When Cassie responded "yes" she was shot, fatally.
The press classified her as a martyr. Rachel Scott, one of the first two students
killed, was quickly given a prominent place in press narratives. On the day of

the event, the brother of victim Rachel Scott, who had himself been in a room where he watched others murdered, including an African-American boy who was racially targeted, was interviewed on live television. Classified as "all-American" the pretty Caucasian Rachel Scott would become one of the press' most written about victims, (in fact Oprah Winfrey would later refer to her as "the face" of Columbine). The use of survivor accounts and interviews with the bereaved, allowed the press to focus on the exceptional qualities of the victims, and by contrast—the villainous act of the killers, in a way that appeared natural.

In service of the terror script, newspapers included maps of the school in order to visually represent how the events unfolded. Additionally, beyond articles describing injuries, typical in the reporting of school violence, the *Denver Post* included a photo of the victim (also typical) next to a sketch of a body marked with black dots to indicate the location of gunshots (not typical).

This very disturbing visual representation located amidst stories of "terror" and "massacre" served to create a sense of severe social significance similar to that, typically witnessed in the war genre. Likewise, such reporting made the villains' individual "evilness" an almost untouchable subject because it was, by connotation, so clear. This is not to imply that evil is necessarily an inappropriate category of interpretation but that such a narrative by definition, fails to consider systemic or situational factors that contribute to violence. I merely mean to point out that a highly individualistic narrative of good and evil was the *only* mainstream interpretation. Likewise, victimization can be represented without transforming victims into heroes and martyrs. Again, this does not mean that these concepts are inappropriate, but rather that they have been constructed to the complete exclusion of other possibilities.

Initial Columbine reporting becomes significant when examining the appropriation of Columbine for other political and cultural uses, which is detailed in the following chapters. For now, let's turn to Pearl Harbor and September 11th initial press representation.

September 11th: Instantly Iconic

As the American public came to learn of the events of September 11th, 2001 in a multi-media explosion of press narratives, they too, quite explicitly, bore witness to the making of an iconic event. September 11th received saturation coverage appearing in a multi-media loop for weeks, completely dominating the mediascape; however, differing from the Columbine High School shootings, the events of 9-11 unfolded almost entirely on television. Much like Columbine, many initial journalistic interpretations of the event were already infused with political agendas. With this said, this chapter focuses on how the press initially marked the event with social significance and the major frameworks used to convey meaning to the public. However, from the outset, the press narrative was based on patriotism, which was also a part of the official state response to the event. In this vein, and others, the initial reporting of the event was never totally free from political spin. Beyond this, several components of how the press presented 9-11 to the American public are also reviewed, including multi-media, saturation coverage, the script used to narrate 9-11, the human interest angle taken by the press, and the validating of the Bush administration's response to the events (which becomes significant in chapter four—when considering the political appropriations of September 11th).

Most American citizens learned about the events of September 11th on morning television. Morning programs either redirected their focus to the unfolding event or were suspended and changed to news coverage. The event was also immediately reported on radio and Internet news outlets. The initial reporting, primarily on live television, is central to how citizens came to view and remember the event. This is an important part of 9-11 collective memory. During the first forty-eight hours, 81 percent of Americans tuned into television for "crisis" coverage.[47, 48] This is significant because during a "state of emergency" the first representations are the ones to stick.[49] Furthermore, live moving images create a different impression than the kinds of illustrations that were found in newspapers in 1912, for example, when Titanic sunk. Many Americans later mused that they initially thought they were watching a clichéd Hollywood action film as in the absence of journalists delivering information, the initial moving images were reminiscent of standard movie scripts involving the destruction of national landmarks. In addition to watching the event unfold live, and mostly devoid of commentary as newsmakers too, were stunned and clearly did not know what was happening, the event initially took on a historic quality, because of its monopoly of the cultural space.

According to American journalists, on September 11th 2001 there was no other news story. It was a day in which one thing happened: "terrorists" attacked the United States. The first major way that the press and state imbued the event with historicity was labeling the event simply by the date. The event was immediately named "9-11" or "September 11th." This is historically unique as typically events are labeled by their genre or a combination of the location and date. By naming the event by the date alone it was implied that on that day, nothing else happened. This is even more significant as 911 is known by Americans as an emergency number. Once named, September 11th immediately took on extraordinary historicity because of how it was represented, receiving non-stop "saturation coverage." Interestingly, much of this early reporting was not based on providing citizens with new information, but rather, looping previously viewed images and commentary. Most of the early 9-11 reporting consisted of journalists in a live feed saying that they didn't know what was happening. Rather than discontinue coverage until new information emerged, the American press engaged, for several days, in a looping of the images of the World Trade Center Towers being struck and then collapsing.[50] As one scholar noted, "Into this void the networks rushed, to provide transparency without depth, a simulacrum of horror . . ."[51] In addition to the repetition of disturbing images, journalists framed the event in particular ways, using space and language to denote historical significance.

Newspaper Coverage of September 11th

Newspapers represented the event in ways that served to mark it with unprecedented national significance. First, the event entirely dominated newspapers, filling them for weeks. By the end of September 2001, 9-11 had so overtaken newspapers that *The New York Times* engaged in one of many reporting innovations (the publicizing of journalistic "innovations" also marked the event with meaning), by eventually deciding to return to covering other events, while still devoting ample space to the ongoing reporting of 9-11 and its aftermath, via the creation of a section called "A Nation Challenged" that dealt exclusively (and separately) with stories connected to 9-11 and its aftermath. This section ran until the end of that year. Newspapers broke with other formatting conventions that also signaled the singularity of the event. For example, for the first time in its nineteen-year history *USA Today* did not have its front-page ears and the *Atlanta Constitution* ran only one front-page story, breaking with its own established format.[52]

Journalists employed a range of storytelling techniques that presumed the magnitude of the event, including enlarging editions, providing bigger and bolder headlines, and using larger typeset and more pictures than typically found in newspapers.[53] When comparing newspaper typeset, 9-11 and Titanic headlines were clearly larger and bolder than in the reporting of all of the other events covered in this book, as well as normal daily newspaper reporting. Furthermore, for a two-week period following the event, *The New York Times* used more pictures than usual in their coverage of the event. Media scholars Zelizer and Allan note: "Every available resource was used to capture and convey the enormous scale of what was transpiring."[54]

Many newspapers across the country opted for one word headlines such as: "Attack!," "Outrage," and "Infamy"[55] (the latter of which is reminiscent of the political framing of Pearl Harbor). The *San Francisco Examiner* editor-in-chief viewed the event through the social memory of Pearl Harbor and, trying to come up with a creative headline chose "BASTARDS,"[56] *The New York Times* headline on September 12, 2001 read: "U.S. ATTACKED."[57] Front pages also showed disturbing images of the Twin Towers in various phases of the attack including with the planes striking, on fire, people jumping out of the towers, and the towers crumbling. These images, the same as were looped on television screens, became the primary images of the event.

As noted earlier, the use of imagery in newspaper reporting is an important part of how journalists narrate an event. In the case of 9-11, there was, it seems, a disjuncture between the images presented and the major stories that the images were meant to illustrate. Analysis of the "paper of record," *The New York Times*, indicates a contrast between the headlines and images, which seem to tell different stories with different emphases. The images selected do not necessarily illustrate the headlines but rather, make connotations between the words and the images which in many cases could be read as focusing on different aspects of the event. The front-page headline on September 13th 2001 read "Stunned Rescuers Comb Attack Sites, But Thousands are Presumed Dead; F.B.I. Tracking Hijackers' Movements."[58] The image underneath the headline was of rescuers going through the rubble in NYC, with an additional photo underneath of a firefighter who was crying. There weren't any photos of the hijackers or FBI officials. On September 14th the front-page headline read "Bush and Top Aides Proclaim Policy of 'Ending' States that Back Terror; Local Airports Shut Down After an Arrest."[59] Despite an emphasis on government policy and a 9-11 related event at an airport, the photo depicted signs of missing people from the Towers, with NYC residents mournfully reading the posters; beneath was a photo of a man waiving an American flag. Without any justification whatsoever regarding the appropriateness of the images used, as one can clearly understand a focus on the victims and plight of the bereaved, one can note a disjuncture between the focus of the words, and the images selected. Newspaper photographs are assumed to illustrate the story in a clear way; however, in much of 9-11 reporting, the imagery focused on the victims regardless of the focus of the stories. This is meaningful for several reasons not least of which is a connotation being created between peoples' pain and loss and other aspects of the event including foreign policy and war rhetoric to be borne out of the event (as seen shortly). Furthermore, the press kept loss and human suffering front and center in the public space.

The front page on September 15th exposes a slightly different issue regarding the placement of words and images. The headline read "Bush Leads Prayer, Visits Aid Crews; Congress Backs Use of Armed Force,"[60] and there was a picture of President Bush, Mayor Giuliani, and the Fire Commissioner at the site of the Towers. There was also a picture of three rescue workers crying and offering a salute. While the headline mentioned Bush's visit and did show that visit, the primary headline about "armed force" is not depicted by the illustration, but rather the imagery again focused on the anguish of loss. On the 16th the headline read "Bush Tells the Military to 'Get Ready': Broader Spy Powers Gaining Support."[61] The corresponding image was an aerial view of the site of the fallen towers. On the 17th the front-page headline read "Nation Shifts Its Focus to Wall Street as a Major Test of Attack's Aftermath."[62] Again, the image shown was the site where the Towers fell, an image of death and destruction. It was not until the 18th that the front-page photograph was not of the fallen towers, and literally illustrated the headline (which was about Wall Street reopening). What is of note here is not simply the choice to use images of what was labeled "ground zero," but rather, the fit between the images and the headlines as well as the perpetuation of horrifying images in the public sphere. It seems that the press opted for the most sensational images which may be linked to the commercial imperatives that drive their industry.

Beyond headlines and images, journalists also used particular kinds of language during their reporting. Winfield et al. found that newspapers uniformly used superlatives to identify the event as transformational for the United States and correspondingly constructed the event's historic quality.[63] Using "expert" commentators as they ascribed meaning[64] the press captured people's attention with remarkable statements such as: "the city changed forever;" "for the first time the nation's airspace was shut down;" "a defining day in US history, unlike any other."[65] Claims that the world had forever changed and that the nation was at war were immediate to the attacks, when officials didn't have a handle on the death count, the causes of the attacks, or future of the country (like in all of the iconic events in this book, the death count was initially overestimated and has been adjusted numerous times).

The press also used historical metaphors to imbue 9-11 with particular meaning. Winfield et al. explain that newspaper journalists selectively used history in order to ascribe 9-11 with meaning in multiple ways, including providing context and analogies to further denote the event's singularity. Journalists most commonly evoked Pearl Harbor as a historical metaphor through which to view September 11th.[66] Despite the absurdity of comparing 9-11 and Pearl Harbor, the American press repeatedly referenced Pearl Harbor in order to reify the turning-point quality they had afforded the event.[67] Furthermore, drawing on Pearl Harbor allowed the press to seamlessly evoke war rhetoric that was consistent with the state's response to the event. Arguably, the strength of using Pearl Harbor as a historical light-post was less about similarities between the events and more about tapping into a pre-existing repository of collective memory. This can itself be conceptualized as a mini "memory-project." The press intentionally activated Pearl Harbor collective memory which is deeply embedded in the American collective conscience allowing for the use of resonant phrases like "a date that will live in infamy" and "Ground Zero" as well as images such as the flag raising at Iwo Jima (itself a copy).

The effect of the saturation coverage, and repetition of images of destruction matched to a host of superlatives, is threefold. First, the event took on un paralleled significance in a way that appeared natural and thus, went largely unquestioned. In other words, the monopolistic media coverage imbued the event with a "turning point" quality characterizing it as a "historic marker."[68] The "world has changed forever" quality given to 9-11 by the press allowed the American government to do the same, and then, use the "these are new times" route as a means of pursuing, with public support, an otherwise risky and unlikely political agenda. Second, due to the unmatched significance that the event took on, it became normal to see it pop up in political and popular culture way beyond war rhetoric. Third, the tale of terror and evil that was also simultaneously promoted by the press and state (discussed later) was rhetorically legitimized by the looping of images of horror.

Beyond the "turning point" quality that the press afforded 9-11, they uniformly represented the event through a particular narrative frame, reliant on a standard American-centric script.

An Act of Evil: Terror, Heroism and Patriotism as Journalists' Narrative Frame

Beyond signaling the singularity of the event, journalists also informed the public as to the nature of the event and were therefore integral in explaining what had happened. Journalists uniformly presented 9-11 through a particular narrative frame that was consistent with the official response to the tragedy. The Bush administration, in cooperation with the press, labeled 9-11 an act of evil. Evil and "evil doers" were to blame and therefore eradicating "evil" became the nation's top priority.[69] Despite the American-centric claim that 9-11 was the worst thing to ever have happened, and an assault against freedom itself Bush used his televised State of the Union address to involve the global community by stating that regimes supporting terror "constitute an axis of evil." The press supported and fostered this spin on the event in several interrelated ways, including depoliticizing the roots of the event, presenting stories through a hero-villain narrative frame, focusing on particular kinds of human-interest stories, focusing on the term "terror" in a decontextualized manner, and promoting one-dimensional ideas of patriotism within the hero-villain narrative.

This frame of good versus evil also seen in the reporting of the other events in this book, is standard fare in American storytelling. These oversimplified, dualistic stories are dependent on the clear construction of oppositional heroic and villainous figures. Clearly, the terrorists as well as "regimes that support them" were uniformly vilified in the press. Even the use of the term "terrorist" by American journalists must be acknowledged as a choice, and an interpretive category. This is exposed when comparing American journalists to BBC reporters who tried to avoid the word "terrorist" as a label for the hijackers because what one might label a terrorist another might label a freedom fighter (Nelson Mandela comes to mind). This is not to imply that the press' use of the term "terrorist" was or was not appropriate, but rather, to point out that this was in fact a choice (the perpetrators of the act could also be labeled hijackers which is what the BBC favored). "Hijacker" describes the action which could be labeled as fact and is consistent with "objective" reporting. "Terrorist" describes the motivation behind the action which is more subjective—an opinion which is open to bias. The news media presented the attacks as "senseless" violence (much the way that school shootings like Columbine have been represented where similar superlatives were used, including "terror"). By referring to the attacks as "horrific" and "world altering", without any substantive investigation into the root causes of the events (which is not to exonerate criminal acts but rather to help understand and thereby attempt to prevent them), the event was "placed outside of political discourse."[70] Furthermore, the geo-political roots of 9-11 were completely unexplored by mainstream American journalists.[71] In this way, the American media uniformly robbed the hijackers and their supporters of political voice and also denied the American public an opportunity to explore the histories that resulted in the massively violent protest that was 9-11. It was only much later that ideas relating to "why they hate us" were at all advanced.

In addition to the rush to vilify without political engagement, heroes were quickly constructed, thus making the good versus evil narrative internally consistent. Hero construction happened in several ways. One example is the rush by the media to label all those who died in the attacks as American heroes. Police officers, firefighters and other rescue workers were then classified as the ultimate heroes in a hierarchy of heroism. The (now iconic) image of the firefighters carrying the body of their deceased chaplain out of the "ground zero" rubble appeared in many newspapers, magazines, and on television news, including appearing on the second page of *The New York Times* on September 12th. Another example of hero construction involved the passengers aboard United flight 93 that went down in Pennsylvania, who were quickly constructed as heroes despite any hard evidence at that time (such as recordings from a black box). The quick belief that "our guys" thwarted one of the four attacks and that Lisa Beamer's husband Todd said: "Let's roll," had the effect of turning everyday good guys into national heroes, and is but one example of how 9-11 was given a human face.

Newspapers throughout the country listed the missing, often including pictures and in this way, individualized the dead while maintaining the group identity of "Americans" as well as a human-interest angle in their reporting. However, journalists were confronted with a problem that differed from Titanic and

Columbine reporting. Namely, there wasn't an official list of the dead, as most remains had not been found and identified. In order to deal with this *The New York Times* created what ultimately became a famous section called "Portraits of Grief." Each portrait was about 200 words and was generally accompanied by a photograph. These pieces eulogized the dead in a way that focused on the every-day, highlighting banal parts of their lives as well as and their mundane person-ality characteristics. Pointing to their popularity, these portraits have been re-ferred to as an unconventional national shrine. According to Jenny Edkins, these were also a part of the press de-politicizing the September 11th attacks:

> . . . they brought out the commonplace, the ordinary, and the unoriginal. This
> borders easily on trite, but, more importantly . . . what it does is depoliticize. In
> emphasizing people's ordinary, everyday lives, it glosses over any political
> commitments or affiliations they may have had and fails to mention anything
> that might be controversial . . . it presents them . . . without a political voice.[72]

Magazines focusing on the pregnant women whose husbands died and later the "9-11 babies" (as termed by the press) are another example of how images of senseless loss are constructed by focusing on subgroups of the victim popula-tion. These are examples of creating emotional connections with news consum-ers by individualizing the dead, while also drawing on the power of the number of dead as "Americans," to legitimize their extensive coverage of the event.

During these critical early weeks when journalists were framing the event for the public, there was also a strong focus on two concepts that were often juxtaposed: patriotism and terror. This is also the space where we can see the intersection of the press and government spin on the event. A review of the first weeks of 9-11 reporting gives an overall impression of these two dominating concepts, with images and stories about a surge in patriotism often juxtaposed with the most popular concept to be employed in the press' narrative: terror.

Journalists expressed ideas about patriotism in several ways. First, many news programs included graphics with American flags flying, news anchors wearing red, white and blue ribbons and flag pins[73] and, showing little or no separation between church, state and journalism, many news personalities ended stories with statements like "God bless America." One news director banned flag pins as a clear breach of the role of journalists as objective information bearers and was ultimately pressured into apologizing due to a public outcry. During the coerced apology he said that he was "proud to be an American."[74] While many have critiqued journalists as playing to the public mood or senti-ment, the more interesting question is: to what extent did journalists' spin on the event *create* the public mood and sentiment? Other examples of journalists modeling a particular kind of patriotism include journalists openly displaying emotion and support for the official story during their coverage, despite a failure to disavow their privileged status in the culture as neutral conduits of information. Journalists both displayed their emotions and maintained their professional autonomy. Dan Rather's comments on the David Lettermen show are perhaps the most infamous example of this kind of behavior, though really, Rather's comments were illustrative of the way many (less famous) journalists situated themselves in relation to the official narrative. On September 17th Dan Rather, a guest on Letterman, said: "George Bush is the President, he makes the decisions, and, you know, as just one American, he wants me to line up, just tell me where. And he'll make the call." Of course the American public doesn't look at Rather as just a citizen, if they did he would not have been appearing on Letterman. These kinds of statements by journalists not only reinforced a limited idea of patriotism as a part of the larger hero-villain narrative, but also further marked the event with a "turning-point" quality (when even famed news anchors are "just Americans" and journalists are openly weeping during on-the-street reporting, the event is further marked as one-of-a-kind). Newspapers also displayed countless photographs involving American flags. There is the iconic flag-raising at "ground zero" which circulated repeatedly in newspapers and magazines, as well as the flag hanging at the Pentagon, and also many images of civilians raising and/or waiving flags. A review of newspapers in the weeks after 9-11 reveals an interesting phenomenon through which ideas about patriotism and heroism circulated, and that has remained outside of most analyses. I am referring to the dozens of full-page ads taken out by various sponsors to show support for the victims and rescue workers. These ads, most of which in *The New York Times* included American flags and many of which showed images of firefighters, occupied an entire section of the newspaper for weeks.

While some of the political outcomes of this kind of "patriotic" reporting are discussed in the next chapter, it was clearly an integral part of how the press narrated this event from the outset. According to both the press and the Bush administration, September 11th was an act of "terror" and patriotic Americans from then on, lived in a world plagued by "terror." As philosopher Slovaj Zizek wrote, terror became "the hidden universal equivalent of all social evils."[75] The outcome of the good-versus evil meta-narrative, simultaneous with the rush to declare a state of "terror" by the government, which went unchallenged by the press, served to de-politicize the events of 9-11. The next chapter deals with how this kind of reporting allowed the event to be appropriated into a controversial military response and a host of other conservative political projects. Due to the surge of patriotism promoted by the press, "protected zones of language" began to emerge—as evidenced by a press threat to boycott a news agency that questioned the overuse of the term "terror," which they claimed, had the effect of rendering the word "blunt" or without meaning.[76]

Both September 11th and Pearl Harbor have been historicized as surprise attacks on American soil. In this vein what follows is a very brief review of initial Pearl Harbor press narratives.

Pearl Harbor as a "Surprise" Attack on American Soil
The New York Times and the *Denver Post* represented Pearl Harbor in consistent ways focusing on the following themes for a straight two-week period: the violence of the attack, casualties, criminality, and war. The Japanese, referred to in headlines as "Japs", were immediately constructed as racialized villains (though as a group and not through particular biographical figures) and the American male victims were framed in patriotic hero and martyr language. The heroes and villains of the press' Pearl Harbor narrative were primarily faceless (as in the Shirtwaist case to be reviewed) and thus citizens were not compelled by the exceptional qualities of the individuals involved but instead, by the idea of a general mass.

Newspapers covered the events of Pearl Harbor in the context of a larger war effort. On the first full day of reporting, December 8th, 1941 *The New York Times* front-page headline read: "Japan Wars on U.S. and Britain; Makes Sudden Attack on Hawaii; Heavy Fighting at Sea Reported."[77] This was consistent with President Roosevelt's famous address in which he labeled December 7th "a date that will live in infamy" and went on to list the other countries attacked by the Japanese. For weeks newspapers were dominated more by general World War II stories than by Pearl Harbor per se. The majority of articles about Pearl Harbor went beyond the reporting of a timeline of the event, and explicitly and repeatedly linked these events to an "Assault on Democracy" and "Shift in Power." Because the press so explicitly capitalized on the villain, hero and martyr concepts by linking them to an overall assault on the country's values, it is fair to say that Pearl Harbor was at once represented by the press and made political. On December 9 *The New York Times* front-page headline began "U.S. Declares War"[78] and on the 10th the front-page headline began with "Roosevelt Sees a Long, World-Wide War."[79]

The Shirtwaist Factory "Triangle" Fire: A Negative Case

How are events that do not become mythic, initially reported by the American press? As stated earlier, in order to understand the process by which some events become iconic, a negative case must also be considered.

The Shirtwaist Factory Fire of 1911 was the largest industrial fire to date, causing one hundred and forty-six deaths. The event was interlinked with many social phenomena including, the rapidly developing capitalist infrastructure and ideology, worker health and safety issues, and gender and ethnic inequality in the workplace. *Shirtwaist was a classic middle-range event.* Journalists recognized it as newsworthy; however, Shirtwaist never received the kind of reporting that would propel it into the public consciousness in a way that parallels the other cases. What was it about the reporting of Shirtwaist that differed from the interpretive practices surrounding the other events under discussion?

Shirtwaist, like Titanic, was brought to the public's attention via newspapers. While the story did receive press coverage, the volume was far lower than that of the other cases. The story appeared on the front page of both *The New York Times* and the *Denver Post* on March 26, 1911, day one of representation, but after that there are only a handful of stories in the *Denver Post*, indicating that Shirtwaist, despite being record-breaking, was primarily categorized as a local event. While *The New York Times* afforded the event considerably more space over a two-week period, the volume of the reporting was significantly lower than for the other events in this book. In order to fully understand this it is important to look at several aspects of journalistic coverage including: the quantity of coverage, placement of stories, illustrations, the narrative frame employed in storytelling, and human-interest stories.

In terms of quantity, *The New York Times* breakdown is: for three consecutive days (March 26th, 27th, 28th) Shirtwaist was one of the lead stories. While Shirtwaist did receive prominence on the front page, being the largest story (and the only one with a photograph) it was one of three major stories and was thus not framed as singular. One of the front-page stories that then mediated and perhaps trumped the Shirtwaist Fire was ironically White Star's successful transatlantic use of wireless technology (remember this is a year before the Titanic sinking). The third story to headline was a controversial mayoral election. On March 29th and 30th there were some brief Shirtwaist stories but it was not mentioned on the front page nor was it mentioned in the March 31st edition. It was again covered in brief articles on April 1st and 2nd but not on the front page. There was then a lull in reporting until April 6th when it again turned up on page one for the final time.

On March 26th, 1911 *The New York Times* front page featured a photo of the factory building with a small X marking a window from which people jumped. The headlines read:

"141 Men and Girls Die in Waist Factory Fire; Trapped High Up
In Washington Place Building; Street Strewn With Bodies; Piles
Of Dead Inside"[80]

There were thirteen subheadings and it wasn't until the eighth that "Only One Fire Escape"[81] was reported. The twelfth subheading read "Mob Storms The

Morgue"[82] which is the first of many times that the victims' families, who were primarily immigrants, were referred to by journalists, in subjective and arguably degrading language. This is similar to the animalistic imagery and mob language used to describe third-class passengers aboard Titanic. Despite leading with "Men", implying that men were the primary victims, on March 27th, day two of interpretation, *The New York Times* presented a summary of the coroner's findings in very small print (located inside the edition) reporting that only thirteen of the dead were in fact, men. The *Denver Post* was significantly more accurate in reporting the gendered nature of the deaths, but overestimated the death toll. "175 Women And Girls Are Killed In NY Factory Fire"[83] Ironically, journalists at the *Denver Post* were much more critical about the causes of the event but nonetheless did not produce many stories about it.

On March 26th, newspapers stories were about death, attempted male heroism, and queries as to the cause of the fire. There were many photos of firefighters carrying away corpses and police numbering bodies, attached to stories about how they had "desperately" tried to save lives. The *Denver Post* ran a front-page story about male heroism. Journalists credited the "elevator boy" for "heroically" saving girls until his elevator failed. In this way some press narratives promoted an image of anonymous male heroism. Page four of *The New York Times* consisted of three photos depicting rescue workers put together as a montage with the center, privileged photo, depicting firefighters carrying away the body of a female worker who had jumped to her death. For me, this recalls the famous image of 9-11 firefighters at "ground zero" carrying away the first documented victim, the firefighters' Chaplin.

There were several photographs of dead bodies on the sidewalk and lists of both identified and unidentified victims. There were only two human interest stories, where a specific individual was linked to the event, both appearing on page four. The first story was about survivor Hyman Meshel who had an arduous escape but was still able to make his way to freedom. The other was a report about the escape of Shirtwaist owners Harris and Blanck (Blanck escaped with his two daughters ages 5 and 12 as well as their governess). The remainder of the stories, between pages four and six, all focused on how the fire broke out and who or what was responsible, but the stories conflicted with each other. There were small stories about fire drills, the danger being known due to a fire nine years earlier, and a quick grand jury fire investigation. Differing from the *Denver Post* which reported on page one that criminal negligence was the cause, journalists at *The New York Times* did not explore this storyline. It is significant that neither paper vilified the factory owners, who, reminiscent of Titanic's Bruce Ismay who was vilified in newspapers, had both escaped. Both newspapers, raised questions, although differently, about culpability (even criminality in the case of the *Denver Post*) but in neither case did journalists do so through the construction of specific villain figures. The absence of villainous figures and the construction of anonymous depersonalized heroism failed to produce the standard good versus evil narrative that is characteristic of the coverage of the other events.

The tone of reporting in *The New York Times* shifted on the second day, March 27th, and stories focused on mass mourning, political protest, and culpability. The Shirtwaist narrative also became gendered as the press acknowledged that the majority of victims *and* protesters were female. Front-page headlines read:

"Locked In Factory, The Survivors Say, When Fire Started That Cost 141 Lives." [84]

A subheading reaffirmed this by reporting "Two Doors Still Locked In Ruins and Others Burned Away Where Many Victims Fell."[85] All in caps, the following subheading reported that the owners denied allegations of having locked the doors. Story headlines such as "Doors Were Locked Say Rescued Girls"[86] became increasingly gendered. There were several stories about violations and firetraps found at the scene as well as more photos of the fire, destruction, and the crowd of fifty thousand people that gathered at the site.[87] One story titled "Sad All-Day March To Morgue Gates"[88] contained the subheading "Many Women Collapse."[89] Finally, there was a story about a protest organized by the Women's Trade Union League who asserted that Shirtwaist employees were underpaid. There was one short human interest story in small print with the lead "Heroic Deed." This was the only newspaper story about female heroism and recounted the experience of survivor Annie Sprinsock who saved her friend's life.

On March 28th there was another shift and *The New York Times* reported that there were multiple "blames" but fire drill laws were listed as the primary issue. The *Denver Post* was considerably stronger in their response to the event calling it the "NY Holocaust" (though not on the front page which seems curious). Likewise, reporters at the *Denver Post* demanded "death proof" and not simply "fire proof" buildings.[90] However, these were the only stories about the event in the *Denver Post* and they were buried amongst unrelated stories, failing to mark the event with historicity. The March 29th edition of *The New York Times* only mentioned the death-list and that 300,000 people marched in the funeral procession. Up until this point journalists had based their narratives on nameless heroism, mourning, and general questions about responsibility; however, there were no guiding narratives and no central figures (including the owners who were absent from most press reports). From March 30th to April 6th the *NYT* narrative became explicitly gendered with articles focusing on two distinct themes: hysteria and militant protest. Within this framework, women dominated the news, but were described as being either hysterical, or combative—a dualistic frame intended to help the public categorize female responses to this event in highly stereotypical ways.

The press constructed the hysteria narrative by using weighted language to describe female survivors, mourners, and protesters. Reporters focused on certain aftermath occurrences at the exclusion of others and framed them in highly gendered ways. For example, headlines focused on women fainting, being carried out of meetings and being generally hysterical and uncontrollable. Accompanying stories defined women by these terms, often further feminizing narratives by adding extraneous information about women's clothing and hairstyles. Some headlines are as follows:

"Faint In A Frenzy Over Tales of Fire"[91]
"Hysteria Piled On Hysteria"[92]
"Hair and Dress Aflame, They Drop To Pavement and Are Killed"[93]
"Fifty Shirt Waist Girls, Upset by Socialist Oratory, Carried Out Of Central Palace Meeting"[94]

While *The New York Times* circulated the female hysteria narrative reporters failed to address substantive aspects of the "socialist oratory" (which was a meeting where speakers demanded an end to what Americans now classify as sweatshop conditions). This was one of many opportunities for the press to link Shirtwaist to issues of import, such as worker health and safety, by addressing the substantive issues circulating within the event's aftermath. Yet this did not occur and later events were trivialized through the use of feminizing language and poor placement within the newspapers.

The second gendered narrative spun by newsmakers was of militant women protesting (unsafe worker conditions) and demanding change (legal reform). It was reported that the female protesters blamed everyone from the "Shirtwaist Kings" Blanck and Harris, to greedy capitalists in general, to the public at large for their indifference to the conditions under which poor women labored.[95] Headlines included:

"Dollars Against a Life"
"Army of Workers, Most of Them Women, March Through the Downpour of Rain"[96]

Beyond the headlines, journalists used very specific and weighted kinds of language to convey their narratives. For example, the narratives were framed in combative and unsympathetic language with words like "army" used to describe the female protestors. Additionally, suffragists were incorrectly reported to have been among the thousands. After constructing these two gendered narratives, and linking suffrage to Shirtwaist, the event all but disappeared from main-stream newspapers.

While Shirtwaist would be the subject of counter-dominant and otherwise resistive interpretations, it would never be used politically or commercially within the dominant culture. It was contained and represented only in its moment, scantly, and ending with "fluffy" and antagonistic gendered stories unlikely to garner public sympathy.

So it came to be that, though many Americans would know something about Titanic and Columbine, very few would recognize Shirtwaist as a part of national identity.

Conclusion: The Role of the Press in Initial Memory Construction

On a basic level, what analysis up to this point reaffirms is that the media plays a significant role in constructing versions of events. As the first source through which citizens come to know of world events, everything newsmakers do, helps frame and give meaning to the event, including the very fact that they are report-ing on it. Additionally, newsmakers spin other ideas for the culture even as they attempt to document world events—ideas about race, class, gender, and nation-ality that extend beyond what is central to the event itself. The questions in terms of this work then become: what is the process by which events become "represented" in a way that gives the press the ability to circulate other ideas within the society? What techniques are routine within this process? What is the role of events within larger processes of cultural interpretation? How does this process differ when contrasting iconic events with those that never captured the public imagination in a meaningful and lasting way? How does technology im-pact the interpretive process?

It is clear that there is a basic pattern that journalists follow as they narrate current events that eventually become iconic within the society. Journalists communicate the importance of an event in many different ways. One area in-volves space and how an event comes to monopolize the journalistic landscape. Techniques for this include enlarged newspaper editions, enlarged print, bolder headlines, enlarged front page photographs, repetitive front page coverage, the exclusion of other front page stories, many stories throughout newspapers and for a prolonged period of time, and in contemporary society—saturation cover-age, allowing the event to appear on a 24-hour audio-visual loop in addition to extensive newspaper coverage. Beyond a monopolization of cultural space, journalists also mark events by applying storytelling conventions. The particular frame in which an event is narrated, also communicates meaning. In this regard journalists often employ a hero-villain or good versus evil narrative, complete with specific or generalized heroes, villains, and martyrs that serve to afford the event a "human" angle. Additionally journalists seem to overestimate the loss of life as reporters overestimated death counts in all of the events covered, with the exception of Pearl Harbor, and provide certain kinds of context for making sense of current events in lieu of other kinds of information.

Journalists often employed superlatives in their initial reporting, also marking the events with significance. The scope or degree to which the press report on an event also signifies the importance of that event in relation to other current events. For example, *The New York Times Index* indicates that Titanic was more extensively covered in terms of numbers of stories on its first day of reporting than all Shirtwaist representations in *The New York Times*. As a result of advances in systems of mass communication Columbine and September 11th received "saturation coverage"[97] and appeared to citizens in a burst of multi-media forms, the volume of which itself, called significance to the events. The real-time live broadcast of these events, which interrupted regularly scheduled programming, reinforced their importance in an anticipatory manner, where one might have had the feeling of not knowing what would happen next. In the case of 9-11, this anxiety was reinforced by journalists' initial silence which they attempted to cover with extreme images. Dayan and Katz analyzed preplanned "media events" that bear similarities in that they too, break with routine and accordingly interrupt the flow of television programming which is itself symbolic of their importance.[98] This interruption, much like the extensive airing of Columbine and 9-11, is monopolistic and if one happens to be plugged into mainstream media, they are receiving coverage. Such an intense flood of event coverage is technologically enabled and thus, Columbine and 9-11 initial reporting differs considerably from the earlier events. Contemporary events are "represented" much faster and the same images appear simultaneously in many mediums. Dayan and Katz show that media events, distinguished from "great news events" which deal with accidents and disruption of the normative order, are purported to be "historic" at the time of their airing.[99] Though in a different genre, with exception of Shirtwaist, all of the events covered in this book were immediately classified as "markers." In this way the press imbues the event with a "turning point" quality. On day one, reporting in both the Columbine and 9-11 cases, the media informed the American people that a historic moment had occurred, a turning point in society—and that things would never be the same. Given the vast difference in lives lost and economic, political and global significance, the instant reporting of these events through similar lenses is very revealing about the larger journalistic process at work. Even in the very early stages of event representation, the media infuses historic significance into an event by projecting it onto all available screens within the cultural landscape and claiming its significance. In this way Columbine upstaged Kosovo which was normalized by the press from a very early point. Likewise, 9-11 became the event *of all events* in the United States.

The high-speed, repetitive, and monopolistic manner in which the press represented Columbine and 9-11 fostered unprecedented audience consumption. "Media events" boast the largest audiences in human history by allowing citizens to watch the events at the time of their "emission."[100] The televised funeral of Princess Diana is one example of a preplanned television event with an unprecedented global audience. However, a comparison of Titanic to Columbine and 9-11 shows that it is only recently that iconic events have been experienced, at least partly, in real-time and within multi-media. In other words, Titanic shows that an event can become mythic in the culture even without this real-time explosion of representations—which apparently simply allow for this to occur at an accelerated rate.

The volume of event reporting, and the mediums in which it occurs, has an impact on how an event will be represented and what meaning will initially be associated with the event. The form and content of these first-generation journalistic representations also contribute to event collective memory.

Because journalists operate within a commercial system, it is imperative that the public consumes their version. In order to capture the public's imagination, newsmakers opt to tell a story that will resonate with powerful themes in the culture.[101] The media however have played a role in what the themes in the culture *are*, and are able to reaffirm these ideologies through event reporting, completing the cycle. As stated, journalists, who are at the forefront of initial event interpretation, have a stake in telling their versions powerfully. As Zelizer illustrated in her analysis of how journalists covered the John F. Kennedy assassination, collective memory is central to the formation of journalistic authority. As such, Zelizer shows that journalists are a particular community of memory-makers who promote their legitimacy by claiming authority over real-world events. "Critical incidents or hot moments"[102] or "cultural flashpoints,"[103] many of which become iconic, allow journalists an opportunity to negotiate the boundaries of their profession and reassert their authority over world events.[104] In other words, these events serve as a site of "rhetorical legitimation"[105] giving journalists an opportunity to claim a unique and authoritative place within the society. This was made explicit in the case of 9-11 when top newsmakers assumed it appropriate for journalists to display emotions in the context of an event deemed particularly horrific. This public renegotiation of the boundaries of objectivity which as a community they have helped create, served to reinforce the magnitude of the event. This is particularly clear in the case of September 11th. But to say that the media are interpreters and have a vested interest in the reporting of world events is only part of the story.

Amy Binder explains that the media appropriates certain frames to make their stories convincing and to help them resonate with the public.[106] In their compelling analysis of the media and public perception of nuclear weapons, Gamson and Modigliani illustrate that the media engages in a selection process whereby they employ frames that draw focus to certain aspects of a story.[107] Boorstin describes how media orchestrated or "pseudo-events," often involve a hero narrative.[108] The press uses the same technique when constructing representations of unplanned and even tragic events. Schudson shows how journalists used the same narrative frame for Watergate stories that he ultimately describes as "a grand national myth" complete with "villains and saints."[109] In this regard he says that the Watergate Hearings were like a soap opera with "instant heroes and instant villains."[110] The speed and completeness with which people were transformed into heroes and villains is also evidenced in all of the positive case studies, particularly Titanic, Columbine and 9-11 where specific people and images were consistently used to reinforce these categories.

In terms of Titanic, journalists transformed a carefully selected array of white upper-class male passengers into heroes and so the story was consumed through the frame of male heroism. Some heroes were also martyred. Stories about certain heroic figures such as John Jacob Astor came to dominate event reporting. In journalistic plots, these kinds of hero stories always rely on the construction of villains and in the case of Titanic, the immigrants who were actually the most disadvantaged, were also transformed into the least sympathetic "characters" in the press story. This narrative form normalized social class biases while creating a personal emotional connection between the public and the event through personal tales of sacrifice and loss. The hero-villain narrative resonates with citizens as stories of good and evil are deeply embedded within American culture. It is then, not surprising that the same narrative form dominated the reporting of all of the positive cases, most explicitly in the cases of Columbine and 9-11—where people were actually classified by these terms thus ensuring the events would be remembered that way. In the case of Titanic, a focus on a small set of individuals allowed the press to all but ignore the severe social class differences in those who lived and those who died, while simultaneously positioning the public to accept that version of events by transforming the steerage passengers into a mass of villains and the wealthy into individual heroes. As Dayan and Katz note, "The hero's daring seems to invite admiration and identification even from those who are disadvantaged by his triumph."[111] A questioning of the dominant version then becomes less likely as the press not only put a particular spin on what happened, but also implicitly justified it. Perhaps this is why *The New York Times* ran stories about Columbine near stories about large-scale racial violence and never made any links or provided any substantive social analysis from expert commentators. In Columbine stories, journalists focused on characterizing what happened and those involved in terms of hero, martyr and villain categories of interpretation. Both the Kosovo and racial profiling stories lacked personal hero and villain depictions and so the press failed to give a "human face"[112] to those stories or tap into timeless themes of good and evil. Shirtwaist reporting did produce several nameless heroes, such as rescue workers and an elevator boy, but the stories were impersonal, failing to produce characters, which, compelling narratives are dependent on.

Despite these differences in reporting, there is a striking similarity between Shirtwaist and Titanic newspaper stories. In both instances, two gendered narratives were constructed. These narratives served as the frame through which women involved in or vocal about the event, were filtered. This exemplifies how the press used Titanic and Shirtwaist as a vehicle for reinforcing ideas about gender—the events are merely the instrument for reifying cultural ideas, even at a time when the events are in fact, most relevant. The press portrayed women in highly stereotypical ways and relied on stereotypes of women as the weaker sex, or as being combative and/or self-serving. This illustrates how the press uses events to circulate dominant ideology.[113] It shows how the press not only reinforces dominant ideology but also spins additional beliefs for the culture. In this case, the narratives that categorized women as combative, tapped into larger fears in the culture—at a time when women's suffrage, and their participation in all spheres of public life, appeared inevitable and therefore challenged the institutional and cultural structure of power in American society.

When analyzing the press meta-narrative of 9-11, what is most significant is that in the critical early days and weeks, the American press uniformly legitimized the Bush administration's "evil/terror" script. The press was complicit in the mass distribution of this narrative in several ways. First, in claiming "national transformation" the press looped images of horror, contextualized only with war rhetoric and inappropriate historical metaphors. Second, the press narrated 9-11 through a good versus evil script reliant on the overuse of the term "terror", and by extension, the "evil doers" were "terrorists" to be thwarted at any cost. In this way the causes of the event were completely depoliticized. Finally, the press reported Bush's response to 9-11 (his evil-doer narrative) but did not analyze or interpret it. The two sources from which the American public could expect to gain reliable information about this event (the press and the government) were both reinforcing the same good versus evil script. The press and the administration served and by extension, legitimized each other. The press played a significant role, as further explored in the next chapter, in the low level of dissent that was publicly deemed permissible in the wake of 9-11 and in this way, ironically (given their professional reliance on freedom of speech), ultimately linked patriotism with very limited kinds of responses to the event, helping to create a mood where patriotism in other forms, such as resistance, was met with great hostility.

The press is the first group that gets to transmit interpretations of world events to the public, thereby laying their claim to events. Journalists claim the singularity of an event and then position themselves as the conduits of information about that which they have deemed urgent. In this way, as Zelizer underscores, journalists inevitably use current events to mark their own profession with authority as they tell us what is "historical."[114] Through these "historic" events, journalists are able to construct and circulate other ideas about social life. But this is only one stage in the making of an iconic event. How do other interest groups then appropriate these representations, with the complicity of the press? How does an event go from a way to spin dominant ideas into a vehicle for directed political use? How and why do some "represented events" become political pawns?

The next chapter revisits the main press narratives and then considers how special interest groups seized these narratives for their own ends. As will be seen, the press continues to have a role in the appropriation of events. Beginning with Titanic, an event with which many people to this day, remain interested in or fascinated by, but also have a personal detachment from, as a result of sufficient time having passed, it becomes clear if not shocking how an event can become linked to an entirely different issue, as evident when looking at how the "ship of dreams" was used in a systematic effort to deny American women their right to vote.

Notes

1. Hayden White, *Metahistory: The Historical Imagination in Nineteenth Century Europe* (Baltimore, Md.: Johns Hopkins University Press, 1973).

2. Daniel Dayan and Elihu Katz, Media Events: *The Live Broadcasting of History* (Cambridge, Mass: Harvard University Press, 1992) 30.

3. Herbert J. Gans, *Democracy and the News* (Oxford: Oxford University Press, 2003).

4. Barbie Zelizer, *Covering the Body: The Kennedy Assassination, The Media, and the Shaping of Collective Memory* (Chicago: University of Chicago Press, 1992).

5. Justin Lewis; Sut Jhally and Michael Morgan, "The Gulf War: A Study of the Media, Public Opinion and Public Knowledge," *Department of Communication, http://www.umass.edu/communication/resources/special_reports/gulf_war/index.shtml* (March 23, 2006).

6. Michael Schudson, *Discovering the News: A Social History of American Newspapers* (New York: Basic Books, 1979).

7. Gans, *Democracy and the News*; Schudson, *Discovering the News.*

8. Michael Schudson, *The Sociology of News* (New York: W. W. Norton and Company, 2003).

9. Dayan and Katz, *Live Broadcasting*, 39

10. Zelizer, Covering the Body.

11. Gans, *Democracy and the News*, 31

12. Iwona Irwin-Zarecka, *Frames of Remembrance: The Dynamics of Collective Memory* (Somerset, N.J.: Transaction Publishers, 1994).

13. Schudson, *Sociology of News*, 185

14. Consider how family members of passengers may have felt when eventually learning the truth. In this vein, the recent mining tragedy in which families were misinformed that their loved ones were safe, comes to mind.

15. The *Denver Post* had a circulation of anywhere from sixty-six thousand to upwards of ninety thousand during the month of April 1912.

16. The false reporting of survivors is similar to the 2006 mining tragedy in which families and the press were initially told that everyone had survived the collapse when in fact there was only one survivor.

17. Because of the importance of wireless telegraphy in the Titanic experience, initial representations, the Senate Investigation, and eventually related reforms based on the Titanic disaster (including the Continental Morse Code and SOS signal), it is important to bear in mind just how new this technology was. In 1886 German physicist Heinrich Hertz was able to prove the existence of electromagnetic waves. In 1897 Italian physicist, and future Nobel Prize winner, Gugliemo Marconi organized a wireless telegraph company in England and in 1901 he received the first transatlantic wireless signals. At the time of the Titanic tragedy, only four American ships were equipped with wireless telegraphy (radio), each with one operator. The importance of wireless technology in the first phase of Titanic interpretations again becomes evident when the Senate Investigation holds the liner California responsible for, in their estimation, failing to swiftly respond to Titanic's wireless signals. This led to the largest reform of water travel safety to date including 1) the monitoring of all ships at sea, 2) uniform distress signals, and 3) mandated responses to distress signals.

18. "World's Largest Steamer hits Iceberg on Her Maiden Voyage," 15 April 1912, *Denver Post*, 2.

19. A similar phenomenon occurred with the 2001 World Trade Center attacks as the initial death toll was also wrong and subsequently, altered several times. Likewise, casualties of the Columbine shootings were also initially misreported as being 25 fatalities.

20. "Noted Names Missing," 16 April 1912, *New York Times*, 4.

21. "Rule of the Sea," 16 April 1912, *New York Times*, 4.

22. "Women and Children First," 16 April 1912, *New York Times*, 4.

23. "Kings of Finance, Captains of Industry; World-Famed Men Who Went Down in Titanic," 16 April 1912, *Denver Post*, 1.

24. "List of Dead Includes Notable Men of Affairs," 16 April 1912, *Denver Post*, 2.

25. "Bravery Shown by Men Passengers," 16 April 1912, *Denver Post*, 2.

26. "585 Women and Children Aboard," 16 April 1912, *Denver Post*, 2.

27. Irwin-Zarecka, *Frames of Remembrance*, 171.

28. John Storey, *Cultural Studies & The Study of Popular Culture. Theories and Methods* (Athens, Ga.: University of Georgia Press, 1996), 81.

29. "Portraits of Grief," 16 September 2001, *New York Times*, 9(A).

30. "Wives Dragged From Husbands to Safety," 16 April 1912, *Denver Post*, 1.

31. "Scantily-Clad Women and Children float to safety as they watch their loved ones perish," 16 April 1912, *Denver Post*, 1.

32. "Bravery of Those Facing Certain Death Makes Chapter in History," 16 April 1912, *Denver Post*, 1.

33. "Two Prominent Women Saved and Two Men Who Were Drowned," 16 April 1912, *Denver Post*, 4.

34. Frances Wayne, "Men of Brains and Millions Sacrificed for Lowly Women: By the Inexorable Law of the Sex, Which Demands Salvation of Women First, Nation Suffers Untold Loss," 16 April 1912, *Denver Post*, 1.

35. While the Senate Inquiry ultimately found the ship Californian's captain/crew accountable for the loss of so many lives, because, in their estimation the ship had failed to promptly respond to wireless signals for help and subsequently lied about their location in relation to Titanic, the Senate Investigation did not fault Ismay. Nevertheless, the Senate twice called Ismay to testify fueling media representations of his "cowardice." The Senate was dissatisfied with his initial testimony as to how he survived when so many women and children had died. Ismay repeatedly claimed that there weren't any women or children on deck when he entered a lifeboat. He also testified that he helped row a lifeboat (thus saving lives). However, Ismay also testified that he did not see the ship sink (or else he would have returned for more people). The Senate Investigation concluded that his testimony was not credible because given the corroborated position of Ismay's lifeboat, had he in fact been rowing he would have been *facing* the sinking ship. Nonetheless, with an external ship primarily blamed for the loss of lives, the only reforms to come from Titanic were regarding uniform laws for wireless technology (including codes) and lifeboat requirements.

36. The *Denver Post*, and similar local newspapers such as the *Detroit News*, used significantly more illustrations than *The New York Times* (and other nationally circulated papers such as *The Boston Globe*).

37. The term "bloody rampage" was frequently used as well.

38. Mark Obmascik, "High School Massacre," 21 April 1999, *Denver Post*, 1(A).

39. "The Colorado School Slayings," 22 April 1999, *Denver Post,* 30(A).

40. "Racial Profiling in New Jersey," 22 April, 1999, *Denver Post*, 30(A).

41. Tina Rosenberg, "Keeping Ethnic Tensions From Turning Violent," 22 April 1999, *Denver Post*, 30(A).

42. Steven Biel, *Down With the Old Canoe: A Cultural History of the Titanic Disaster* (New York: W. W. Norton and Company, Inc., 1996).

43. "True Courage in Time of Terror," 22 April 1999, *Denver Post*, 14(A).

44. "In The Face of Evil, Human Decency Triumphs," 22 April 1999, *Denver Post* 27(A).

45. "Courage in the Face of Evil," 22 April 1999, *Denver Post*, 10(B).

46. "Carnage Puts Spotlight on Trench Coat Mafia," 21 April 1999, *Denver Post*, 17(A).

47. 11% of the American population used radio as their primary source of information in the first days following the 9-11 attacks.

48. Daniel Martin Varisco,. "September 11: Participant Webservation of the 'War on Terrorism,'" *American Anthropologist* 104, no. 3 (September 2002): 935.

49. James Der Derian, "9/11: Before, After, and in Between," in *Understanding September 11*, ed. Craig J. Calhoun, Paul Price and Ashley Timmer (New York: The New Press, 2002): 182.

50. The damage at the Pentagon and at the field in Shanksville, Pennsylvania received significantly less media coverage as compared with the World Trade Center Towers. Marita Sturken explains that the focus on "Ground Zero" constructed New York as the symbolic center of the event (2002, p. 75).

51. Der Derian, "9/11," 183.

52. Barbie Zelizer and Stuart Allan, *Journalism After September 11* (New York: Routledge, 2002), 7.

53. Zelizer and Allan, *After September*, 7.

54. Zelizer and Allan, *After September*, 7.

55. Zelizer and Allan, *After September*, 7.

56. Zelizer and Allan, *After September*, 7.

57. Serge Schmemann "U.S. ATTACKED," 12 September 2001, *New York Times*, 1(A).

58. Robert D. McFadden, "Stunned Rescuers Comb Attack Sites, But Thousands are Presumed Dead; F.B.I. Tracking Hijackers' Movements," 13 September 2001, *New York Times*, 1(A).

59. Clifford J. Levy and William K. Rashbaum, "Bush and Top Aides Proclaim Policy of 'Ending' States that Back Terror; Local Airports Shut Down After an Arrest," 14 September 2001, *New York Times*, 1(A).

60. Brian D. McFadden, "Bush Leads Prayer, Visits Aid Crews; Congress Backs Use of Armed Force," 15 September 2001, *New York Times*, 1(A).

61. James Risen, "Bush Tells the Military to 'Get Ready': Broader Spy Powers Gaining Support," 16 September 2001, *New York Times*, 1(A).

62. Richard W. Stevenson and Jonathan Fuerbringer, "Nation Shifts Its Focus to Wall Street as a Major Test of Attack's Aftermath," *New York Times*, 1(A).

63. Betty H. Winfield, Barbara Friedman, and Vivara Trisnadi, "History as the Metaphor Through Which the Current World Is Viewed: British and American Newspapers' Uses of History Following the 11 September 2001 Terrorist Attacks," *Journalism Studies*, 3, no. 2 (April 1, 2002): 292-7.

64. Winfield, Friedman, and Trisnadi, "History as the Metaphor," 298.

65. Winfield, Friedman, and Trisnadi, "History as the Metaphor," 292.

66. Winfield, Friedman, and Trisnadi, "History as the Metaphor," 294.

67. Though comparisons to Pearl Harbor may be absurd, even odious—many voices in the media, desperate to establish some relativity saw their comparison as a way of "fixing" scope and magnitude of this "violation" overlooking how their generalized ex-

ample failed in their rushed attempt to make sense out of what appeared to be "sense-less."

68. Dayan and Katz, *Live Broadcasting*, 12–15.

69. Der Derian, "9/11," 178.

70. Der Derian, "9/11," 177.

71. While Bush clearly had an agenda for providing this simplistic narrative frame the news media also relied on such a narrative and thus were complicit in Bush's appropriation of 9-11 into a range of political actions including the Iraq War and underlying attempt to alter the power balance in the Middle East.

72. Jenny Edkins, "The Rush to Memory and the Rhetoric of War," *Journal of Political and Military Sociology* 31, no. 2 (Winter 2003): 239-40.

73. Zelizer and Allan, *After September*, 11.

74. Zelizer and Allan, *After September*, 11.

75. Slovaj Zizek, *Desert of the Real: 5 Essays on September 11 and Related Dates* (New York: Verso, 2002), 111.

76. Der Derian, "9/11," 183.

77. "Japan Wars on U.S. and Britain; Makes Sudden Attack on Hawaii; Heavy Fighting at Sea Reported," 8 December 1941, *New York Times*, 1.

78. "U.S. Declares War," 9 December 1941, *New York Times*, 1.

79. "Roosevelt Sees a Long, World-Wide War," 10 December 1941, *New York Times*, 1.

80. "141 Men and Girls Die in Waist Factory Fire; Trapped High Up In Washington Place Building; Street Strewn With Bodies; Piles Of Dead Inside," 26 March 1911, *New York Times*, 1.

81. "Only One Fire Escape," 26 March 1911, *New York Times*, 1.

82. "Mob Storms The Morgue," 26 March 1911, *New York Times*, 1.

83. "175 Women And Girls Are Killed In NY Factory Fire," 26 March 1911, *Denver Post*, 1.

84. "Locked In Factory, The Survivors Say, When Fire Started That Cost 141 Lives," 27 March 1911, *New York Times*, 1.

85. "Two Doors Still Locked In Ruins and Others Burned Away Where Many Victims Fell," 27 March 1911, *New York Times*, 1.

86. "Doors Were Locked Say Rescued Girls," 27 March 1911, *New York Times*, 2.

87. The tone is so serious that while reading it seems as though a public Shirtwaist discourse will continue for an indefinite period of time, which of course did not happen.

88. "Sad All-Day March To Morgue Gates," 27 March 1911, *New York Times*, 2.

89. "Many Women Collapse," 27 March 1911, *New York Times*, 2.

90. "We Must Have Death-Proof as Well as Fire-Proof Buildings," 27 March 1911, *Denver Post*, 1.

91. "Faint In A Frenzy Over Tales of Fire," 30 March 1911, *New York Times*, 1.

92. "Hysteria Piled on Hysteria," 30 March 1911, *New York Times*, 1.

93. "Hair and Dress Aflame, They Drop To Pavement and Are Killed," 26 March 1911, *Denver Post*, 3.

94. "Fifty Shirt Waist Girls, Upset by Socialist Oratory, Carried Out Of Central Palace Meeting," 30 March 1911, *New York Times*, 1.

95. In one article the press reports that some victims' families refused to accept the monetary compensation offered by the Shirtwaist owners, but this article fails to address their reasons.

96. "Army of Workers, Most of Them Women, March Through the Downpour of Rain," 6 April 1911, *New York Times*, 1.

97. Lewis, Jhally and Morgan, "Gulf War."

98. Dayan and Katz, *Live Broadcasting*, 5.

99. Dayan and Katz, *Live Broadcasting*, 12.

100. Dayan and Katz, *Live Broadcasting*, 14.

101. Amy Binder, "Constructing Racial Rhetoric: Media Depictions of Harm in Heavy Metal and Rap Music," *American Sociological Review* 58, no. 6 (December 1993); William A. Gamson and Andre Modigliani, "Media Discourse and Public Opinion on Nuclear Power: A Constructionist Approach," *American Journal of Sociology* 95, no. 1 (July 1989); Iwona Irwin-Zarecka, *Frames of Remembrance: The Dynamics of Collective Memory* (Somerset, N.J.: Transaction Publishers, 1994); Michael Schudson, "How Culture Works: Perspectives from Media Studies on the Efficacy of Symbols," *Theory and Society* 18, no. 2 (March 1989): 153–80; Michael Schudson, "The Past in the Present Versus the Present in the Past," *Communication* (1989): 105–13.

102. Zelizer, Covering the Body, 4.

103. Michael Schudson, *Watergate in American Memory: How we Remember, Forget, and Reconstruct the Past* (New York: Basic Books, 1992), 66.

104. Schudson, *American Memory*, 191.

105. Binder, "Racial Rhetoric," 189 is drawing on the work of Weber and Habermas.

106. Binder, "Racial Rhetoric."

107. Gamson and Modigliani, *Media Discourse*.

108. Daniel J. Boorstin, *The Image: A Guide to Pseudo Events in America* (New York: Harper and Row, 1964).

109. Schudson, *American Memory*, 12.

110. Schudson, *American Memory*, 29.

111. Dayan and Katz, *Live Broadcasting*, 39

112. Irwin-Zarecka, *Frames of Remembrance*.

113. Binder, "Racial Rhetoric,"; Gamson and Modigliani, "Media Discourse,"; Lewis, Jhally and Morgan, "Gulf War,"; Storey, *Cultural Studies*.

114. Zelizer, Covering the Body.

Chapter Four

The Representational Event:
Political Appropriations

Government officials at the local and national level, immediately put their spin on major events as they unfold. Events are highlighted and classified by genre—including criminal, technological, war-related, or any number of standard categories. State spokespersons display either surprise, indicating an "acute crisis" has occurred or react as though the event was inevitable, implying a persistent problem. Initial government responses to events may include the rhetoric of war, the language of horror, or moral indignation. Jenny Edkins questions whether political communities sustain themselves by scripting events as emergencies through which they can barter (future) security for patriotism.[1] Iconic events provide the state an opportunity to reify or redefine national identity, to promote a set of national priorities, and to tighten the (imagined) link between the individual and "the nation." In this way, the representation of events is never free from political appropriation. The state does not however, act alone in shaping public perception of world events.

As stated in earlier chapters, the press interprets events as they report on them. This mundane social process results in a repository of event representations that constitute the "represented event." This is the journalistic version of the event which is largely constructed with state sponsored information. It is this media constructed version of the event that comprises base-line collective memory and that becomes available for recollection and rescripting. The represented event is what, under certain conditions, becomes purposefully used in political discourses, or becomes what I term a "representational event." While the press continues to be a part of the "political life" of events, once representational, the event is no longer being reported for "documentary" purposes, but is now explicitly used as a vehicle for something else.

There is no clear border between the government's "official" story and the press' version of events, which are typically consistent, largely because the press acquires much of their information from official state sources and also offers the government an unlimited platform to broadcast the information they deem relevant. The consistency between press and official accounts is a site where journalism's role with regards to democracy, reveals itself. An informed citizenry is necessary to the execution of democracy, especially in the information age, and the relationship between the press and other groups in the formation of collective versions of events, is paramount. Because they are protected by the rhetoric of journalistic practice which claims objectivity, professional authority, and autonomy the press are able to transmit the state's message without analyzing the constituent components, invariably serving to authenticate it.

The political appropriation of events by special interest groups continues to involve the press in several ways, begging the question: what happens to the press narrative during the political use of an event?

The represented event, or press narrative, becomes available for "use," transplant or appropriation. In other words, it is the journalistic narrative of the event, in part or whole, that is co-opted, transforming it into a "representational" event. The event narrative isn't necessarily transferred out of the realm of journalism and into political culture (though it can be), but rather the appropriation of the event for political purposes reveals the interplay between journalistic practice and the day-to-day "happenings" of political culture.

Not all current events become directly politicized in these ways, but the collective memory of selected events becomes activated by interest groups that typically operate in conjunction with the media. When a particular collective memory is activated for a specific political use, which may be completely removed from the event itself, it can be understood as a "memory project."[2] By memory project it is meant that interested parties activate initial memory in a purposeful way.[3] So then, who creates memory projects?

There are many different "communities of memory" that all have differing interests in the event and different avenues for creating their memory projects. When thinking about communities of memory, there are two major genres into which groups may fall. First, there are those with organic ties to the event. These groups may include event survivors; the bereaved who lost loves ones in the event; and the perpetrators of the event. These groups may be particularly interested in how the event is first marked with significance and then how the event is "officially" commemorated. This may include national remembrance, memorials and the like (often involving a state response that is publicized by the press). The communities of memory that I am primarily concerned with are those that are *not* organically linked to the event, those for whom interest extends beyond traditional commemoration. These kinds of communities of memory, which may activate a repository of collective memory for political purposes, are special interest groups or sponsors which either reside in, or have access to the media sphere.

The press has a role in creating "communities of memory."[4] Likewise, Schudson explains there is a "memory industry" and "memory professions" within which the media and other interest groups reside.[5] When Gamson and Modigliani explain that the media use particular packages to frame world events, as we saw in the last chapter, they go on to point out that some packages have sponsors who not only advocate particular narratives but actively promote them.[6] When investigating how events are used as vehicles for other political purposes we will see how certain interest groups, or "sponsors," aided by the media, actively promote some narratives transplanting them into other arenas.

This chapter considers examples of how Titanic, Columbine, and September 11th have been inserted into other political discourses, occurring in different ways. In some instances, journalists have brought events into other political conversations. In other cases, special interest groups have appropriated the event and used commercial media to communicate their narratives. Using case studies that span different genres of events, also proved interesting in that the politicizing of events can run counter to a logical hypothesis as to how certain events might play out in political culture. For example, in the cases of Pearl Harbor and September 11th the state and the press went out of their way to *depoliticize* the events portraying them as shocking acts of senseless violence, rendering the political roots of the events invisible. As a result, the American public perceived 9-11 as fanatical fringe violence rather than violent political protest, a huge distinction. These events were then used to further many political agendas, though the actual political nature of the events themselves were entirely glossed over. On the other hand, Titanic and Columbine which had social roots and were not, by nature, political, were immediately infused with political spin. The political space created by traumatic events also allows for unpopular or marginalized interpretations to surface. How have counter-culture or otherwise resistive groups responded to the appropriations covered in this chapter? In the case of Shirtwaist, the event was activated politically by marginalized groups though the event itself was never appropriated in the mainstream.

The issue of resistance to dominant press and state narratives as well as their misappropriation is important to the chapter because this particular stage of representation, is critical for putting forth alternative or oppositional narratives that may have initially been overlooked by journalists. When challenging the "official story," the burden of creating powerful alternatives rests with resistive groups.[7] It is during this "representational" stage that a push-pull dynamic emerges between official and resistive representations. The speed by which an event is co-opted is vital to the timeframe in which resistive representations may emerge. Accordingly, technology plays a central role in how events are *re-scripted*.

As described earlier, initial Titanic reports were narrated through a hero-villain frame that demonized the steerage passengers and praised a finite selection of wealthy white men. The overall press story focused on two competing gender narratives: "survival of the fittest" and "the rule of the sea." The gendering of initial Titanic reporting gained significance during the transition from historic event to vehicle of political culture at the end of April 1912 when Titanic — the represented event — was brought to directly bear on the women's suffrage movement.

Votes for Women

The Women's Suffrage movement was in a critical time of growth and promise when Titanic went down. Even a cursory glance at newspapers from 1912 suggests that the press consistently reinforced the dominant (implicitly anti-feminist) discourse regarding the movement. In the case of Titanic the press did not simply recount the politicizing of the event, they created it—as it was journalists that made the link between Titanic and Suffrage. While not explicitly anti-suffrage, newspapers create(d) a cultural space where the prevailing power structure is maintained and in which women's issues in 1912 were marginalized.

Five days into interpreting Titanic, as contradictory gendered narratives circulated, on April 19th, the day the United States Senate began its official inquiry into the disaster, The New York Times linked Titanic to the Suffrage movement. Titanic, the represented event, became an explicit vehicle of and for political culture: a representational event. This is also where and when a space for resistance to the press story emerged.

Towards the back of the April 19th, 1912 edition of *The New York Times*, amidst an array of articles under the heading "Topics of the Times,"[8] there was an article about "English suffragettes of prominence"[9] responding to the Titanic tragedy. The article specifically focused on how these women viewed the first-class men who died aboard Titanic, purportedly so that women would be saved.

The article reported that the suffragists were *responding* to a question posed: how do you feel about the men who died aboard Titanic so that women and children might be saved? The reporter referred to the men who died as "magnificent." Clearly the women interviewed were jumping into a dialogue that had already been framed by the journalist. These particular suffragists did not deny the "fine" actions of men; however, they asserted that these actions did not merit any particular praise because the men were simply fulfilling their duty. The suffragists explained that women are more integral to the human race, and therefore, as more valuable members of society, they *ought to be saved first*. The journalist reported that this position was "scientifically" unfounded. Conversely, the reporter posited that men are more valuable members of society as evidenced by their dominance in the economy (though gender inequality was not linked to male economic dominance). Chinese law was then used as an example of rea-son-driven survival of the fittest policy—where women are categorized as the least valuable citizens. There is a clear tension here as earlier press accounts demonized male Chinese Titanic passengers with racialized and animalistic language.

The Associated Press picked up the Suffrage story and within two days it was widely circulated.[10]

Two days after *The New York Times* piece, the *Denver Post* linked Titanic and Suffrage using famed anarchist Emma Goldman's presence in Denver as its point of departure. On April 21, 1912 the *Denver Post* published an article by Goldman titled "Suffrage Dealt Blow By Women of Titanic."[11] The sub-heading, anonymously authored read: "Emma Goldman Inquires to Know If Equality in Demanded Only at Ballot Box   Human Nature Came Into Own in Men."[12] Goldman began the article by acknowledging "conflicting reports" re-garding what occurred during the Titanic disaster but used this as a segue to assert that the role of women in the "terrible disaster" had been overlooked. Goldman's analysis is interesting in that it contains both dominant and resistive aspects while she was of course perceived as a counter-culture thinker. Goldman argued that women's conduct aboard Titanic was pathetic, her argument resem-bling the dominant social Darwinist analysis from many initial press stories, while at the same time she invoked history as the cause of this latest exhibition of female incompetence. In terms of the latter, Goldman argued that women aboard Titanic enacted the typical needy feminine role *but* attributed this to women's social training as "mere female[s]." In this way the article was situated within a larger web of gendered power relations. Goldman simultaneously delved into the mainstream by comparing the conduct of women to that of "ba-bies" while also asserting that women's obligation to "do better" was because women have a "higher goodness"—a tradition of "love and self-sacrifice." She persecuted women and essentialized them for her own political purposes, but nonetheless her article was rooted in the gendered historical inequities that came to bear in the lived Titanic disaster—as seen in chapter two. It is doubtful that such a subtle counter-dominant undertone would have been widely recognized by the public, particularly since she was conveniently mislabeled a feminist when in fact she was an anarchist. My assumption is corroborated in that later representations responded only to Goldman's statement—that Titanic harmed the Suffrage Movement, failing to credit her for presenting a multi-dimensional historical analysis. In other words, by publicly criticizing the women aboard Titanic, Goldman, popularly and incorrectly defined as a "feminist", strengthened the dominant narrative that Titanic's female survivors behaved badly and did so as a result of their "femininity."

The response to Goldman's piece was swift. On April 22nd the *Denver Post* ran an article by Frances Wayne titled "Titanic Disaster Furnishes No Proof That Women Are Unfit for Suffrage."[13] The article is clearly resistive. Similar points (in the form of "feminist" quotes) contained predominantly within male authored articles, also circulated in newspapers throughout the United States. Wayne made three main points.

First, in a clear response to Goldman, Wayne makes perhaps the most analytically interesting claim to emerge in a commercial publication. She argued that the women who were saved in the Titanic disaster might not have "tainted their little white hands" to bring about Suffrage because women of privilege were not the movement's stronghold, implying that their behavior should not have any bearing on the movement because as a group, they were not actively involved in the political cause of suffrage. Wayne was implicitly acknowledging the class distinction between the women saved and those who died. Since the press had not previously engaged in a class-based discourse, this exemplifies how the directed political use of an event can create a space for those marginalized, to put forth previously silenced narratives. In this case, the social class issues conspicuously absent from initial press reports made their way into the press' discourse only via the event's appropriation into the Suffrage Movement. Wayne also clearly made a distinction between women involved and those not involved in the suffrage movement. She implicitly claimed that it is suffragists who must be held accountable for enacting typical gender roles, if they do so. The actions of other women should not be held against the movement. Unlike Goldman, Wayne did not employ the essentialist category of "woman." Feminists continue to debate the political value of this form of essentialism.[14] Interwoven within these points is the assumption that women of the lower socioeconomic classes were more likely to be politically active. This is interesting, as generally speaking, only prominent feminists had access to systems of mass communication.

The second point in Wayne's article, strangely absent from the Goldman piece, is that women aboard Titanic had not been told that the ship was sinking. Men (who knew the situation) didn't want to worry women, and had said that the occupation of lifeboats was just a precautionary measure. Therefore, in an informed sense, women's behavior did not represent a choice. In order to crystallize this point Wayne, as did Goldman, drew on historical modes of gendered power and the construction of "the feminine" in order to explain that "during the ages it has been accustomed for women to believe men." If women entered the lifeboats it was because men told them to. While Goldman and Wayne create radically different analyses, both invoked history in order to contextualize their points. Historical context was not provided in any of the press' initial narratives and in this respect their professional authority over the event was simply assumed.

Third, Wayne mused: "should women club men into boats to prove their equality?" This view, also prominent in many resistive suffragist responses to the disaster, again posited that women merely followed men's orders. Additionally, the only alternative would have been to resort to the violence purportedly perpetrated by the male crew towards the steerage passengers. These issues were addressed in articles such as, "Universal Suffrage would not have changed the occurrences on board the Titanic, neither will the Titanic disaster affect suffrage." The process of naturalizing a relationship between dissociated subject matter, such as Titanic and Suffrage, is central to how power relations are maintained and it is this phenomenon that makes the study of iconic events interesting. Wayne's article, early on within this social process, attempted to denaturalize the relationship between Titanic and Suffrage in order to challenge the gender narrative upon which this association was built. This article illustrates beautifully, how the press' appropriation of Titanic into Suffrage allowed, unintentionally, for the mainstream circulation of feminist theorizing. And this was only the beginning.

Linking Titanic and Suffrage Through Myth Appropriation[15]

By the time Titanic and Suffrage found themselves in conversation, the association between these two subjects, at least, to the public—seemed natural. How could this have been? Titanic was a contained industry disaster. The Suffrage Movement was an ongoing political struggle of fifty years, characterized by its own specific range of victories and losses. The common thread was gender. But did gender define the Titanic experience—and if it did, to what degree? In terms of cultural outcomes it simply doesn't matter, the question is misleading. Titanic collective memory was gendered, thus creating a common ground between the event and the larger political suffrage struggle and this is what is relevant from here on. As reviewed in chapter three, this collective memory grew out of initial press practices that constructed the represented event, with the dualistic "good versus evil" meta-narrative through which the press framed Titanic stories, relying heavily on the construction and repeated circulation of the mythical concepts Hero, Villain, and Martyr.

This brings us to the most significant aspect of myth: appropriation. A single myth can be appropriated and subsequently "transplanted" into any number of discourses. Once a myth develops in a way that appears natural to those positioned as "believing subjects,"[16] the mythical concept can then be used in ongoing social processes without seeming artificial, without appearing constructed. This enabled the press to link Titanic to the Women's Suffrage Movement: the public perceived the link to be natural. During initial interpretive practices, journalists produced a wide array of narratives and images that signified heroism. The resulting mythical concept (heroism), appearing natural, became the most appropriate category for describing events. This, of course, relies on a cultural tautology or "rhetorical legitimation" with the heroism concept seeming to have a natural correlation to larger societal issues pertaining to gender such as stereotypes that in some instances, linked masculinity with the protection of women. At the time, the Suffrage Movement epitomized struggles over gendered political power. If we think back to the first link between Titanic and Suffrage, *The New York Times* article of April 19th, the article directly uses the hero myth in order to bring Suffrage and Titanic together: Suffragists were asked to respond to the good deeds of male heroes aboard Titanic, taking for granted that there *were* heroes and not questioning whether or not the press had *created* them. This is not to necessarily imply that there were not "heroes," but rather, to point to the *construction and naturalization of this terminology*.

The cultural appropriation of myth into a directed political use constitutes the transformation from a represented event into a representational event. This phenomenon also creates a space for resistance. Roland Barthes explains:

> myth can always, as a last resort, signify the resistance which is brought to bear against it. Truth to tell, the best weapon against myth is perhaps to mythify it in its turn, and to produce an *artificial myth*: and this reconstructed myth will in fact be a mythology . . . All that is needed is to use it as the departure point for a third semiological chain, to take its signification as the first term for a second myth . . .[17]

When resistance to dominant historical representation occurs, it is necessarily reactive and thus, entering a discourse that has already begun. In order to most effectively accomplish this task—where memory-makers do not begin on equal footing, the myth appropriated to maintain current power relations must be again appropriated — *transformed to mean something new* — and inserted into counter-dominant or otherwise resistive narratives. So, while the commercial press used Titanic to weaken Suffrage, they simultaneously opened up a space for Titanic to be used in order to *aid* Suffrage. This process, that began with the Goldman and Wayne articles, was to later emerge fully in resistive venues, primarily suffrage publications.

It is often theorized that the domination of a cultural space (literally) reduces resistance within that domain by virtue of monopolization; however, further consideration, although perhaps counterintuitive, reveals that dominant and resistive forms are mutually dependent in so far as each dominant narrative creates a space for what it has concealed.[18]

Titanic and Suffrage Revisited: Resistance by Second-Tier Myth Appropriation

This section explores the Titanic narratives that circulated in resistive venues, specifically two feminist pro-suffrage publications: *The Common Cause* and *Woman's Journal*. While both texts responded to Titanic after it had been brought to bear on the question of Suffrage by the commercial press, both were weekly publications. Editions were not slated to come out until after the press had already begun covering Titanic. It is therefore impossible to know who would have chosen to first link Titanic and Suffrage, it is only possible to analyze the narratives as they were published chronologically. When doing so, these counterculture journals are reactive.

The Organ of the National Union of Women's Suffrage Societies produced *The Common Cause*. This Suffrage journal, registered as a newspaper, identified itself as "Non-Militant." While certainly a resistive text, it was far tamer than *Woman's Journal*. On April 25th, 1912 the journal addressed Titanic on its front page in an article titled "The Wreck of the Titanic."[19] The anonymous author begins by expressing collective grief over the tragedy and then goes on to articulate two main points. The first issue raised is the difficulty with which women must have entered the lifeboats knowing that their loved ones were going to die. The author then suggested that perhaps they *didn't* know that their loved ones would die and that their subsequent survivor grief must have been overwhelming.

The style in which *The Common Cause* communicated its resistance to dominant press interpretations is congruent with the overall style of that publication. While the text was pro-suffrage and the content, necessarily resistive, the form was very similar to that of mainstream newspapers. The text was presented as a series of information-bearing reports. In accord with the "non-militant" mantra, the journal implicitly questions dominant discourse—but not in the form of a clear and directed challenge. Specifically, their narrative counters dominant images of women immediately "choosing" to enter the boats ahead of others— free from concern, confusion, or remorse. Here, resistance was posed subtly. Within the first two sentences of their response to the Titanic-Suffrage link, the journal suggested that women had experienced unspeakable tragedy commenting on 1) how difficult entering the lifeboats would be if one knew her loved ones were going to die, and 2) that women may not have been informed that the ship was sinking. In a concise and arguably non-confrontational manner, this journal took the dominant gender narrative and appropriated it to mean something else: women who entered the boats were presented as strong, not weak. Throughout their Titanic reporting *The Common Cause* never challenged how Titanic events had been reported, they accepted that the press had accurately reported the event, but they consistently took the "facts as reported" and interpreted them from a feminist standpoint in order to alter their meaning. This is one particular way resistive groups can challenge dominant discourse. Images of women entering the boats were reconstructed to represent tremendous personal challenge and fortitude. Images of men placing women into boats represented women not being informed about the situation. The same dominant images and mythical concepts, now readily available for recall as a part of base-line collective memory, were used to construct new meanings. In this case, the text created a new connotation using a shared memory-image (men helping women into the boats). Despite accepting the dominant reporting of "facts," for example, that women had entered the boats before men, this method of creating new meaning *within* the confines of an openly pro-suffrage journal, illustrates political resistance through re-interpretation.

The second and larger part of the article was a tribute to Titanic passenger W. T. Stead. There was a large photograph of Stead in the center of the page and the article reported that he was an extraordinary person who would be greatly missed. Beyond having worked as an editor at *Northern Echo*, he was a social activist who fought against white slavery and child labor. Stead was a strong supporter of women's equality in all areas of social life including education and the economy. Despite his links to the movement, it might seem strange that a Suffrage publication chose to devote so much of their interpretive space to a man. This may have been a very clever strategic move. By memorializing Stead, they were able to bring his political views—under the umbrella of the hero myth that subsumed his story in dominant press narratives—to the public consciousness. This is a different kind of example of second tier myth appropriation. The press had already included Stead among lists of "notable men" who died aboard Titanic, and while he did not receive as much coverage as Astor, he was nonetheless constructed as a hero. Suffragists were then able to use this mythic image of Stead *for their own political purposes*. Once he had been firmly implanted into collective memory as embodying heroic qualities, his "liberal" political tendencies regarding equality could be used without fear of rebuttal by the public or conservative political groups. By using the vision created by the press, suffragists were able to jump into a preexisting discourse and use it to their own advantage. The mainstream press was so successful in constructing Stead (and others) as heroes that no one would then dare to challenge an article that detailed the heroic acts of his lifetime. On page 37 of the same edition of *The Common Cause*, there was a full-length feature article that memorialized Stead by listing his political affiliations, all of which advocated equality for women and children. These are the *only* discussions of Titanic within the April 25th edition.

Produced by The Official Organ of The National Woman Suffrage Association, *Woman's Journal* took a decidedly more aggressive approach to responding to the Titanic-Suffrage link in their April 27th, 1912 edition. The front page of the journal read: VOTES FOR WOMEN TO THE RESCUE.[20] There was a large illustration of Titanic labeled "Ship of State" and a savior ship (a take on the Californian) emitting the slogan "Votes for Women." The illustration equated Titanic to the Nation having lifeboat capacity for only half of the people. In the water surrounding the troubled "Ship of State" were life preservers and sea creatures labeled with the social issues that feminists were concerned with. The political labels included: "white slavery," "consumption," "social diseases," "gambling," "child labor," "fire traps," "sweatshops," "impure food," and "poverty," The majority of the labels were placed on snake-like creatures. Historically, the snake has been a symbol, within dominant discourse, of female weakness with mythic roots in Genesis.[21] The strategic use of the snake was a part of the political challenge being posed.

This powerful resistive image is a prime example of how suffragists took the link made between Titanic and Suffrage and used it in order to reclaim their own historical representation. The piece not only challenged dominant Titanic reports, but it went further by actually taking the Titanic image and re-implanting it into the Suffrage Movement in order to expose the very social-political oppressions that suffragists opposed. In terms of critique, mainstream journalists merely questioned whether there was inadequate lifeboat capacity. *Woman's Journal* took that critique, which was also a widely shared public sentiment, and compared it to the treatment of women and other minorities in the United States. Ultimately the illustration asked the public: if you have a problem

WOMAN'S JOURNAL

OFFICIAL ORGAN OF THE NATIONAL AMERICAN WOMAN SUFFRAGE ASSOCIATION

VOL. XLIII   NO. 17   SATURDAY, APRIL 27, 1912   FIVE CENTS

VOTES FOR WOMEN TO THE RESCUE

WHEN WOMEN CANNOT VOTE THE SHIP OF STATE IS LIKE THE STEAMSHIP "TITANIC" WITH ONLY HALF ENOUGH LIFE BOATS.

WOMEN PARADE, RAIN OR SHINE   **BIG NEWSPAPER SETS EXAMPLE**   **TO HEAD CHILDREN'S BUREAU**

with a ship carrying lifeboats for only half of its passengers, then how do you feel about a country that protects less than half of its citizens?

Beneath the Titanic piece there was an article announcing an upcoming Suffrage Parade predicted to be the largest in U.S. history. In fact, that parade turned out to be the largest in world history, demonstrating the momentum of the movement at that time. Held on the day of John Jacob Astor's memorial service, parade participants marched directly outside of Astor's New York memorial service illustrating the importance of the Titanic narrative within the ongoing Suffrage Movement. Again, suffragists took the hero myth constructed by the press and married it to their own political objectives. This was only the beginning.

In the same edition of *Woman's Journal*, three other Titanic articles, all authored by Alice Stone Blackwell, were presented column to column on a single page. The first article titled "The Lesson of The Titanic"[22] was a feminist reinterpretation of the hero narrative. The hero myth was acknowledged and transformed via four steps. First, the acts of heroism during the tragedy were highlighted. These included the conventional narrative of husbands saving wives, but extended to wives who refused to be saved so that they could die with their husbands as well as daughters, who gave their place in the boats to their mothers. For example the story of Mrs. Straus that had been used in the mainstream to signify the sanctity of marriage, was reclaimed and transformed into a story of female equality. After broadening the scope of those who acted bravely in order to include women, the article challenged the press' construction of heroic figures. Specifically, Blackwell questioned how Astor became the central figure of the event, as opposed to Stead.

> It is strange to think of William T. Stead and John Jacob Astor clinging to the same cake of ice until their hands froze and they went down! It was touching to see how many people were able to die bravely though they had not been able to live bravely; but that has been shown before, in every war and in almost every great catastrophe. Life is harder than death.[23]

While not challenging the claim that "notable men" had acted bravely in terms of staying to die so that others could be saved, these suffragists challenged the press' construction of hero figures based solely on one's actions aboard Titanic and noted the press' failure to situate heroic actions within the context of how a person lived the rest of his life. Stead, friend of the movement, may have died in the same manner as Astor but they had lived very differently.

The article then addressed the lessons of chivalry brought home by Titanic, asserting two meaningful ways that this newfound knowledge could be applied in society, more specifically—to the shipping Industry. The first was to make

certain that all human life be protected—through strict legislative policies requiring complete lifeboat protection, wireless technology mandates, and the abo-
lition of "reckless speed of rival lines racing for record passages." It is within
the second lesson of chivalry that suffragists directly reclaimed their own historical representation by appropriating the myth promulgated by the commercial
press, thereby altering, even transforming its meaning. After concurring that
chivalrous acts were abundant during the Titanic disaster, Blackwell (re)defined
"chivalry" as *people in a position of strength being ethically obligated to help
those who are weaker or less situationally empowered.* Blackwell contended
that this form of heroism occurs between varied individuals and groups and not
just men towards women. Furthermore, the cultural value of chivalry could ap-
ply not only to individuals, but to society as a whole.

> It is a question not merely of helping a lost child, but of stopping child labor;
> not merely of guiding a stranger, but of securing protective legislation for im-
> migrants; . . . not merely of putting forth personal influence to save a weak
> brother from falling, but of grappling with the white slave traffic; not merely of
> easing an old man's steps, but of getting old-age pensions; not merely of con-
> tributing to a servant's self-respect, but of improving industrial conditions. To
> promote all these things the ballot is needed. Opponents of equal rights do not
> realize that there is actually a strong element of chivalry in the suffrage move-
> ment. Thousands of women . . . are seeking a vote for the sake of helping the
> less fortunate—men, women and children. When we remember Titanic, let us
> not only try harder to put forth the new chivalry in our own personal dealings
> with those weaker than ourselves but also work harder to secure the ballot, the
> prime weapon in the modern warfare against oppression and wrong.[24]

In this piece, suffragists transformed the hero myth by broadening cultural understandings of chivalry, and extending the concept to the very social causes
they had long been fighting for. The Titanic myth created by journalists fostered
a new public appreciation for chivalry, by grabbing hold of this constructed public sentiment, suffragists were able to use the collective feelings conjured up in
the mainstream for their own political ends. "Chivalry" per se, was not previously a part of the suffragist agenda. By adopting the dominant term at that precise historical moment, feminists were able to build upon press-created public
sentiment and expose its oppositional possibilities. Ironically, the male-centered
narrative produced within dominant discourse, created resistive groups' access
to the power of collective memory construction. In other words, the journalistic
authority that allowed the press to put forth their version of Titanic was eventually co-opted and used as a challenge to their own (press) spin, unwittingly pav-
ing, via the printed word, the way for feminist resistance.

The second article was titled "Suffrage and Life-Saving."[25] Four key points were raised. First, Blackwell recapped that the press used chivalrous acts aboard Titanic as a reason to deny women the right to vote. This argument stated that chivalry, at the time revered as a high cultural value, would disappear if women had the vote. In a direct rebut Blackwell stated that one had nothing to do with the other, and she offered a series of historical examples of chivalrous acts committed by those without the right to vote (including male soldiers). Second, it was explained that in China, women live in "extreme subjection," and by extension, Chinese law should not be taken as evidence that American women were better off without voting rights.

Next, Blackwell accepted that the men aboard Titanic undoubtedly committed chivalrous acts; however, this did not eradicate the thousands of non-chivalrous acts men routinely commit against women and children, such as white slavery and other forms of exploitation. This is the third time within the same edition that this organization chose to take the hero myth (in the form of its constituting concept chivalry) in order to expose the multiple social conditions that suffragists were trying to change. It is the second example of suffragists calling on the American people to look not only at the acts that spontaneously occurred during an anomalous industrial accident, but to consider how individuals lived day-to-day and to examine large scale social patterns of inequality.

The final point was a call for women's Suffrage. Blackwell critiqued the pursuit of financial gains "which too largely rules the world today"[26] at the sacrifice of human life and asserted that if women obtained the right to vote—they would be able to "mitigate" such occurrences. She pointed out that women best understand the value of human life because they are its creators and raised the point, had there been proper safeguards in place, the high loss of life would have been prevented. The article concluded; "There will be far fewer lost by preventable accidents, either on land or sea, when the mothers of men have the right to vote."[27] Just like in the front-page illustration, and the "Lesson" article, this piece took the myths that constituted initial Titanic collective memory and breaking them down, transformed them in order to change their meaning, ultimately using this new interpretation as a call for women's Suffrage.[28]

The third Titanic article was a tribute to Stead. Using a similar format to the Common Cause, Stead was defined as brave because of his pro-equality political affiliations. This tribute, not as purely glowing as a typical eulogy, posited that his "eccentric" personality also caused him to engage in unwise politics such as his support of the Russian government towards the end of his life. Nonetheless, Stead was pro-women and pro-children and represented a true hero lost. This article reads as an attempt to combat the one dimensional portrayals of heroes, found in mainstream newspapers.

The Common Cause continued to write about Titanic for three more weeks while Titanic only made its way into the pages of *Woman's Journal* once more.

The cover of the May 9th edition, using the imagery of a ship (heading towards the "Bright" land of suffrage) seems to symbolically invoke Titanic imagery although no textual explanation was given. The May 16th edition contains the last two Titanic articles to make their way into *The Common Cause*. The first was another tribute to Stead, written as a letter endorsed by over five hundred women. The second article authored by Wex Jones was written as a poem and titled "Woman and Children First."[29] This piece blamed nature as a "traitor," referred to repeatedly in feminine terminology, "with her half-bared fangs" claimed the lives of people so heroic that they died by the "creed of women and children first." This article, reprinted from the *N. Y. Journal*, is a dominant narrative circulating within a resistive publication.

On May 4th *Woman's Journal* printed its last Titanic article similarly titled: "Women and Children First"[30] by Mrs. Rheta Childe Derr. The only difference in the title of the two pieces is the word "women" instead of "woman." The former was generally used in suffragist texts as a method of de-essentializing women. The use of the essentialist category "woman" in *The Common Cause* illustrates the tensions within that self-proclaimed resistive text. The "Women" article tells a very different story. Here, the author narrates (in the first-person) a story of women working in a factory. While the Shirtwaist Factory was not mentioned by name, it seems clear that this was a mixed historical-fictive account of that tragedy and Titanic. Figuratively speaking, readers were walked through the factory from the perspective of the immigrant women who labored there, and were introduced to the many forgotten women, many elderly, who earned their living there: "All they were fit for was sorting over the debris of civilization."[31] The article raised gendered labor oppression as the silenced, repressed, ignored effects of industrialization. Written as prose, the narrator juxtaposes ferocious noises of the machines with the desperate faces of the female employees.[32] Signs of a hierarchical organization of the workspace abound:

> There were signs about: "No Smoking." But more than once during the day a buyer strolled through accompanied by the boss, both smoking big cigars. The most disconcerting thing about that factory was the locked doors. As soon as the girls were inside and the power was turned on, the foreman closed and locked the doors.[33]

The author wrote that one woman had to leave to nurse her newborn child, described as "awful thin and sickly."[34] She tried to escape through a window and broke her neck. Consistent with other articles in *Woman's Journal*, this unfolding story was used to respond to the stories of heroism aboard the Titanic, put forth by the press, (that were so powerful that, as noted earlier, they had made their way into some suffragist publications).

"The law of the sea: women and children first.
The law of the land—that's different.
Yet it is known on land as well as at sea that the race is carried on by children, and that women are needed to care for the children."[35]

Without any mention of Titanic, by using a negative iconic event (or non-iconic event) to expose social conditions rooted in inequality, *Woman's Journal* attempted to debunk the hero myth by exposing what it marginalized. This form of critical deconstruction occurs by taking the myth constructed in the mainstream and asking for equal application. It is interesting that this journal used Shirtwaist imagery so explicitly since, as we shall soon see, they were far less responsive to Shirtwaist in its own time and on its own terms.

The use of Titanic in the Women's Suffrage Movement, in so far as the larger cultural processes at work, is quite revealing. The dominant press narrative that began to form immediate to the event, was gendered in highly stereotypical ways—even overlooking the important role that social class played in that experience. The way that journalists reported on Titanic, reified cultural stereotypes about gender, normalizing the idea that women were inferior to men. This allowed them to then link Titanic and Suffrage in a way that may have appeared natural to many. This was the beginning of a "memory project" where the Titanic press narrative was employed in service of the anti-suffrage lobby—which had benefited from the press' initial gendered reporting. Suffragists then responded to the use of Titanic against them by turning the event into a call for women's Suffrage.

The politics driving early journalistic interpretations, and how those ideas may be appropriated for political causes, becomes clearer when comparing Titanic to contemporary cases.

Contemporary Positive Cases

The Columbine school shootings and September 11th immediately generated an intense and multi-media interpretive process or what Dayan and Katz call intense "hermeneutic activity."[36] The event was initially represented in an explosion of multi-media forms—a frenetic attempt to make sense of, while attempting to document the events which the process itself, imbued with a "turning point" quality. As seen when looking at initial press interpretations, Columbine and September 11th produced simplistic meta-narratives of good versus evil based on the mythical concepts: hero, martyr, villain and in the case of 9-11, patriotism. Distilled concepts are easily stored in memory[37] and as a result, their intense repetition in the media quickly solidified them within the press' version and the public's understanding of Columbine and 9-11. The reporting of these events was never free from political spin. For example, 9-11 reporting was immediately framed with war rhetoric, limited notions of patriotism, and reified the administration's "official" story. Differing from Titanic, Columbine and 9-11 were at once documented and "used" politically, in purposeful ways. In this way, real-time journalistic responses to the events were limited to their political use.

How was Columbine explicitly appropriated into ongoing political struggles? How did this occur in ways that appeared natural? What is the relationship between the press' initial construction of Columbine and the appropriation of the Columbine narrative? Put differently, who "sponsored" certain press narratives at the exclusion of others and how did special interest groups work in the context of media to create political projects out of Columbine? In the case of 9-11, we can also ask how did the media production of patriotism allow for the immediate directed use of the 9-11 press narrative? Given the bombardment of representations in the cases of Columbine and 9-11, and the immediate political uses of the event images, when and how did resistive narratives emerge? Columbine and 9-11 are also engaging because of the ways in which they *weren't* used—in order to promote social change and challenge the commercial media (the notion of a "free" media with commercial imperatives that operates from "objectivity" is itself, highly contradictory). This raises the question: what is the selection process by which events become co-opted into some political discourses and not others?

In short, how did the press, in conjunction with other special interest groups, spin political propositions vis-à-vis these events? How does this process compare to the political appropriation of Titanic into the Suffrage Movement?

Columbine

Columbine was used to further several political agendas. It was appropriated into the national debate over gun control, conservative demands for media censorship, an attack on the "breakdown" of the family, and demands for more surveillance. Journalists and politicians however did not use Columbine to address the widespread phenomenon of male violence or the country's historic epidemic of racism. So, Columbine, the represented event, was turned into a directed political use many times over, but in the interest of a certain set of politics, to the exclusion of others. How did this happen?

As discussed in the last chapter, during the first day of interpretation, two main images dominated television screens: students running outside of the school with their hands on their heads and a bloody boy dangling from a broken window during his rescue. The repetition of those particular images highlighted them as the images most linked to Columbine and in turn, the images most associated with school violence in the United States. As the press continued to narrate the event, three concepts dominated their stories: Villains (the two gunmen), Heroes (the coach who stayed to save students), and Martyrs (the two girls who said "yes," I do believe in god and were killed). These reduced concepts were quickly appropriated within the dominant discourse to signify a range of meanings. In particular, "villain" images, deeply entrenched in the language of the "trenchcoat mafia" were juxtaposed with "hero" and "martyr" images, making the villain narratives more ominous and thus more evocative to the public. These emotionally charged concepts were then transplanted into ongoing political discourses about: 1) surveillance, 2) the family, 3) gun control, and 4) censorship. In a marked shift from Titanic newspaper reporting, the public saw the immediate political uses of these concepts, *citizens tuned into the various media were actually watching the process of Columbine becoming representational, mythic, and soon, iconic.* With the exception of creating a space to renegotiate gun control and stage the "million mom march", (issues which are organically linked to the school shooting), all of the appropriations of Columbine centered on conservative politics. Even the gun control narrative was overshadowed by the other political uses of Columbine and was not the dominant story spun in the mass media (although Columbine was used to create new legislation and place gun control visibly in the public domain).

Before addressing the various ways that different interest groups as well as journalists, co-opted Columbine as a vehicle for pushing their political agendas, there are strong examples of how political leaders, seperate from the press, infused Columbine with particular social significance. For instance, the day after Columbine, political leaders at the Statehouse, publicly offered the victims and community a moment of silence, and also cancelled their work day as a sign of respect: "At the Statehouse, the mood was unusually solemn as the Senate and the House both opened with morning prayers, followed by a moment of silence for the victims and their families. The legislature then shut down for the day."[38] This, in conjunction with the saturation coverage the event was simultaneously receiving, marked it with political significance, from the outset.

Columbine and Surveillance

Surveillance became a major political topic after Columbine—and reporters covered it extensively. There were many newspaper stories about new town curfews nationwide, increased surveillance in schools, and the availability of commodities like clear backpacks aimed at reducing instances of weapons being carried onto school property. This level of coverage, normalized an increase in surveillance. (The *Star Tribune* carried an article that praised companies such as Tactical Alliance, which employs professionals trained in SWAT, for creating methods that better protected American schools.) It was reported that local Minnesota schools were contemplating using this company's services which included: "Digital photography, of schools, taken by experts, attempting to emulate the path of would-be snipers, to pinpoint weak spots. The company would request school floor plans and details of crawl spaces so that police would have them available, perhaps on computer discs or training manuals."[39] This article is just one of many national and local stories, documenting the measures taken all over the United States, after the shootings at Columbine High School. Responding to bomb threats was another example of this call to action: "Schools are reacting strongly, doing everything from evacuating buildings while they are searched to canceling classes for the day."[40]

Columbine and Guns

The use of Columbine with respect to gun control, exhibits how an event can be appropriated into a political discourse for disseminating messages, or how it can be employed directly in the service of policy change. While these outcomes are usually interrelated in one memory project (the press and anti-suffrage advocates communicated ideas about women *and* attempted to stunt the Suffrage Movement), Columbine's place in gun control, presents a different configuration. The image of Columbine was seized by multiple groups that were at the time interested in gun legislation. Columbine was used as a directed political use by liberal groups in the service of 1) changing gun control legislation, and 2) putting pressure on political candidates and raising gun control as a national priority through the "Million Mom March" (which contrary to public opinion was not inspired by Columbine, only fueled by it). Both appropriations were moderately successful and constituted the only "liberal" uses of Columbine that occurred shortly after the event. Interestingly though, the majority of press reporting I examined, spun pro-gun discourses. Furthermore, while gun control legislative changes flowed from Columbine, gun control was not the dominant politicized story in Columbine reporting, censorship, (as seen later) was.

Columbine was swiftly used by gun control advocates. President Bill Clinton took action three weeks after Columbine proposing a legislative package which included: " . . . raising the age of handgun ownership to 21, requiring background checks for buyers at gun shows and holding parents criminally responsible for allowing a child access to a gun that is later used in a shooting."[41]

While the "Million Mom March" is at times mistakenly assumed to have been inspired by the events at Columbine High School, in actuality, though the march may have gained support as a result of Columbine, it was a school shooting later that year that motivated one mother to start a protest. In August of 1999, Donna Dees-Thomases, a New Jersey mother, read about the shooting of school children in Granada Hills, California. One week later, on August 17, She applied for a permit to march on Washington to protest weak gun legislation in the United States. Dees-Thomases connected with a group at a news conference where the million mom march was announced, and was supported by the Brady Campaign to Prevent Gun Violence, as well as the public support of celebrities like Rosie O'Donnell (who was very vocal about her feelings that Columbine resulted from poor gun control). On Mother's Day, May 14, 2000, approximately 750,000 protestors marched in Washington D.C. as well as 150,000 to 200,000 who marched in linked events around the country. So while Columbine was used to gain support and publicity for the grassroots social movement, it was not the impetus for the protest.

Beyond these two politically "left" uses, *the press* made Columbine a political story through its gun-control coverage. Two patterns are of note. First, journalistic coverage primarily relayed a pro-gun discourse. Second, the press generally evoked gun-control as a means for talking about *other* social and political issues. Most frequently, journalists used gun-control as a vehicle for arriving at issues pertaining to popular culture, censorship, and the image of the teen killers as "outsiders."

The *Denver Post* summed up the media sponsored political "uses" of Columbine in a cartoon that appeared in the Friday April 23rd, 1999 edition. The cartoon played off of the press coverage from day one and brought Columbine to bear on gun laws, the family, violence in popular culture, and an impersonal school system. (Ultimately, Columbine would have little bearing on how Americans think about public schools in the U.S. beyond issues of "safety.") The cartoon appeared right in the middle of two gun control articles indicating that gun control, also privileged as the first topic in the cartoon, was the primary issue. The article above the cartoon was titled "Rethink the Second Amendment"[42] and appeared to be the "anti-gun article;" however, this was not the case. While the article, taking a shot at NRA President Charlton Heston, did proclaim that the second amendment was "not the ten commandments" and should be reconsidered given the nation's "epidemic" of violence, the journalist ultimately chose to critique popular culture—blaming singer Marilyn Manson, the producers of the film *The Matrix*, and the makers of the video game "Mortal Kombat" for the Columbine shootings. The article reported that the two gunmen, identified as "trenchcoat mafia members," were fans of all of these forms of entertainment (though people who knew the gunmen would later dispute that they were fans of Marilyn Manson). So, the article that at first glance appeared to be a pro-gun reform piece, was actually a conservative attack on American popular culture. The article beneath the cartoon was titled "Making Schools Safe for Criminals"[43] and was a pro-gun piece that took the position that society is much safer when "law abiding citizens" maintain the right to bear arms. Furthermore, taking an extreme right-wing stance, the reporter argued that it was because of "gun control advocates" that none of the victims at Columbine were able to defend themselves (by having guns in school). So, the newspaper page that at first appeared to present both sides of the gun debate, in which the cartoon illustration was enmeshed, was really a pro-gun and pro-censorship call.

Using Columbine's link to the issue of gun control in order to create a discourse about popular culture, was widespread and shows a partnership between conservative politics and the media that promotes them. One day before this cartoon appeared, in the April 22nd edition, the *Denver Post* ran an article titled: "Denver: Ground Zero in the Gun Debate."[44] Most interesting, are the other articles that appeared on this page. On the opposite side of the page is a pro-gun control article in which the journalist repeatedly claims that his opinion, as with the pro-gun side, could not be proven because statistics are not trustworthy. This had the effect of diffusing the gun-control piece. The article across the bottom of the page rounded it out and was titled "Demonizing and Scapegoating Won't Save Kids' Lives."[45] This oddly titled article was a pro-gun and pro-censorship piece. The journalist attacked popular culture which he called "the real roots of violence" for producing "cultural garbage vomiting from our TV screens." Analytically, what should be considered is not so much the conservative politics that this article promotes (as individual journalists may be known for their particular political leanings), but rather, the conservative politics promulgated *throughout* the newspaper. At first glance it appeared that articles with different political bents were juxtaposed in the form of a balanced debate; however, this was not actually the case. Returning to the cartoon illustration from April 23rd, though the picture emphasizes gun-laws and reinforces this by showing the multiple social "guns" to the country's head, a genuine discourse about guns is not the lasting story to come out of Columbine's press coverage.

Columbine and Conservative Discourses about "The Family"
When considering how Columbine was co-opted into a conservative discourse about "family" it is important to bear in mind that the family is a social institution and therefore the manner in which it was written about, fueled ideas not about the specific families involved, but rather the "state of the family," in general. Such discourses necessarily are grounded in a particular set of assumptions

about what constitutes "family," ideas that are linked to cultural constructions of gender, class, and sexuality. The *Denver Post* circulated cartoon imagery that blamed everything from "parental apathy" to "broken homes", for the tragedy. The newspaper spun these conservative ideologies *as if they were neutral.*

Columbine, "Goths," and Censorship

The primary political appropriation of Columbine placed it within a preexisting debate over censorship. The conservative media-fueled focus on censorship, both created a site for right-wing politics and simultaneously introduced the big Columbine scapegoat to the public, a public that was primed by the press to want answers, and/or someone or something to blame. The use of a scapegoat parallels how the press' gendered Titanic narratives were later co-opted, allowing the link between Titanic and Suffrage to be made—in a way that appeared natural. In both the Titanic and Columbine cases, there is a blame element that is crucial to the eventual political appropriation. In other words, in both cases, initial reports spun very particular ideas about who was to blame for the event they simultaneously labeled as historic. As such, the event is both used directly for a political cause (anti-suffrage and media censorship respectively) and is also being used to divert attention away from other pressing social questions that could be a part of the interpretive and healing process. From the outset, the press consistently linked the attack on "goth music" to stories about "outsiders." This systematic use of an "othering" spin on Columbine is particularly troubling because, as we saw in chapter three, the press never used Columbine as a vehicle to address racism in the United States despite the racialized attack and link to Hitler. This is reminiscent of the press' failure to address the issues of race and class that were critical to the Titanic experience. Likewise, the commercial press did not use Columbine to address the epidemic of male violence that Columbine signifies. While a gun control story did emerge out of Columbine, it was largely conflated with discussions about censorship and family. This indicates that the politically conservative appropriations of Columbine imagery, being the most pervasive, were the ones to stick.

From day one of representation, the media, spinning dominant conservative ideology, created narratives that were quickly used to legitimize a right-wing discourse about censorship. The press was thus complicit in distributing a narrative that would, ironically, ultimately challenge the freedom of the media, though not journalists themselves, who self-immunize against such connections. Marilyn Manson and others, within what the press haphazardly labeled "gothic subculture," were targeted. On Friday April 23 the *Denver Post* reported: "Area schools tighten security, ban trench coats."[46] Several pages later the paper also ran a resistive article titled: "Goth-fashion crackdown seen by some as fascism"[47] which reported that teenagers were ticketed by the police for wearing trench coats and one student had hers confiscated by a teacher. There was a photo of a ticketed student. The photo appeared between two stories. The student was wearing all black, including a trench coat, with his head low and hair disheveled. He appeared sullen. The photo resembled that of the two Columbine killers. On the right of the photo was a story titled "Copycat threats spook schools across nation."[48] One need only look at the photo in relation to the two stories, framing it, to get the picture. The mapping of this page serves to dilute the potential resistive power of the "fascism" article. Several pages later in the same newspaper, there is an article titled "Manson concert called off."[49] The placement of these articles also contributes to, and influences how the narrative develops. It is not just individual stories, but also a larger Columbine narrative that is more than the sum of its parts.

Focusing on the dark dress and reported musical taste of the two Columbine gunmen, dominant narratives claimed that Marilyn Manson promoted hate, death, suicide, and mass murder.[50] Soon after the Columbine shootings, this quote appeared in the *Star Tribune*: "Manson whose angst-filled lyrics some have loosely linked to last week's school shootings in Littleton, Colorado, has cancelled an upcoming Friday night show near Denver."[51]

Rather than addressing the social causes from which school violence flows, the media and conservative politicians were quick to blame Manson and his music, pressuring him to cancel a show and not play in Denver for years to come. In the same article, one parent also referring to Manson's music said "Our teens don't need a message of hopelessness."[52] In a resistive text one writer referred to Manson as the "Trenchcoat Scapegoat Superstar."[53] Via the Internet, magazines and television, Manson denied any link to the Columbine killings. Moreover, he began a resistive dialogue about censorship, the uninformed attack on "gothic culture", and the poorly chosen focus of "official" energies aimed at preventing future violence. In terms of the latter, Manson pointed to a culture of fear, fostered by politicians and the corporate-driven mass media, for creating such high rates of violence and fear cycles in the United States.[54] Through Internet websites, blogs, personal web pages, and counter-culture magazines, many stories with similar alternative interpretations by those who would otherwise not have had access to technologies of mass communication, were able to circulate. Void of an ongoing directed political cause, such as the Suffrage Movement, resistive groups in this case, did not have their own publication(s); generally speaking however, increases in systems of mass communications, of which the mass media is only one part, and the very nature of media texts themselves, is changing this. The Internet is central to this shift but should not, at least at the time of Columbine, be taken as equivalent to the commercial mass media. Despite an ability to react more rapidly in resisting the dominant discourse, the anti-censorship and anti-scapegoating campaigns that emerged, were wholly reactive and responsive to ideological uses of Columbine. In other words, the resistance wasn't aimed at its own political end(s), but rather, to rebutting the use of Columbine in a conservative discourse about censorship.

In an attempt to ban Manson from performing in Denver (which occurred twice after Columbine), Governor Bill Owens and youth pastor Jason Janz argued that his lyrics legitimize acts such as Columbine by promoting murder and suicide. With wit and irony, Manson responded that he could mix his songs with Bible stories about murder, suicide, adultery, disease, and child sacrifice. The simplistic myths used by the right-wing were then again appropriated by Manson and resistive groups in order to challenge the dominant interpretation.

After Columbine, there were many groups not only blaming Marilyn Manson, but also the producers of the film *The Matrix*, and the makers of the video game "Mortal Kombat." It is noteworthy that none of the press' reports about violent media, made connections to the wars occurring at the time of each shooting (and the media coverage of those wars which could also be argued had a desensitizing effect). Furthermore, journalists failed to address media violence as a gendered phenomenon perhaps more aptly categorized as male violence, instead choosing to leave it ambiguous and thus appearing gender-neutral.

Scholars Jackson Katz and Sut Jhally responded to the press' coverage of Columbine by complicating the Manson and bullying stories in order to try and spark a national conversation about gender and violence. Katz and Jhally, drawing on feminist scholarship, asserted that media and political analysts had "missed the mark" when talking about Columbine as "kids killing kids" when in fact all of the 39 cases of school violence in the proceeding two years were "boys killing boys and boys killing girls."[55] Jhally recalled that Jackson Katz had called Columbine a "teachable moment in the U.S. that the media ignored."[56] In fact, the gender neutral language that the media chose to use in framing the event, fostered an invisibility of one of the main issues Columbine may have flowed from, namely the social construction of masculinity in the United States and how it promotes male aggression and violence. On May 2, 1999 a story titled "The National Conversation in the Wake of Littleton is Missing the Mark"[57] appeared in the *Boston Globe*.

> the way in which we neuter these discussions makes it hard to frame such questions, for there is a wrong way and a right way of asking them. The wrong way: "Did the media (video games, Marilyn Manson, 'The Basketball Diaries') make them do it?" One of the few things that we know for certain after 50 years of sustained research on these issues is that behavior is too complex a phenomenon to pin down to exposure to individual and isolated media messages. The evidence strongly supports that behavior is linked to attitudes and attitudes are formed in a much more complex cultural environment. The right way to ask the

question is: "How does the cultural environment, including media images, contribute to definitions of manhood that are picked up by adolescents?" Or, "How does repeated exposure to violent masculinity normalize and naturalize this violence?"[58]

Katz and Jhally used the same concepts created during initial press coverage (that converged into a censorship narrative), in order to accomplish three objectives, (only the first of which has already been seen in other resistive representations): 1) to respond to the attack on certain sectors of the mass media 2) to appropriate Columbine in order to generate a national conversation about the construction and normalization of violent masculinity, and 3) to call attention to the press' initial (and inaccurate), framing of the event in gender-neutral language.

The focus and exploitation of the "goth" and "outsider" narratives by the commercial press and politicians also made invisible the racial and social class aspects of Columbine. In the June 7th edition of *The Nation*, scholar Patricia J. Williams authored an article titled "Smart Bombs"[59] in which she considered Columbine in relation to issues of racism and classism. She criticized the press for normalizing the issue by ignoring the race of the killers—as if their "whiteness" was not a race, and she questioned how these events would have been dealt with, had others perpetrated them, as these kinds of mass killings are typically committed by white males.

> It began to dawn on me why all of those kids in Colorado could go on and on about how "normal" Eric Harris and Dylan Klebold were. I began to appreciate why the authorities might find it hard to pick out any further suspects from a student body whose poetic sensibility is suffused with the metaphors of blood lust . . . I think of the long, tragic history of what happens to minority kids who wave toy guns in public. I think about Dylan Klebold touting around town in his BMW with a trunk full of bombs, and I can't help thinking about the black dentist who was stopped by the highway patrol more than a hundred times over four years before he finally traded in his BMW for something more drably utilitarian. Perhaps the power of "the normative" to induce moral blind spots can be appreciated for its depth and complexity only when the world for some reason gets turned upside down.[60]

This kind of race and class interpretation, similar to the gender narrative, was highly marginalized and never made its way into the public discourse.

September 11th

The attacks of September 11th have been brought to bear on many ongoing political movements and continue to be transformed into a vehicle of representation and a call to political action. The last chapter alluded to how the press laid the groundwork for the Iraq War by depoliticizing the causes of 9-11, promoting a limited view of patriotism, using war rhetoric, and failing to pose any challenge to the administration's official account.

While "chivalry" was the center of the Titanic hero narrative, "patriotism" is the strongest current within the September 11th national mythology. The nation-state relied heavily upon this public sentiment which itself was systematically created by journalists and state officials. In particular the Bush Administration exploited this mass hysteria to garner support for pursuing a specific political agenda—public support fueled by a new form of patriotism entangled in notions of heroism and visions of "evil" and "evil-doers," within which there was nearly no room for dissent. Globally, there is little doubt that the War in Iraq is a result of conflating 9-11 narratives with the administration's agenda (which Bush has all but said). A prime example of this conflation was when Bush released an official statement regarding how he mourned the loss of the first 1,000 soldiers in Iraq, " . . . and those who died on September 11th." Using the fear-based hero-villain narratives of 9-11, Osama Bin Laden's image was strategically fused with the image of Sadam Hussein. All "terror" became the same and Bush was able to use 9-11 in order to gain public support for a war which otherwise, would have been very difficult to sell to both Congress and the American people. Resistive and counter-dominant politicized narratives, such as those put forth by the political left and scholars like Noam Chomsky, as well as the host of books which suddenly appeared, also emerged through the direct appropriation, adaptation, transformation and interrogation of dominant patriotic hero narratives.

While the war in the Middle East is globally the most significant appropriation of 9-11, the two issues have been so deeply conflated that, for my purposes, it may not be the clearest example of an event co-opted and then transplanted into a political campaign *with which it had no inherent link*. Though true of the war, there are other examples, namely, the pro-life and anti-drug campaign uses of 9-11. These political campaigns obviously do not have any direct link to the events of September 11th. It is important to recall the good versus evil, or hero versus villain grand narrative that emerged out of the press' reporting and that centered on the core term "terror." Ultimately, terror and patriotic heroism, were the ideas most used by journalists to frame discussions of September 11th. This chapter focuses on two "smaller" directed uses of 9-11 sponsored by 1) the pro-life movement, and 2) the anti-drug campaign.

September 11th and Abortion

The Pro-Life Movement, a campaign of three decades, existed independently of the events of September 11th, and is run by conservative and religious special interest groups that support George W. Bush, himself openly anti-choice (adopting an extreme anti-abortion stance). Several months after September 11th, the Pro-Life Movement used the 9-11 narrative of evil and terror toward their own very specific political agenda. Appropriating the image of 9-11, the Pro-Life campaign released a television commercial showing images of destruction, almost identical to images of the collapsed Twin Towers at Ground Zero. The montage-style commercial included images of rescue workers, who at the time epitomized "patriotic heroism" in the American media. The message that appeared at the end of the ad was: "Choose Life." As a part of this particular 9-11 inspired campaign, the pro-life faction also created bumper stickers with the same theme. The bumper stickers displayed an American Flag on one side—the ultimate 9-11 signifier—and on the other side the caption: **Every year 3,200 people are murdered by the TERROR of abortion.** This is a clear example of a political special interest group co-opting images of patriotism and terror, already established as central to the official and press narrative—and forever linked to 9-11. Using these concepts, the movement appropriated 9-11 into the national abortion debate in a way that may have seemed natural to some; however, the events of 9-11 are not organically connected to reproductive legislation. This is a clear example of the transformation of 9-11 from a reported event, into a representational event—an event that takes on a directed use in a political struggle that has in fact no meaningful connection to the initial event. How was the pro-life movement able to co-opt 9-11 in what most people, regardless of their abortion views, would likely agree is a clear *mis*appropriation of a tragic event in American history?

There is a relationship between the press' coverage of the event, which just about uniformly reinforced the official government response, and the subsequent use of 9-11 imagery and ideology by right-wing special interest groups. In this regard, several components of press coverage converge in this anti-abortion, 9-11 inspired campaign. First, the dominant 9-11 narrative of terror, evil, and patriotism put forth by the Bush administration and the press is a quintessential conservative, biblical interpretation of an event. This framework is consistent with the politically conservative, religion-driven, pro-life lobby in the United States. Second, the extent to which the press provided Bush a platform to deliver his interpretation and agenda without challenge, furthered a conservative political spin on September 11th. It thus becomes important to recall the context in which the press represented 9-11, and how they were pressured into a particular discourse about patriotism and terror. Journalists who attempted to stray from publicly espousing this patriotic outlook were forced back into line. Consider for example how the refusal to wear flag pins at one television station was met with public outcry fostered by a right-wing discourse that linked patriotism with an acceptance of the official version of events, causing journalists to act as public models of patriotism. Finally, many citizens might not have even noticed the widespread conservative political uses of 9-11, or at least, the extent to which it was used. The press reporting was so extensive, that seeing 9-11 in the media was completely normalized and people may have come to think of seeing 9-11 images flashing on television or appearing on bumper stickers as "normal."

The process of appropriation that we see with regard to 9-11 and abortion bears similarities to the use of Titanic in the Suffrage debate; however, there is a difference. In the case of Titanic and Suffrage, it was the commercial press that made the initial link which anti-suffrage and pro-suffrage groups then responded to in their own publications. In the case of 9-11 and the pro-life movement, a political organization, using the media as its co-conspirator, made the initial link. Resistive efforts, as with Titanic and Columbine, followed. (Differing from the other cases, the response of the National Women's Organization, NOW, may have actually been less reactive to the pro-life use of 9-11 and more responsive to the changed public support of President Bush in a post-September 11th political landscape.)

During the 2000 presidential election that culminated with George W. Bush taking office, NOW sponsored a rigorous Pro-Choice television add campaign urging American citizens to protect reproductive choice. Clearly NOW was fearful that if Bush were to become president, Roe v. Wade would be vulnerable. Once Bush was declared President, these ads stopped circulating. Again, this was not out of the ordinary. After 9-11, following the administration's military response in Afghanistan, and patriotism reemerging as a dominant cultural value—Bush's approval ratings soared, and NOW began to rebroadcast the same pre-election campaign that had been out of circulation for months. This was a clear message to the American public that even in the aftermath of 9-11, which for some, included supporting Bush's military response to the attacks, life and politics goes on. The government continues to make decisions that impact our daily lives, issues such as reproductive rights and need not be blurred with national sentiment regarding a single tragedy. Quite simply, other things are still happening.[61] This potential "overshadow" effect, which is part and parcel of the intensive remembering period that surrounds iconic events, is a common concern for resistive groups and was clearly a major concern for many liberal groups after September 11th.

The overshadow effect emerges in other ways too. For example, the American public's changed sentiment towards George W. Bush after 9-11, illustrates how a tragic event can alter public mood and even silence pre-existing conversations within the society. This was particularly strong in the case of 9-11 with the administration benefiting from the way the press constructed the event as a war story, from the outset. This made any kind of dissent appear unpatriotic despite the inherent irony contained in that line of thinking. In the case of 9-11 the media reconstruction of Republican Rudy Giuliani is a clear example of how hero transformation suppresses previous media stories. Giuliani, New York City's former Mayor was transformed from an adulterer and failing politician, into *Time* magazine's "Man of the Year:"[62] he became America's top hero in a media-made hero hierarchy. Just weeks before the deadly attacks, Giuliani was tabloid material for committing adultery and publicly acknowledging his mistress as his girlfriend, for whom he'd left his wife. His wife responded, in a press conference, that he had also had a long-term adulteress relationship with an intern. He was even publicly attacked for allegedly having emotionally scarred his children. All of this, followed the public protest of his many "broken window" policies that demonized the poor, attacks on art and street artists, and other failed right-wing policies. At the time, Giuliani was repeatedly characterized in negative terminology. Post 9-11, all the press represented was Giuliani as leader, healer, Hero. September 11th had rendered him "symbolically deadly," annihilating his preceding mass-mediated image, and replacing it with a technologically imaged version of a national hero. This is reminiscent of the press' construction of John Jacob Astor as a hero after the Titanic sinking. Suffragists charged that the press focused solely on their interpretation of how he had died, and reported very little about how he had lived. Likewise, when commercial journalists memorialized Stead as a hero, the "radical" politics at the end of his life were completely excluded. Of particular concern for non-dominant groups is that the major public transformations after 9-11 were of politically conservative men, this falling on the heels of the Bush-Gore election debacle and a divisive time in the history of the nation.

9-11 and the "War on Drugs"

Beyond the pro-life appropriation, a prime example of 9-11 succumbing to a directed political use outside of what could at all be considered within the scope of the event itself, is the anti-drug advertisement that I opened this book with. Only months after 9-11, the following public service announcement began airing on American television. Children one by one recite the following lines:

> **I helped kill a police officer.**
> **I helped kill a judge.**

I help terrorists.
I help bomb buildings.

Over the black screen an announcer says:

Drug money supports terror. Talk to your children.

The terror concept that developed during initial spin was co-opted and transplanted into a twenty-plus year right-wing anti-drug campaign, a campaign initially directed at Colombian-U.S. drug production and trade, far removed from current "conflicts" in the Middle East. This directed political use signifies, like the abortion campaign, two important shifts regarding 9-11 representations. First, September 11th became a site through which highly diffuse political cultural representations began to circulate. Second, the (mis)appropriations of 9-11 imagery fostered some counter-dominant discourses, drawing the public's attention to this often hidden process of appropriation.

What remained consistent between initial 9-11 reporting and these (mis)appropriations is that they support conservative political agendas.

Shirtwaist Politics

In order to understand the process by which some events become iconic, it is helpful to look at a negative case: the Shirtwaist Factory Fire. With the loss of one hundred and forty-six lives in one of the worst industry fires in American history, the press deemed Shirtwaist "newsworthy" and accordingly produced stories about it. Blanck and Harris, the factory owners, later referred to as "the Shirtwaist Kings," were indicted for first and second-degree manslaughter, and by mid-April 1911 were acquitted of all charges.[63] As reviewed in the last chapter, Shirtwaist received press coverage but considerably less than the other events. The press also treated Shirtwaist largely as a local event. Nonetheless, there were initial commercial press interpretations of this event. Given their nature, it also seems likely that resistive narratives would have been produced, and, in fact, this is true, as counter-culture Shirtwaist narratives were and continue to be written. Analysis of some of these resistive texts sheds light on why Shirtwaist never became mythic in American culture.

Labor Unions and Women's Labor Organizations produced a proliferation of stories that countered the dominant press spin on the event. Uniformly referring to the Shirtwaist owners as mass murderers, some labeled the event "the Shirtwaist Holocaust." These narratives all focused on the "sweatshop" conditions under which working-class Americans, as well as many poor immigrant

girls, endured on a daily basis. These stories were published in highly specialized journals and papers and never made their way into the mainstream, or, at
least, they never made their way into the public's consciousness.

In May 1911, *Life and Labor* published a commentary by Martha Bensley
Bruere titled "What Is To Be Done." The haunting piece began as follows:
"Well, the fire is over, the girls are dead, and as I write, the procession in honor
of the unidentified dead is moving by under my windows. Now what is going to
be done about it?"[64] She then described the march of working-class men and
women walking in the rain without the pomp and ceremony of a military pag-
eant (pointing to the failure of the government to have a presence in the public
mourning). Bruere criticized the factory owners for offering the victim's families one week's pay as if their loved ones were given a vacation, and also blasted
Blanck and Harris for running an advertisement in the trade papers just three
days after the fire listing their new address (9-11 University Place) and letting
customers know they were in good working order. Her chilling piece concluded:
"It is four hours later and the last of the procession has just passed." Many similar responses were published. On April 8th, 1911 *The Survey* published an article by Rose Schneiderman situating the Shirtwaist "murders" in a broader context of working-class exploitation. She urged a "strong working-class
movement" as the only means to make work-life more bearable. *The Ladies
Garment Worker* and *American Federationist* published many similar articles,
the former—all the way through autumn of that year, actually exceeding feminist representations of Titanic the following year. Into the twenty-first century
"The Union of Needltrades, Industrial and Textile Employees" continues to
commemorate the event annually at the site of the fire.

Perhaps what is most revealing about the larger process at work here, is not
merely that resistive narratives were abundantly produced, but specifically suffragists' public response to Shirtwaist, bearing in mind the kinds of representations we know in hindsight, that suffragists would create in response to Titanic,
a year later. Shirtwaist, arguably, had a much clearer direct connection to the
Suffrage Movement and was emblematic of the working conditions of an immigrant female labor force, already a central issue within the women's movement.

When looking at *The Common Cause*, which reacted to Titanic multiple
times, there was absolutely *no mention* of Shirtwaist. The journal completely
ignored the event, despite the fact that their March 30th edition focused specifically on labor. *The Woman's Journal* had a very powerful visual representation
of Shirtwaist on their April 1st 1911 cover. The illustration posits the deadly fire
as the result of capitalist greed and argues that the courts had also betrayed
workers.

Herein, is a link to Suffrage, and a woman's right to participate in the political and legal system. Beneath the illustration was an article titled "Women to

Burn," clearly a resistive response to the event. However, the article was small and placed adjacent to several other stories. So, differing from the exclusive front-page coverage of Titanic, *The Woman's Journal* represented the fire as the lead story but not the only story, thus failing to mark the event with singularity and thus significance, (as some other events) just as the commercial press had done. Only two more brief Shirtwaist articles appeared in the journal.

In the end, Shirtwaist received considerably less coverage than Titanic without the creation of any individual heroic figures, which is vital to the construction of an iconic event. Differing from the repeated use of lists and names in all of the other cases, the press' failure to personalize Shirtwaist impacted later counter-culture narratives.

Given that the commercial press did cover the event, and that there was a proliferation of counter-culture representations, why didn't it capture the public's imagination? First, the political appropriation of the event occurred in marginal resistive discourses and *not* in mainstream venues. This was the opposite in the cases of Titanic, Columbine and September 11th. *The New York Times* made the first link between Titanic and Suffrage. Commercial media outlets also first linked Columbine to censorship, popular music, surveillance, dress style, gun control, and the family, while 9-11 was linked to war rhetoric, a particular discourse about patriotism, and other issues. Resistive efforts were reactive and responsive to mainstream uses of event images (at least initially). Second, in the case of Shirtwaist only one clear storytelling concept developed, that of the "villain", and it too was constructed within resistive venues. In contrast, Titanic, Columbine, and September 11th inspired multiple constructs ranging from those with "positive" associations ("hero" and "martyr") to those with "negative" connotations ("villain" and "coward"). Most importantly, these mythical concepts first developed in dominant press and state narratives and were later appropriated by resistive groups, not the converse. Here again, we see the key role that journalists play in collective memory building.

Resistive discourses are at a clear disadvantage because they do not initiate the public interpretation of the event; however, this can also, ironically, create a space for challenging cultural norms. Resistive groups who want to put forth an alternate interpretation of an event are able to draw on the ideas produced by the media and transform and transplant them in order to challenge prevailing power relations. In this circumstance, counter-culture groups actually have the advantage of building on widely circulated ideas that are already in the public domain. By going second, they also get to adjust and strategize, taking advantage of unforeseen opportunities created. Nevertheless, they still have to counter positions which may already be widely accepted.

THE REAL TRIANGLE. (BY COURTESY OF THE NEW YORK CALL.)

Conclusions about Political Appropriation and Resistance

Historical events can be used to serve political agendas that are far removed from the event itself. When this occurs, the event goes from being "represented," which is a normal cultural practice, to becoming "representational." This means that the event is intentionally co-opted into ongoing political struggles. Whether or not an event is used politically, and in which ways, depends on several factors: the quick development of a meta-narrative with mythical concepts, how (and by whom) events are initially appropriated, the legitimacy given to the press' initial interpretation, and the technologies of mass communication available to circulate competing narratives.

In all of the positive cases, the press created stories that centered on heroes, martyrs, and villains (at minimum) which when strung together, constitute the event meta-narrative of "good versus evil." While these myths were the result of routine interpretive practices they then became available for transfer into a range of political discourses. As Schudson notes, myths are necessarily polysemic.[65] In addition to having multiple meanings, they explore a culture's "central dilemmas" versus revealing the simple truths they may appear to present.[66] Despite contradictory narratives, such as in the case of the two gendered Titanic narratives, what ultimately emerges from initial press coverage is an overriding event narrative.

Because the press initially puts forth their interpretation of an event, the development of concepts occurs within a commercial venue, a pathway to the general public. In terms of Titanic, lists, narratives, and photographs of wealthy men who died, were used to signify male heroism. This relationship, between the image and the meaning assigned by the press, was presented as natural.

> what allows the reader to consume myth innocently is that he does not see it as a semiological system but as an inductive one . . . the signifier and the signified have, in his eyes, a natural relationship . . . myth is read as a factual system, whereas it is but a semiological system.[67]

The image of men remaining to die so that women could be saved, by its very nature seemed to represent heroism. Likewise, the image of firefighters and police officers rushing into the World Trade Center prior to collapse seemed most inherently to represent heroism. The narratives and images (signifiers) used to demonstrate this relation (the signified) appear to have a natural correlation; however, as seen in chapter three, these initial stories were produced from very particular viewpoints and were spun at the exclusion of probing other major issues. While this helps illuminate how citizens consume the press' narrative, it also indicates how resistance emerges. Collective memory is a contested site.

It is plausible that in the case of tragic events there is, to some extent, a repression of questions that might otherwise challenge the press' construction of good and evil as it pertains to heroism. Perhaps in the case of Titanic, heroes were constructed in order to (on some level) avoid complex "why" questions that would call for a meaningful reexamination of national identity during a time of rapid economic, technological and social change and hence, heightened stress. The same could be true for Columbine where victims were instantly transformed into god-loving heroes and martyrs who sacrificed for others. This may also be true in the case of 9-11 where passengers aboard United 93 were quickly constructed as heroes. Within those stories, tensions, doubts and contradictions are rife. Herein is where resistive efforts may emerge. Once contradictory event narratives and concepts are co-opted for uses beyond initial reporting, counter versions may be quick to emerge.

The official interpretations of all of the events under discussion were challenged and alternative narratives produced. In the cases of Titanic, Columbine and Shirtwaist, resistive groups attempted to "use" the events for their own political purposes, including but extending beyond contesting the dominant version of events. In the case of events that have captured the public's attention, the grand story spun by the press was appropriated into other political discourses. Resistive groups then responded to the appropriation of the event by challenging how it had been "used", sometimes necessitating challenging the press' version of the event. Some groups would mount their challenge by taking the same mythical narrative and reconceptualizing it to mean something else. Shirtwaist differs in that the press' initial reporting, far more scant, did not produce a clear good versus evil narrative or individualized heroic figures. Furthermore, the mainstream press did not co-opt the event for political purposes or assist other interest groups in circulating counter-dominant stories. Shirtwaist was used politically, only within marginalized communities of memory. So while the event memory was in effect activated, there was no mainstream appropriation which is generally the point of entry for resistive groups.

By the time events are recognized in relation to a few reduced concepts like heroism or patriotism, which are recalled by powerful images, the history of how the "represented event" came to be is essentially concealed. This is partly due to the journalistic authority afforded the commercial press. Arguably the entire process by which an event becomes iconic and is used to further unrelated political agendas, rests with the press—including how they choose to represent an event and the extent to which the state's position is legitimized. The scope and duration of reporting as well as the language that the press initially uses, to describe/mark the event, is critical. Beyond this, the narrative frame through which the event is reported, determines the kinds of concepts that circulate and the extent to which broader issues about gender, race, class, and nationality become associated with the event. This is why the press relies on resonant storytelling techniques such as personalized examples of heroism. Building on Zelizer's work to better understand the process by which journalists legitimize their authority vis-à-vis iconic events, consider that once the press has marked an event as important they are then more committed to re-asserting their version of the event.[68] The press is deeply implicated in how events are *mis*appropriated by those with political agendas, as in the example of the use of Titanic against Women's Suffrage or the fusion of 9-11 and Iraq. In terms of the latter, while the Bush administration created this link, it was journalists who legitimized it. In all of the positive case studies, it was conservative groups that used the concepts and narratives created by the press, for their own ideology-driven purposes.

Technologies of mass communication foster the repetition of event images in the public domain. Due to increases in mass communications (mass media), Columbine and 9-11 were used almost simultaneous to initial representation, while Titanic and Shirtwaist underwent two distinct phases of representation. The speed of this process created a historically unique situation. The event may take on a quality of historic significance by virtue of the many mediums in which it is represented—everywhere a citizen turns, they may be confronted by an image of the same event. An informed citizenry is necessary to democracy. This raises concerns about the explosion of multi-media narratives that blur the line between press reporting, state response, and political appropriation. The public may be less likely to see a political proposition as such and rather consume it as "news." This is vital in the case of September 11th because as reviewed in chapter three it was immediately used in a military effort—first in Afghanistan and later in Iraq. However, the faster an event is "used" within the dominant political discourse, the faster counter-dominant and otherwise resistive interpretations may spring forth. Likewise, the event may then be appropriated into discourses with social justice oriented objectives such as using Columbine to address racism and sexism in the United States. Newer technologies such as the Internet provide more democratic access to mass communication and assist counter-dominant groups in circulating alternative versions of events (though truly democratic access is clearly not yet a reality). In the case of September 11th, the atmosphere of patriotism fueled by the press in compliance with the government, made dissent within the mass media very difficult if not impossible; however, the Internet opened up a space for dialoguing about alternative views in the form of blogging and the like.

After political appropriation, the event is ready to become commodified and transformed into entertainment for the masses. During this final stage in the "making and life" of an iconic event, the simplistic press narratives are further reduced, flattened, and glorified. The events in this book have all undergone an extraordinary transformation, being turned into objects for sale and entertainment to be viewed by citizens turned voyeurs. The following chapter traces how all of these (now) politicized events have been made iconic within consumer culture.

Notes

1. Jenny Edkins, *Trauma and the Memory of Politics* (Cambridge, U.K.: Cambridge University Press, 2003).

2. Iwona Irwin-Zarecka, *Frames of Remembrance: The Dynamics of Collective Memory* (Somerset, NJ: Transaction Publishers, 1994.

3. Irwin-Zarecka, *Frames of Remembrance*.

4. Barbie Zelizer, *Covering the Body: The Kennedy Assassination, The Media, and the Shaping of Collective Memory* (Chicago: University of Chicago Press, 1992).

5. Michael Schudson, *Watergate in American Memory: How we Remember, Forget, and Reconstruct the Past* (New York: Basic Books, 1992).

6. William A. Gamson and Andre Modigliani, "Media Discourse and Public Opinion on Nuclear Power: A Constructionist Approach," *American Journal of Sociology* 95, no. 1 (July 1989).

7. Gamson and Modigliani, *Media Discourse*, 7.

8. "Topics of the Times," *New York Times*, 12 April 1912, 1.

9. "English suffragettes of prominence," *New York Times*, 12 April 1912, 1.

10. In *Down With the Old Canoe: A Cultural History of the Titanic Disaster* Steven Biel presents an array of dominant and resistive narratives that bring Titanic directly into the public discourse regarding Suffrage. As I am drawing from a limited number of texts I need to be clear that other fascinating representations exist and an interested reader would be well served by reading Biel's book. However, I am interested in the transformation of an event (in its represented form) into a representational event and not necessarily all of the "uses" of Titanic. Given this point of difference I present a smaller selection of Suffrage materials that ultimately speak to the directed political use of historical events.

11. Emma Goldman, "Suffrage Dealt Blow By Women of Titanic," *Denver Post*, 21 April 1912, 8.

12. "Emma Goldman Inquires to Know If Equality is Demanded Only at Ballot-Box—Human Nature Came Into Own in Men," *Denver Post*, 21 April 1912, 8.

13. Frances Wayne, "Titanic Disaster Furnishes No Proof That Women Are Unfit for Suffrage," *Denver Post*, 22 April 1912, 6.

14. Contemporary feminists whose work is central within the continued essentialism debate include (but are not limited to) Susan Bordo, Judith Butler, Lisa Cosgrove, Marjorie DeVault, Nancy Fraser, Nancy Hartsock, Patricia Hill-Collins, and Alison Jaggar.

15. In his 1996 book, *Down with the Old Canoe: A Cultural History of the Titanic Disaster*, author Steve Biel discusses the linking of Titanic with Suffrage and how suffragists responded to the Titanic event. Although I did collect my own sample of data, and conduct a reading of that data, there are several sources of data that we both use, and I come to many of the same conclusions as Biel. For example, Biel thoroughly reviews how some suffragists took the mainstream notion of chivalry and gave it an alternative meaning. While I have conducted my own research and reached these conclusions on my own, I have read and am influenced by Biel's terrific book and he certainly came up with this analysis before I did. For readers interested in the use of Titanic in the Suffrage Movement, as well as the many cultural uses of Titanic, I again highly recommend his book.

16. John Storey, *Cultural Studies & The Study of Popular Culture: Theories and Methods* (Athens, Ga.: University of Georgia Press, 1996,) 78.

17. Roland Barthes, "Myth Today," in *A Barthes Reader*, ed. Susan Sontag (New York: Hill and Wang, 1982), 123.

18. In his post-9-11 text, *The Spirit of Terrorism*, (London: Verso, 2002), Jean Baudrillard makes a similar contention by asserting that a growth in goodness does not reduce evil as traditionally philosophized, but rather "good" and "evil" grow in direct proportion to each other. Foucault (1976) has also written extensively about power and resistance growing in direct proportion to each other.

19. "The Wreck of the Titanic," *The Common Cause* 4, no. 159 (April 25, 1912): 1.

20. "Votes for Women to the Rescue." *Woman's Journal* 43, no. 17 (April 27, 1912): 1.

21. Many early Goddess religions (and Ancient mythologies) used the imagery of the snake as a symbol of female and earthly power within creation stories. In Stone Age times the symbol of the snake was always linked to water. The image of the snake was not co-opted and transformed into a negative symbol until the creation story of Genesis. For a complete discussion on this complex history please see Monica Sjoo and Barbara Mor. *The Great Cosmic Mother. Rediscovering the Religion of the Earth* (San Francisco: Harper and Row, 1987), 57 – 62.

22. Alice Stone Blackwell, "The Lesson of the Titanic," *Woman's Journal* 43, no. 17 (April 27, 1912): 2.

23. Blackwell, "Lesson of the Titanic," 2.

24. Blackwell, "Lesson of the Titanic," 2.

25. Alice Stone Blackwell, "Suffrage and Life–Saving," *Woman's Journal* 43, no. 17 (April 27, 1912): 2.

26. Blackwell, "Suffrage," 2.

27. Blackwell, "Suffrage," 2.

28. This process as an impressive use of critical deconstruction aimed at cultural transformation. This approach resembles later feminist strategies such as Luce Irigaray's method of "jamming the theoretical machinery", which is a critical methodology aimed at disrupting the normative social system in order to create space for analysis and change. Luce Irigaray, " The Sex Which is Not One," (Ithaca, N.Y.: Cornell University Press, 1985), 78.

29. Wex Jones, "Woman and Children First," *The Woman's Protest* 1, no. 1 (May 1912): 6.

30. Mrs. Rheta Childe Dorr, "Women and Children First," *Woman's Journal* 43 no. 18 (May 4, 1912): 141.

31. Dorr, "Women and Children First," 141.

32. Despite a radically different subject and medium, the experience of reading this article was reminiscent to me of Lars Von Trier's 2000 award winning fictional film *Dancer in the Dark* in which the audience watches the desperate faces of 1960s immigrant factory workers in the US, as quite literally in the film, the noises of the machines become so loud and omnipresent that they sound like an orchestra.

33. Dorr, "Women and Children First," 141.

34. Dorr, "Women and Children First," 141.

35. Dorr, "Women and Children First," 141.

36. Daniel Dayan and Elihu Katz, Media Events: *The Live Broadcasting of History* (Cambridge, Mass: Harvard University Press, 1992), 15.

37. James Fentress and Chris Wickham, *Social Memory* (Cambridge, Mass: Blackwell Publishers, 1992).

38. Pat Doyle, ""Community struggles in aftermath; Some survivors wrestle with having escaped while others died," *Star Tribune,* 22 April 1999, 18(A).

39. Joy Powell, "Schools may hire firm that has SWAT know–how." *Star Tribune,* 11 May 1999, 1(B).

40. Allie Shah and Joy Powell, "After Littleton, School Grapple With Bomb Scares," *Star Tribune,* 30 April 1999, 1(B).

41. Davis Westphal and Tom Hamburger, "Clinton: Gun Industry to Back Controls; He Also Call on Parents, TV to Fight Teen Violence," *Star Tribune,* 11 May 1999, 1(A).

42. Dottle V. Lamm and Richard D. Lamm, "Rethink the Second Amendment," *Denver Post*, 23 April 1999, 11(B).

43. Linda Gorman, "Making Schools Safe for Criminals," *Denver Post*, 23 April 1999, 11(B).

44. Caroline Schomp, "Denver: Ground Zero in the Gun Debate," *Denver Post*, 22 April 1999, 11(B).

45. Bob Ewegen, "Demonizing and Scapegoating Won't Save Kids' Lives," *Denver Post*, 22 April 1999, 11(B).

46. Cate Terwilliger, "Area schools tighten security, ban trench coats," *Denver Post*, 23 April 1999, 2(A).

47. Susan Greene, "Goth-fashion crackdown seen by some as fascism," *Denver Post*, 23 April 1999, 5(A).

48. Jim Hughes, "Copycat threats spook schools across nation," *Denver Post*, 23 April 1999, 5(A).

49. Mark Harden, "Manson Concert Called Off," *Denver Post*, 23 April 1999, 21(A).

50. Manson did not appear in Denver for two years following the event, and even at that point his appearance was marked by political protest. This is interesting particularly because the National Rifle Association (NRA) held meetings in Denver almost immedi-

ate to the Columbine "massacre." Until Michael Moore's 2002 resistive film *Bowling for Columbine*, the NRA meetings in Denver received very little criticism in the commercial media—with Manson's cancellation itself, causing more of a stir that the NRA meeting that did occur.

51. Curt Brown, "Protestors Fail to Block Manson Show," *Star Tribune*, 27 April 1999, 4(B).

52. Brown, "Protestors Fail to Block Manson Show," 4(B).

53. Sly Spurling, "Trenchcoat Scapegoat Superstar," *Rock Out Censorship Incident Updates* 2003, *http://www.theroc.org/updates/mm-denver.html* (22 March 2006).

54. *Bowling for Columbine Special Edition*, DVD, directed by Michael Moore (Santa Monica, Ca: MGM Home Entertainment, 2003).

55. Jerold J. Katz and Sut Jhally, "The National Conversation in the Wake of Littleton is Missing the Mark," *Boston Globe*, 2 May 1999, 3(E).

56. Sut Jhally, speaking on the Tough Guise: Violence and the Social Construction of Masculinity, on November 3, 2003, to Stonehill College.

57. Katz and Jhally, "National Conversation," 3(E).

58. Katz and Jhally, "National Conversation," 3(E).

59. Patricia J. Williams, "Diary of a Mad Law Professor: Smart Bombs," *The Nation* 268 no. 21 (June 7, 1999): 10.

60. Williams, "Smart Bombs."

61. Scholar Jack Solomon explains that the US entered a period of "national anguish" immediately followed by a "patriotic binge" after both the Viet Nam War and the Iran hostage crisis. Jack Solomon. "Masters of Desire: The Culture of American Advertising," in *Signs of Life in the U.S.A.: Readings on Popular Culture For Writers*, ed. Sonia Maasik and Jack Fisher Solomon (Boston: Bedford/Saint Martin's, 2000), 141.

62. *Time* Magazine gave Giuliani this official title, the highest annual recognition they offer to an individual for world impact. Giuliani earning this title over President Bush and Osama Bin Laden, given the events of the year, is perhaps illustrative of the ability to most easily reconstruct Giuliani's identity to represent a variety of cultural values and histories in a manner that appears less political, than inherent.

63. In 1914 Blanck and Harris were order to pay $75 to each of the twenty-three families who had sued them.

64. Williams, "Smart Bombs," 10.

65. Michael Schudson, *Watergate in American Memory: How we Remember, Forget, and Reconstruct the Past* (New York: Basic Books, 1992).

66. Schudson, *American Memory*, 124.

67. Barthes, "Myth Today," 118.

68. Barbie Zelizer, *Covering the Body: The Kennedy Assassination, The Media, and the Shaping of Collective Memory* (Chicago: University of Chicago Press, 1992).

Chapter Five

Iconic Events in Popular Culture

In contemporary society, commercial culture, and more specifically modern cinema, plays a vital role in the collective memory of iconic events.

> "Filmed 'memories', according to a national survey in the United States on popular sources and uses of the past by Americans, now form an important part of how we learn history: Eighty percent of respondents said they had recently watched movies or television programmes about the past, in comparison with 53 per cent who said they had read a book about the past[1] . . . Film was said to make events 'more Real' . . . "[2]

Although often mistakenly trivialized as a result of the cultural fact-fiction dualism that informs public perception, popular culture has a significant impact on how history is remembered, event narratives are rewritten, and "nation" is re-imagined. Furthermore, it is within the realm of commercial or popular culture that new mass audiences are introduced (or reintroduced) to certain interpretations of major events which may reify or unsettle the historical "record." In this way, commercialized versions may bring an iconic event into the public consciousness long after its passing, and may do so in ways linked to reaffirming or renegotiating the official story or national identity, more broadly. The concepts of collective memory and national identity are themselves interlinked, even mutually reliant. Perhaps the term "national memory" incorporates the notion of both social memory and national identity. While the concept of collective memory always relies on the willful intention to publicly remember and commemorate, group identity is dependent on an imagined community bound by the perception of a shared history or struggle. As Gillis explains, a national memory is shared by a group of people only attached by an assumed common identity resulting from shared history (the record of which is constituted by both systematic remembering and forgetting). Thus, Gillis argues, as new memories are constructed, others must be actively forgotten.[3] This chapter considers the relationship between memory and identity as expressed in the realm of popular culture. Specifically, in this chapter I analyze selected cinematic versions of iconic events as well as commodities associated with them. Given that the focus of this book is on iconic events in American culture, the films selected were (widely) consumed by American audiences, with other lesser known works discussed for specified reasons.

Films have become an important medium for relaying information or generalized ideas about the past. Though they may fly under the radar in so far as people believe they should not be taken as seriously as other texts with historical subject matter, in fact, this represents one of the very reasons that historical films may have a larger impact on collective memory than people might realize. People's "dismissal" of historical films is a result of the long-standing dichotomy between fiction and nonfiction, being particularly pronounced in cinema.[4] The polarization of "the factual" and "fictional" of course assumes there *is* an objective and complete historical record that can be accurately represented, but as discussed throughout this book and in the work of many scholars, this is a fallacy. As historical film scholars McCrisken and Pepper note, films are complex and ideological texts.[5] Films do not recount the "truth" of the past, but rather present a version of truth that is bound to the time and place in which it was produced. Furthermore, film not only depicts some aspect of social reality, it also produces and shapes that reality.[6] Films can also reinforce or challenge general perceptions about an (imagined) past, or as Romanyshyn writes, they can portray "the mythology of an age."[7] In these ways, historical films serve as a means for rescripting collective memory. Films, therefore, are also "memory projects" that activate the repository of collective memory built around a given iconic event. In some respects, films offer an equalizing force with respect to historical "knowledge", as they are typically made to appeal to a diverse audience cutting across class and race barriers, they do not use academic jargon or other prohibitive language, they are low on prior knowledge expectations, and they are not cost prohibitive to most Americans, particularly in the era of low cost DVD rentals, television airing of films, and the like. Given that the success of historical films depends on public consumption, they can in certain respects be viewed as "public history" (ironically, within a commercial system).

Conceptualizing films as a part of "public history" raises several questions. When a historical film about an iconic event is created, what purpose does it serve the public? What is the intent or motivation behind the making of a particular film (challenging the dominant historical record, social resistance, the inclusion of previously silenced histories, disseminating new information or ideas about status characteristics such as race, class and gender)? What are the outcomes, unintended or otherwise, that result from the film's release (such as challenges to the official story, reinserting an older event into the public domain, introducing the event to new generations, transforming history into a vehicle for profit, and so forth). When iconic events are revisited in cinematic forms for the purpose of contesting dominant versions of the past, this too can be a form of political appropriation or social challenge. How does this differ from the forms reviewed in the last chapter?

Before reviewing specific examples it is important to consider the ways in which film is itself a distinctive medium, not to mention the uniqueness of this particular genre (historical film), more specifically those that center on iconic events. There are, of course, also distinctions to be drawn between documentary, docudrama, and narrative film, (and perhaps independent versus commercial film), that bear directly not only on the homogenization of content to fit specific distribution models, but also the role of Hollywood with respect to collective memory practices within shifting national and global contexts.

As noted, films are complex textual forms differing from other texts in several ways, beginning with the most obvious: film adopts a moving audio-visual format. This means there are many interlocking components which shape film, including moving imagery, sound, dialogue, music, color, and so forth. Additionally, film lends itself to narrative and this form of creating and communicating meaning, dominates American cinema. As with other story-telling forms, conventions are often employed in the service of narrative, "…narrative closure, image continuity, nonreflexive camera, voyeuristic observation, sequential editing, causal logic, dramatic motivation, shot centering, frame balance, realistic intelligibility, etc.."[8] In addition to this list, American films with historical subject matter often rely on over-simplistic plots already resonant within the culture, much like journalists use familiar frames in their storytelling.

Cinema also creates a different experience of consumption as compared with traditional texts. Regarding practices of collective memory, films actually create memories for viewers, which then become a part of how he or she might think about the event. In some cases, the film may be the only or prominent part of the social memory stored away by the individual. The nature of these new "memories" is relevant too, as the experience of film creates a different kind of powerful, *visceral*, visual, and emotional memory for the viewer, as compared with other texts, such as books. George Lipsitz explains cinema "overwhelms" the viewer more than other mediums by the spectacle it creates, and in the context of modern film-viewing, this often occurs in silent darkness, on a massive screen, in surround sound.[9] Though the experience of film may be "overwhelming" in the ways Lipsitz proposes, this does not mean citizens are merely passive viewers, nor does it mean that film is an objective text that is consumed equivalently by all that see it.

Film-viewing is participatory and involves a process of projection. Julia Kristeva theorizes that individuals project themselves into what they view.[10] Additionally, I argue, historical films about iconic events depend largely on a process of anticipation. People have very particular expectations as to what they will be viewing, as well as how the plot will be resolved (consider the famous line from *Apollo 13* (1995) "Houston. We have a problem."[11] Or audience expectations at *Pearl Harbor* as they watch those stationed there totally unaware of the impending attack, or audience members at *Bobby* (2006) waiting for the inevitable assassination scene). As such, and as in no other medium or genre of film, the experience of historical film consumption involves active projection and anticipation. The particular process of anticipation that audience members engage in, is grounded in practices of collective memory that involve drawing on a repository of shared images and narratives, and then subjectively projecting oneself into that remembered and simultaneously unfolding narrative. Audience members cast themselves into the different roles, imagining who they might be or how they might react in times of crisis. What would you have done if you were on a sinking ship and you were offered a place in a lifeboat, over others? This combination of recollection, anticipation, and projection makes for a unique film watching experience.

Given the prominent role of American filmmaking in world cinema, it is important to address the production of American films about iconic events. Hollywood's global dominance, appears to raise issues of conflict of interests[12] making America's portrayal of its own shared history, questionable and therefore globally significant. Grainge argues, "Hollywood has functioned strategically in the articulation and codification of the cultural past."[13] Hollywood films are centrally concerned with America and American history.[14] This raises several issues. Hollywood's dominance regarding world cinema and its emphasis on its own past, (or at least, America's understanding of its past), communicates these narratives to both national and international audiences and therefore, provides an opportunity to reinforce official interpretations of the past in American-centric ways while often rescripting dominant narratives in ways that challenge the official record or reveal the contested nature of the record itself.[15] In terms of the latter, films may expose dominant narratives in social memory to a process of demystification, thus resisting earlier versions of historical truth. In this way, when a film brings an event to a new mass audience, or new generation, it may do so in a way that challenges official records (or conversely, may serve to bring that dominant national history into the public consciousness again).

One of the difficulties in analyzing films is that, like all texts, there are always alternate ways of "reading" a given representation. Moreover, scholars have diverse ideas about the properties of historical films and appropriate strategies for interpreting them. This connects to a point alluded to earlier. As suggested at the beginning of this chapter, the public may underestimate the affect of historical films to shape history and by extension, our understanding of the present. Furthermore, the explicit use of melodrama as a narrative tool in films about iconic events, agitates the fact-fiction dualism that leads many to a premature dismissal of historical films. With this said, it is my position that films about iconic events need not be judged on the basis of historical accuracy alone, but rather, the overall narratives or themes and corresponding approaches to filmmaking that facilitate them.

The analysis presented in this chapter is primarily thematic, considering the major narrative choices and dominant themes a viewer might be left with after consuming a particular film, including the extent to which the film reinforces or challenges dominant memory. Particular attention is paid to the interplay of fact and fiction, dramatic techniques, how "spectacle" may serve the narrative, and how meaning itself is imparted.

In addition to films, commodities are another form in which iconic events remain in the public sphere. Frequently, these commodities are linked to another site of memory, such as a film's release, or the opening of a commemorative site (historical societies, museums exhibits, memorials, etc.). The kinds of commodities associated with iconic events can be categorized as "memory objects," and these spaces can be considered "lieux de memoire" in Nora's terms such products serve to link selected understandings of the past with inanimate objects rendering history as a product for sale. The commodification of history via iconic events, also often wrongly trivialized, is a mode of organizing simplified ideas about "a past" and is therefore also linked to the maintenance or transformation of national identity. Furthermore, by extension, the idea that citizens can "own" a piece of history, is another method by which the public is engaged in these larger processes of collective memory and national identity making.

Early Titanic Films

Titanic was rapidly classified as an iconic event not only via initial press interpretations, but also as a result of extraordinarily fast film-making. The first two Titanic films, both silent, were made in 1912, very shortly after the sinking. The immediacy with which films were produced both helped solidify Titanic as an iconic event, while also serving to indicate that it was perceived as such—early on. The first film, *Saved from the Titanic* (1912), was an American production released on May 14, 1912 starring Dorothy Gibson, an actress and Titanic survivor.[16] The second film, made in Germany, was called *In Nacht und Eis* (1912) (translation, *Night Time in the Ice*), and premiered in Berlin on August 17,

1912.[17] Given the different outcome for immigrant versus wealthy passengers, it is worth noting that silent films expunge language barriers that would otherwise prevent immigrant audiences from viewing them (though reliable data on audience makeup is not available and ticket prices may have been prohibitive).

The first talking Titanic film was a British production called *Atlantic*, released in November of 1929. White Star representatives attempted to ban the film, claiming it would directly harm their business and the Atlantic passenger trade in general. White Star was unsuccessful in convincing government officials to ban the movie; nevertheless, filmmakers were ordered to run a disclaimer at the end of the feature stating that liner travel was safe. The name Titanic did not appear in the film.

Two later Titanic film projects were both directly impacted by World War II. In 1938, suspense filmmaker Alfred Hitchcock developed a film project called *Titanic*; however, the film was never made. There is evidence suggesting that White Star attempted to thwart production efforts, although Hitchcock's public statement indicated that he had abandoned the idea because of the war. In 1943 the Nazi Party produced a propaganda film titled *Titanic* (1943). The film portrayed the Titanic tragedy as an example of "capitalist greed and British cowards"[18] and is the first example of a Titanic film explicitly promoting a political agenda. The Nazi Party was not the first to blame the wreck on capitalism. The primary resistive element in Marshall Everett's 1912 book *Wreck and Sinking of the Titanic* was his assessment of capitalism with respect to the tragedy. Everett argued that capitalism created a context in which profit was promoted at the expense of human life. Some suffragists also questioned whether profit was valued more than human life and argued that capitalism was responsible for the "loss of notable men" (and not women, as some press officials had claimed). The idea of cowardice also first emerged in American newspaper stories. As you may recall from chapter three, Bruce Ismay was repeatedly emasculated in newspaper accounts for "sneaking" into a lifeboat ahead of women and children. The failure of Ismay to ultimately be held accountable in the Senate Inquiry further fueled these portrayals. Likewise, women were branded as cowards within the press' "survival of the fittest" narratives. Conversely, hero figures were portrayed as rejecting cowardly behavior, and thus, by tautology, were perceived as heroes. One could therefore argue that both narratives of "capitalist greed" and "cowardice" first circulated in mainstream American discourse and were then co-opted by the Nazi Party via cinematic propaganda to serve their own particular political agenda.

A Night to Remember

After conducting interviews with nearly 60 Titanic survivors, many of whom were crew officers, Walter Lord wrote *A Night to Remember*, which was published in 1956 and produced as a film in England in 1958. *A Night to Remember* served as Titanic's main entrée into cinematic culture with the story being told, primarily from the perspective of Titanic crew officers. Although a British product, this film was widely consumed by American audiences and consequently, serves as the first major cinematic Titanic narrative to impact American collective memory. The film is rampant with historical inaccuracies when compared with the empirical record, and reifies many stereotypes first circulated by the press, with no signs of being affected by the burgeoning women's and civil rights movements. In short, this film reaffirmed the official story ignoring any social changes that had occurred as a result of the Great Depression and/or World War II.

As Titanic is shown striking the iceberg ten minutes into the film, the focus is from that point on. Four themes dominate the story: 1) technological progress, 2) women and children first, 3) Ida Straus' decision to stay with her husband (Macy's co-owner Isador Straus, and 4) the Californian ship, reportedly seen in the distance. Additionally, there are powerful images of passengers stereotyped by social class, as well as stereotypical portrayals of ethnicity throughout the film. The film also mixes fictional characters with depictions of real passengers (as did the later blockbuster, though, as there is no character development, this technique seems less tied to creating emotionality and more explicitly linked to stereotyping).

Via an opening montage portraying passengers heading to the ship, technological progress emerges as a prominent theme. One example comes from a sequence where two couples are traveling to Titanic by train. During a conversation one of the men calls Titanic a "symbol of progress . . . man's final victory over nature." In this sequence the audience is also introduced to a priest telling a crowd of shabbily dressed third class passengers "you'll come back when your fortunes are made," implying that the ideology of the Victorian and American dreams, which in part produced Titanic, is also the reason third-class passengers chose to travel on the ship.

Third-class passengers are systematically portrayed as drunk, incoherent, unruly, and speaking foreign languages—in ways that are "inconvenient" for others. Crew officers refer to them as "hooligans," having the effect of appearing natural given the portrayal of their behavior, and the upper-class passengers stay clear of them. Though the film does depict the crew blocking steerage passengers' access to the second-class stairwell, (the only viable means to the lifeboats), the context of the third-class male passengers acting wildly, makes it appear that crew officers are legitimately protecting the other (female) passengers rather than committing a classed and raced crime. Ironically, the film justifies the very behavior the crew officers had *denied* participating in and can almost be read as a distorted, veiled confession of sorts.

The promotion of stereotypes continues with the portrayal of upper-class women. In addition to behaving "hysterically," these women are depicted as materialistic, selfish, and quite frankly, stupid. There are several scenes showing women complaining that the lifeboats are "uncomfortable." In this vein, many female characters are seen delaying matters by insisting on bringing their jewelry and luggage.

Bruce Ismay is depicted in a lifeboat wearing a woman's shawl, clearly appearing "cowardly." The use of female clothing, never proven to be a part of Ismay's safe passage, serves to reinforce heterosexist and dualistic conceptions about femininity and masculinity. The assumption is that only a coward would emasculate himself by dressing in women's clothing in order to evade his obligation to the "rule of the sea;" this line of thinking can be read as both sexist and homophobic.

The other gender related theme emphasized is Ida Straus' decision to remain aboard Titanic. She is depicted refusing entry into a lifeboat. As the ship sinks, the Straus' are frequently shown embracing. The repetition of isolated images of Ida Straus, powerful visual images that rarely correspond with dialogue, cement this as a main theme. Steven Biel explains that this narrative choice is best understood when situated within the context of rising divorce rates in the United States at the time, while the 1950s American political, social, and cultural realms systematically promoted a nuclear family "ideal."[19] Within this context the focus on Ida Straus "standing by her man" despite the other 1,503 people who died, is not surprising. Mrs. Straus was strategically used to make a statement about the sanctity of heterosexual marriage in a context where many feared the weakening of this institution would alter prevailing gendered norms that favored men.[20]

The last major theme in *A Night to Remember* was that the Californian had been only ten miles from Titanic and failed to respond to Titanic's flair signals and wireless messages. In this film, the audience is ultimately diverted from considering culpability on the part of those employed by White Star as attention is shifted to this other ship. Beyond crew officers reaffirming their earlier story, the focus on external problems is highly characteristic of the 1950s as evidenced in pop culture representations of: communism, fascism, nuclear power, accusations of homosexuals preying on children, and fear of women participating in the public sphere. Science fiction films of the 1950s, such as *Invasion of the Body Snatchers* (1956) and *Attack of the 50 Foot Woman* (1958) center on this kind of blaming the "other," and fear of social change. The emphasis on a "ghost" ship is then highly congruent with the point of production as well as the larger social historical context in which this narrative was written and received.

Though there are many more Titanic films, the next major film is the blockbuster *Titanic* (1997). However, two major developments in the preservation of Titanic history, rescripting of Titanic collective memory, and commodification of the event, must first be addressed (as they also impacted the 1997 film narrative and subsequent flood of commodities): the formation of the The Titanic Historical Society and the discovery of the ship.

Preserving Titanic Memory

The Titanic Historical Society was founded in 1963 to preserve Titanic and White Star Line history and can itself be conceptualized as a long-term "memory project," or "lieux de memoire" in Nora's terms. It is a global non-profit organization with offices in the United States and England[21] and is supported by volunteers, officers and members (for a fee, anyone can join). The Titanic Historical Society was the first, and remains the largest, organization of this sort. In addition to the more recent website, there are three facets of the organization. First, the museum, which houses many Titanic "relics," such as Madeleine Astor's lifejacket, menus, a breadboard, a square of first-class estate room carpet, etc. The creation of a museum space also transformed these items into historicized objects. Second, the journal, *The Titanic Commutator*, has been published quarterly since the organization opened. This journal, available for purchase, routinely contains original articles, illustrations, and survivor biographies. In and of itself this journal ensures the production of new narratives. Third, there is the store, which is discussed in the commodity section toward the end of this chapter.

The Discovery

Right after the 1912 sinking, the families of some of the wealthiest passengers, including Astor, Guggenheim, and Widener, inquired about a possible search and salvage mission. In 1914 an article in *Popular Mechanics* magazine predicted that "one day children of the victims might see photographs of the wreck."[22] Ideas relating to what to do with the ship even included raising it as a floating museum.[23] Many experts believed that Titanic would be found in perfect condition, unharmed by decay. There was a widespread belief that the cold-water temperatures and depth at which it rested would act as a natural preserver.[24] Despite many prior attempts, Titanic was not discovered until 1985 by a team led by Dr. Ballard, and was finally explored and photographed in 1986. The ship, despite hopes, had suffered much decay.

Expeditions to the remains are very expensive thereby greatly limiting access to the site. Many early explorations resulted in looting from the wreckage, as well as objects ostensibly removed, for restoration. The most infamous public display of Titanic artifacts occurred in August 1987. Telly Savalis (the late actor), hosted a "live" program called *Return to the Titanic . . . Live*. The highlight of the program was the opening of a safe recovered from the ship. However, photographs taken prior to the airing, reveal the back of the safe had actually been entirely rusted out, and the safe held no contents. In fact, this early precursor to "reality TV," *was staged*—the safe was filled with artifacts removed from the site and a false back was welded on. From the outset, the discovery and labeling of "artifacts" drew public fascination, and were represented in popular culture serving to enhance public intrigue. Moreover, the commercial possibilities linked to the discovery were immediately recognized and exploited. Some survivors, and those related to survivors, began to protest. Eva Hart, a survivor who was seven years old at the time of the tragedy, was outspoken about what she called the "pirate" act of "grave robbing".[25] As a result of pressure generated by the public, the U.S. government passed a bill stating that objects removed from the Titanic site could not be displayed or sold for profit in the United States.[26] Despite this law, explorations of Titanic remains have never been systematically documented, nor is there any record of where specific items were originally located. To this day, there has never been a complete inventory of all of the items that were ever moved or removed from the site. Neither is there any documentation of damage done to the ship by investigators and their equipment. In short, despite the fetishism surrounding the ship, the area has not been treated as an archeological site.[27]

What is most relevant about the discovery, in addition to the initial spotlight it shone on Titanic, is the impact on the Titanic collective memory repository, both the rescripting of dominant memory and reestablishment of the Titanic as an iconic event to new generations. The discovery prompted interest in the wreck on the part of documentary and commercial filmmakers who, together with the aid of new images and information, began visually reconstructing Titanic narratives. The discovery also prompted filmmakers to document Titanic history while those who bore witness were still living, resulting in stories being shared for the historical record. In addition, explorations of the site enabled many new "scientific" narratives to be debated. For example, a 1987 expedition reconstructed a version of the events, positing that an explosion caused the sinking and *not* an iceberg.[28]

Titanic: The Highest Grossing Film in World History

James Cameron's *Titanic* is a commercial "memory project" that after nearly a century thrust Titanic prominently back into the public domain. This big-budget Hollywood blockbuster, award winner, and fan favorite worldwide, altered Titanic collective memory in several ways. First, the film introduced the event to new generations, and revitalized interest in it on the part of the public, historians, and writers. This kind of reinsertion into the public's consciousness, which also spawned the production of additional Titanic "memory projects" and sites of memory, helped reconstitute Titanic as an iconic event in American culture. Second, the script drew on contemporary understandings of the role that social class played in the event, and the relationship between social class and gender, bringing these new ideas to the public. Other contemporary understandings, along with new information also became part of the narrative. Third, the movie uses technologically enabled footage of the wreckage, offering the public an opportunity to "virtually" tour the famous site. Finally, the success of the film influenced the production of other historical films, most notably, serving as a model for *Pearl Harbor* which is discussed in the next section (as well as other Titanic films, such as *Ghosts of the Abyss*).

As much public adoration as *Titanic* garnered, the film also yielded sharp criticism from historians and other Titanic "experts." This criticism results mainly from the over-utilization of melodrama as the primary storytelling technique in the movie. This approach unsettles the fact-fiction dualism that affects how historical narratives are usually received, particularly by academics. Additionally, the film relies heavily on techniques of spectacle in order to simulate the event. This also served to generate public interest and further professional criticism.

The story is narrated from the perspective of the fictional character Rose, a 101 year old Titanic survivor. In the opening scene, an expedition is searching the remains of Titanic for a lost "treasure": the heart of the sea (a very valuable blue diamond necklace). This is interesting as it could have led to inferences about how the site had been managed over the years, as well as the ethics surrounding the removal of these items, nonetheless, these issues are not raised. Rose is seen watching television as she learns of the expedition. She contacts the explorers claiming to have owned the necklace, and from that point on, proceeds to narrate the film, taking the audience back to 1912.

The film centers on an ill-fated love story between fictional characters who serve as composite representatives of their respective social classes. Rose is an upper-class passenger traveling to New York with her wealthy fiancé Cal, whom she is being pressured to marry by her mother so that they can maintain their social class status. Jack Dawson is an American artist who won his third-class ticket in a poker game. It is not long before the two characters fall in love. Social class supplies us with a lens through which to view the relationship.

More than half of the epic movie occurs prior to Titanic's collision with the iceberg. During this time, the focus is on the relationship between Jack and Rose, and through them, others in their respective classes, including depictions of real historical figures. Melodrama also serves the larger memory project of reinvesting the public in this long-passed tragedy. Arguably, without sympathetic and compelling characters, the audience might not be encouraged to mark the event with the same significance, thereby reaffirming it as a watershed moment in the history of the nation.

Through Rose, the audience is introduced to the upper-class, experiencing the glamour of estate rooms, the first-class dining room, the famous grand staircase, and the upper-class decks. Rose is also a vessel for introducing real-life biographies into the film, including, John Jacob Astor, Madeleine Astor, Molly Brown, Captain Smith, Thomas Andrews, and Bruce Ismay. These formerly prominent figures within Titanic narratives are peripheral to this story. There are also brief isolated images of Mr. and Mrs. Straus and Ben Guggenheim. By following Jack, the audience is introduced to the modest third-class accommodations, and the poor treatment of the third-class passengers. Through an attempt at rescripting dominant class and gender narratives, stereotypes (ironically) flourish in this film, almost serving as a complete reversal from the 1958 film. In this movie, the wealthy are systematically portrayed as frivolous, uptight, and greedy. Rose's discomfort with the gendered confines of being a woman in her social class, allows the upper-class as a whole to (via these stereotypes) be understood. Cal, the representative first-class male and patriarchal figure, treats Rose as if she were his property. Through their relationship the audience gets to experience the rigid gendered separation within the upper-classes as compared within the third-class, implying that the "cult of domesticity" that Betty Friedan later wrote about in 1963, actually only applied to wealthy women. Through Jack, the audience sees third-class passengers celebrating merrily, laughing and dancing. Any tensions or anxieties that poor non-English speaking immigrants might have experienced during the actual voyage, are completely absent, and nearly all of the steerage-class passengers are Italian and Irish (making them white-skinned). Jack, the representative third-class passenger, is himself American thus negating the need to consider the process of traveling to a new country and eventually experiencing a major accident outside of one's cultural comfort zone (as would have been the case with the actual third–class passengers. Arguably, American audiences would find this character easier to relate to, which can itself be read as racist or at minimum an attempt to get audiences to identify more strongly with third-class passengers.

The character of Jack Dawson, who is both the main character and ultimate heroic figure, is significant because of his generalized portrayal of third-class passengers. There are several scenes where Jack tells Rose that he understands "the way the world is" and his place within it. Furthermore, Jack is depicted as being wise and knowing. At one point Rose looks at Jack's sketch book and says: "You have a gift Jack. You *see* people."[29] In another scene, Rose shows Jack some paintings she had bought in Europe by an, at the time, unknown artist, named Pablo Picasso. Cal thinks the paintings are worthless while Jack finds them fascinating. Rose, who transcends gender stereotypes, defines the cubist paintings as "truth without logic." In these ways, these supposedly representative characters, are written as quite exceptional and not in the least bit ordinary. Arguably, Rose's character who so wholeheartedly wants to break the gender norms reserved for her social class could *only* be written in contemporary culture, which can be read as "pure fiction" or conversely, as a means of revealing that which might otherwise remain hidden.

As half of the film occurs prior to the accident, the experience of consuming the film involves high levels of anticipation. Titanic has taken on such mythic status in American culture that to varying degrees viewers wait, in anticipation, to see how several things will unfold, with the most build-up reserved for the moment of collision and it's aftermath. Contrary to the 1958 film, *Titanic* viewers must wait in anticipation. The fictional romantic relationship also creates characters, of remarkable qualities, that the audience is meant to care for. Knowing that tragedy will soon befall the passengers, viewers wonder how Rose and Jack will fare. The public is for the most part, likely to be aware that Astor (and other famed Titanic passengers) will die, but the fate of the fictional characters, is not known. This heightens the anticipatory experience.

While the first half of the film centers on the relationship between Jack and Rose, and through them "the ship of dreams" and its passengers, the climax of the film, is when the crow's nest lookout delivers the famous line "Iceberg, right ahead." From that point on, the focus shifts to the spectacular recreation of the events, emphasizing technological prowess in filmmaking. The major cinematic strategy at this point, is spectacle—a technologically staged recreation with massive special effects aimed at creating an "authentic" view of what happened (though Cameron's version takes great dramatic license often departing from the scientific "record" in service of his story). Through Jack and Rose, and their attempt at survival, (which follows an over-the-top escape from Cal's gun-toting right-hand man), third-class passengers are shown locked behind gates without an opportunity to free themselves. Many first-class passengers, who have not been informed as to what is happening, are shown complaining about going to the lifeboats, and later appear stunned as they row to safety and watch the horror unfold.

The dualistic good versus evil narrative that structures the script via Jack and Cal, also comes to a head in the last half of the film. Jack increasingly comes to embody exceptional heroic qualities, and through his character heroism is allowed to emerge as a dominant theme. Ultimately, while Jack dies in the freezing waters, he saves Rose. Not only does he save her from death, but as she ultimately explains, from being bound to a gender and class defined life she did not choose. By taking the last name Dawson, Rose's family wrongfully assumes that she died in the tragedy, thereby allowing her to pursue a life (supposedly) free from ideas about femininity linked to her social class. In this vein, Rose explains "he saved me in every way a person could be saved."[30] Again, this film is a hero story that also draws heavily on contemporary understandings of gender and class. The use of fictional characters facilitates the challenge to dominant Titanic memory without questioning any of the individual narratives of heroism or villainy that constitute it. Furthermore, though the official story is altered, the film ends up being held hostage by extreme stereotypes. The melodramatic script, although it generated criticism, served the storytelling in so far as it drew the audience in and helped expose the trauma and loss that real passengers undoubtedly experienced, and in this way, perhaps the fiction helped to cultivate the human part of the event that would otherwise not have surfaced. Furthermore, the explicit intermingling of fact and fiction in a film that purports to be the most accurate to date, unsettles the fact-fiction dichotomy with which historical representations are generally judged, and as a result, ends up privileging certain forms over others.

The Hollywood Blockbuster: *Pearl Harbor*

The film *Pearl Harbor* (2001) followed the same model as *Titanic* in order to produce audience anticipation and create an emotional connection between the viewer and fictional "representative" characters. Both films are spectacular epics that center on fictional love triangles and climax with impressive technologically recreated images. Furthermore, while filmmakers generally avoid making a film that is perceived as derivative, *Pearl Harbor* was actively promoted as being similar to *Titanic*, and fans of the former were told that they would enjoy the latter. In publicity press junkets, those involved with the film compared the dramatic love stories and promoted the massive special effects that created "new" images of the past tragedy.

Though both Titanic and Pearl Harbor are iconic events, when considering these two films it is necessary to bear in mind that Pearl Harbor is tied to the events of World War II. Of note, *Pearl Harbor* was released in conjunction with the 60th anniversary of the attack, linking the film to a national commemorative process. The representation of the event is part of a process of nation-building which is not diminished simply because the events are dramatized.

Like *Titanic*, the first ninety minutes of the film depicts a love triangle between three fictional characters, Danny, Rafe and Evelyn (the former two are childhood friends who end up stationed at Pearl Harbor where Evelyn works as a nurse). As noted by film critics, the love story is clearly a quasi-replication of the love story that guided *Titanic*.[31] Through these characters, the audience gets to watch the carefree "fun-in-the-sun" lifestyle of the nurses and officers stationed at Pearl Harbor. This melodrama heightens anticipation for the offensive, as viewers are shown glimpses of the Japanese preparing to attack, interspersed with romantic scenes from Pearl Harbor. The date and time periodically appear on screen as audience members wait for the December 7th assault.

In this film, the ninety minute buildup to the highly anticipated attack scene serves two primary purposes. First, as with *Titanic*, an emotional connection is fostered between the audience and the characters. The use of fictional characters also allows for stories of heroism to emerge without picking real-life biographies to highlight, while on the contrary, villainous characters are presented by real historical figures (in the Japanese military). After poor box office returns in the United States, the film was released globally, with the distributor banking on large Japanese audiences. In the daily *Yomiuri Shimbun*, Japan's most circulated newspaper, an advertisement read: "The world starts moving; the world is caught in a tide of history. With hope for the future and love in their hearts, young heroes battle against the opposition of the times."[32] Another common Japanese trailer proclaimed: *"Pearl Harbor*: love story."[33] The fictional hero narrative made the film viable in a global context, and Japan in particular, the second largest market for Hollywood films.

Second, through following these characters the audience is introduced to the nurses and officers stationed at Pearl Harbor. This storyline also provides the filmmaker with the opportunity to focus on the "fun-in-the-sun" lifestyle that these young adults reportedly experienced prior to the attack. The characters, but not the audience, are clueless as to what will soon occur. (Interestingly, the academy award winning film *Tora Tora Tora* (1970) was criticized by some for portraying the Americans as being unprepared, given the climate of the time.) The film's climax is the thirty-minute technologically-enabled, recreated attack and battle scene.

The morning of December 7th consists of three sub-narratives inter-cut to form one continuous sequence aimed at evoking maximum audience anticipation: 1) shots of the Japanese military ceremoniously preparing for battle, 2) shots of President Roosevelt and his aides attempting to determine what the Japanese are planning, and 3) shots of a beautiful, relaxed day at Pearl Harbor.

This filming technique continues during the thirty-minute battle scene where shots of the attack are interspersed with shots of nurses caring for the sudden onslaught of wounded soldiers. The montage style gives way at moments during the battle scene to a technique of "cinematographic narrativity," where a camera-pan is used to present a scene as an uninterrupted sequence.[34] This filming style presents the content as "what is happening" versus "a *view* on what is happening." During the height of the movie, this style allows the audience to relax and absorb the moving image. After such an elongated period of heightened anticipation, the attack is a strange relief to hyped-up viewers. Furthermore, the technique also emphasizes the point of view of the Americans at Pearl Harbor, focusing on the wounded, the dying, and displays of American courage.

This script, following the official story, proposes that Admiral Yamamoto knew that the United States was intercepting Japanese radio signals, and precedes the surprise attack by sending an array of contradictory signals. At the moment of battle, the United States is portrayed as knowing something is about to happen, but not what or where it will happen. In this, and other ways, this film reinforces the official American version of this event. The dialogue is as follows:

> Yamamoto: "Set up teams of radio operators to send out messages the Americans will intercept, concerning every potential target in the Pacific. Include Hawaii- the clutter will be more confusing that way."
> Genda: "Brilliant, Admiral."
> Yamamoto: "A brilliant man would find a way not to fight a war."[35]

The filmmaker publicly stated his intention to make a film that dignified the Japanese.[36] Despite these claims, there is no historical context provided for the Pearl Harbor battle, the Americans are uniformly portrayed as heroes, and the film ends with the Doolittle Raid (where American soldiers "successfully" attacked the Japanese in a suicide-mission of sorts), allowing the film to end on a note where the United States was victorious (a standard recurring theme in America's official view of its own past).

Thinking about the September 11th films that have been made, reviewed later in this chapter, one wonders if an American filmmaker closer in time to a traumatic historical event, such as September 11th, would aim to dignify the attackers. This has not been the case in any of the 9-11 movies made to date, and arguably was a claim made by those involved with *Pearl Harbor*, at least in part, to account for the radically different economic and political relations between the U.S. and Japan at the time this film was made. Furthermore, if the filmmaker "dignified" the Japanese, as promoted in the United States, then one wonders why a different version of the film was shown in Japan. What can be inferred from this, regarding the reconstruction of collective memory within a global commercial context?

After bombing at the box office in the U.S., *Pearl Harbor* premiered in Japan in the Tokyo Dome, a stadium with a temporary screen erected that was the size of a basketball court.[37] The dome was filled with 30,000 Japanese viewers.[38] This audience saw a different version from American audiences. This cut contained edits, re-shot scenes and voice-overs, which together with an even heavier focus on the love story angel[39], had the combined effect of softening the film. One author remarked, "The billboard image resembles that for Titanic, Japan's highest grosser of all time, and if the ship is smoking rather than sinking, at least its bombed-out glow might be mistaken for a sunset."[40] Many Japanese film goers were dismayed to learn that the film was tailored to specific audiences.[41] Moreover, some audience members were troubled by the one-sided nature of the plot. For example, the Japanese pilots were not depicted as having loved ones like the American soldiers and were thus not portrayed sympathetically or heroically (in the context of patriotic sacrifice).

While *Pearl Harbor* reified official collective memory, the events of September 11th, which journalists and politicians have frequently framed through the lens of Pearl Harbor, has been the subject of films, that, at times purport to take less dramatic license and focus on the real people involved in the tragedy.

September 11th

September 11th was immediately the subject matter of countless books and documentary films. The first theatrical release inspired by the event was called *11-09-01* (2002), which translates to *September 11*. The film was produced in France by Alain Brigand who invited eleven directors from different countries to "create a film lasting eleven minutes, nine seconds and one frame - 11'09''01 - around the events of September 11 and their consequences."[42] The pieces range from documentary footage, political statements, cultural statements, dramatizations of culture wars, and allegory. Though interesting in its intent, if not a bit gimmicky, and diverse in subject matter and film quality, the montage was not widely seen by American audiences. Later, popular culture latched onto more popular tales of heroism spun immediately after the event, focusing on United Flight 93 and New York City firefighters.

Pop Culture and United Flight 93
In the four years following September 11th, United Flight 93, which crashed in a field in Pennsylvania, has been a central focus of 9-11 "memory projects" in popular culture. Already the subject of two films (the first a television movie and the other a theatrical release) as well as many books, significantly, these are the first American made films about 9-11, and those that Americans are most likely to have seen.

Flight 93 (2006), an A & E movie, and *United 93* (2006), a theatrical release, both purport to tell the story of how passengers and crew aboard United 93 attempted to regain control of their airplane, resulting in the crash into a Pennsylvania field, diverting the hijacker's from their presumed Washington DC. target. Both filmmakers claimed to "recreate" the events in "real-time," that is, as they unfolded in actual time, and both relied on public records, interviews, and the assistance of victims' families. Furthermore, *United 93* released in-depth trailers and "behind-the-scenes" promos of the making of the film, in part to show that the families of the victims supported the production. Illustrating just how raw the event remains for many Americans, after receiving complaints from the movie-going public that had gone to the movies and were subjected to traumatic 9-11 images, many movie theaters decided to display warning signs if

United 93 was advertised during the coming attractions for another film. Despite advertisements that each film recreated the events in "real-time," the timeframe for each movie was very different, as were the foci. In short, these were drastically different films. *Flight 93* followed a typical melodramatic Hollywood script much more so than *United 93* which seemed to take less dramatic license and followed a "real-time" sequence more closely (including the 40-45 minutes the flight was delayed on the ground). In this section I interpret the film scripts, content and presentation, as well as the kind of audience experience each film cultivates. I suggest that the dramatic *Flight 93* fostered heightened audience *projection* while *United 93* cultivated higher levels of audience *anticipation*.

Both films focus on the events aboard the flight (primarily from the perspective of passengers and crew, though both films depict the hijackers alone in the bathroom and cockpit). *Flight 93* centers on the families of the victims, as well as others who had contact with people aboard the flight, while *United 93* was filmed mainly from the perspective of the air traffic controllers who watched the events unfold on their radar screens. Both films present a timeline throughout, while additionally, in *Flight 93* people's names are a consistent part of the film (presented on the bottom of the screen along with the time—appearing on their tickets and also in conversations). These conversations serve to individualize characters, more so than in *United 93*.

Flight 93 begins with background music playing as the two pilots get ready for work. Pilot LeRoy Homer Jr. kisses his wife and baby and leaves for work. Next there is an ominous shot of the plane, followed by a depiction of a hijacker shaving his face and chest. The next ten minutes of the film introduces the audience to flight attendants talking about their children, and passengers boarding the plane. The first pilot announces a departure delay and then the scene changes to the American Airlines control office, where flight attendant Amy Sweeny has called in, from American Airlines flight 11, reporting their hijacking. Then, approximately ten minutes into the film, United 93 takes off, immediately after which AA 11 crashes into the World Trade Center with Amy Sweeny screaming through the phone. There is very minimal build-up leading to the flight taking off, and the majority of the film unfolds while the plane is in the air, book-ended with about ten minutes after the crash.

This film focuses on the families of those aboard the plane, and the flight itself. Families are introduced at home watching the events unfold on television and, in some cases, starting to worry about their loved ones, or via phone calls from the airplane (reportedly there were 24 phone calls made from the flight). The young children of male passengers are frequently shown at home with their mothers. This family-focus serves two purposes. First, it fosters an emotional connection with the viewer, as the story unfolds through the fear and grief of loved ones. Audience members feel like they "get to know" something about the passengers in a personal way beyond their shared identity status as "Americans." Second, the script fosters heightened audience projection. As one is watching the film, he or she imagines what it might be like if it were happening to them. The film invites the audience to ask: Who would *you* call? What would *you* say? What message would *you* leave your partner, your mother, your children? Viewers are not just invited to imagine how they would feel and act as a passenger, but also as a family member back home watching the events unfold on television, and in some cases having to receive phone calls from loved ones. Since family members informed passengers that they were on a "suicide mission" (knowledge which prompted them to fight back), these moments are portrayed, thus allowing a viewer to wonder what that heart-wrenching moment might be like for them.

Lastly, the focus on families produces a way to introduce newscasts into the film. This is significant. Within ten minutes, family members are shown learning about the unfolding attacks via television. These newscasts continue throughout the film, including right up to the moment where the ultimate crash of United 93 is reported. Though filmed as if in the background, the clarity of sound is such that this is obviously *not* the case. This technique allows for the introduction of material, and voices, that would otherwise not be possible, (which also frames the experience in the language of the press who evoke terms like "terrorism," from the outset). Of additional significance is that, despite "real-time" claims, the film uses news footage that occurred later in the day, after United 93 crashed. Some of the specific ideas communicated through the news broadcasts, conveniently shown and heard in the houses of worried family members, include: when the second plane hit the towers a news anchor saying "this has to be deliberate folks;" "undoubtedly this is terrorist-related;" "what comes to mind is Pearl Harbor" (in terms of casualties); "the big fear is that there are more attacks coming;" "eyewitnesses saw a plane fly into the structure;" an anchor saying "over 100 stories vanishing before our eyes . . . the horrifying possibility of the North Tower collapsing" (as the first tower collapsed); the scene at the World Trade Center and Pentagon (at various points); a commentator saying there will "be a massive effort. The city will rebuild . . . and no doubt the towers will be reconstructed. I would assume there will be a response, a military response;" and lastly, reporters announce they are "searching for evidence and a voice recorder" at the crash site of United 93.[43]

The comments regarding casualties, the North Tower collapsing, and the speculation about rebuilding and military response, only circulated widely after United 93 crashed, and thus, the implication that the spouses of family members heard this information while their loved ones were still alive is misleading. Many of the ideas communicated via the news footage are actually ideas that commentators had in hindsight, (during the attacks, news anchors appeared mostly stunned), and yet the script presents their musings as a part of that morning's ongoing events.

There are several passengers who, along with their family members represent the main characters of this movie—and as a result, receive more of the focus. (In the case of Todd Beamer, his phone call with Lisa Jefferson, including praying and saying the now famous "let's roll;" is also depicted at length). The audience "gets to know" approximately half a dozen characters, experiencing the event through their eyes, and those of their loved ones. Tom Burnett, one of the passengers who reportedly helped create a plan to take back the airplane, is clearly the main figure in this film. From the beginning to the end, he and his family are emphasized, he serves as the "hero" of this film, and his wife and children serve as representatives of all 9-11 widows and children.

The focus on families, and other people on the other ends of phone calls, and central characters with whom the audience develops a connection, gives the film its emotional charge. Additionally, music is used to create a somber foreboding mood. This is a standard Hollywood technique (yet it is not used in *United 93*). This film shows the plane crashing down fiercely; however, *Flight 93* does not end at this point, nor is it filmed from the perspective of those aboard the airplane. A farmer, in a red barn, witnesses the plane heading toward the ground and shortly thereafter a huge cloud of black smoke is seen. A fighter jet pilot trying to reach the flight also reports the plane is down in a field. The film ends with family members learning the news on television and FBI agents and firefighters searching the crash site. A large black smoldering hole in the ground, where the plane was obliterated, is shown from an aerial view—then the scenes change as the site is shown in autumn, winter, and by summer, the hole is gone, and the grass is green. The film is dedicated to the passengers for preventing the plane from hitting the White House or Capitol (in *United 93* the target is purported to be the Capitol building and the hijackers are shown placing a picture of it in the cockpit).

United 93 was promoted with posters and movie trailers that said:

"September 11, 2001.
Four planes were hijacked.
Three of them reached their target.
This is the story of the fourth."

In the posters, this caption appears beneath a large image of a corner of the statue of liberty's face, with a plane looming in the distance. *United 93* was also rigorously advertised as endorsed by the victims' families, perhaps, to offset concerns the public might have, that the film was exploiting these tragic events. It should also be noted that 9-11 films are perhaps not best read through the endorsement (or lack thereof) of the bereaved who have an understandable vested interest in the way their loves ones are memorialized and remembered. It has been reported (in documentaries and books) that some of the bereaved responded that, thinking of their loved ones trying to take over the plane, had brought them solace to know that at least they had some measure of control in their final moments, and were proud to remember them as courageous and hopeful in the face of tragedy. Additionally, a portion of the ticket sales from this movie went directly to the Flight 93 memorial fund.

United 93 followed a very different script than did *Flight 93*. *United 93* did not focus on any particular passengers, nor did it include the perspective of those waiting at home (or all of the television news commentary seen in the earlier film). Rather, *United 93* was a suspense-filled "real-time" film that followed the events primarily through the perspective of the air traffic controllers who, having suspected hijackings, then watched helplessly as the events unfolded on their radar screens. Several of the people cast in the film were real air traffic controllers and flight attendants, in an attempt to add authenticity to the film (as was also done with *Elephant*, the Columbine film discussed later). The film followed the airplane, not just the people aboard, including many shots of the exterior of the plane. In particular, the film focused on the 40-45 minutes the plane was on the ground, delayed, while the other events of the day were unfolding. Approximately half of this film occurred with United 93 still on the ground, which differed dramatically from *Flight 93*. This allowed for several things.

First, audience members saw the events unfold from the perspective of the air traffic controllers, which had not been portrayed before and was largely a story outside of the public's consciousness. Second, and most importantly in terms of how this film may have been consumed, this created tremendous suspense and anticipation. While one might think that it is difficult to create suspense telling a story where everyone knows the ending, and that it was a tragic "non-Hollywood" ending at that, in fact the movie was extremely suspenseful. Watching it unfold, and particularly as air traffic controllers learn of the hijackings *before* United 93 took-off, one kept having the feeling that the plane could somehow be saved. The storyline also included the disappointing official response to the events as they unfolded not least of which, included the whereabouts of the President and Vice President who were missing in action. After takeoff, anticipation again builds as viewers wait for the passengers to realize they are on a hijacked flight (and "suicide mission"), and then, for the air traffic controllers to realize that United 93 is one of the hijacked flights.

Interestingly, the movie, though powerfully advertised, and suspenseful right to the end, was not as emotionally evocative as *Flight 93* (the film ends with United 93 plummeting down, the screen goes white and then black, and the "facts" of the day are then reported as well as a dedication to the heroic passengers and crew). I saw the film on opening night and the audience was absolutely silent throughout, you could hear a pin drop (it was edge of your seat kind of silence), and yet, no one was crying. It was an eerie film experience, where I felt and heard some others say it was very uncomfortable because of the voyeurism involved in watching these tragic events unfold—an experience not shared with others in the case of *Flight 93* which was a made for television movie consumed privately.

What both films have in common is that they dramatize the events of September 11th in memorable ways. The films also placed United flight 93 back in the public domain, although at the point of release the country was engaged in the Iraq War (which has consistently garnered diminished public support). Furthermore, despite some contradictions with each other, both films reinforce the official account of what transpired on that flight (evidence from the plane's voice recorder cannot confirm whether or not the passengers made it into the cockpit, though by all accounts, this was their intent). Finally, both films reify the conceptualization of the passengers and crew as American heroes, which will likely impact further memorialization and commemoration.

World Trade Center
World Trade Center (2006), an Oliver Stone film that generated controversy from the outset, was released on August 9, 2006. The film, marketed as "A True Story of Courage and Survival", and starring actor Nicolas Cage, is a narrative film that chronicles the experience of two Port Authority police officers trapped in the rubble of one of the collapsed towers. The film follows a typically emotional dramatic Hollywood plot, employing music to evoke mood, and drawing on popular conceptions of police officers as heroes. The film dramatizes the experiences of veteran police officer John McLoughlin and rookie Will Jimeno, both of whom arrived at one of the towers just prior to collapse. The narrative unfolds from the perspective of the two police officers as well as their wives (and extended family), and the rescue workers who worked to save them (particularly highlighting one marine who traveled to New York to aid the search and rescue effort). Though framed as inviting audience members to bear witness to the experience of being trapped in the rubble (not knowing the towers had collapsed), much of the film centers on how the two wives coped with the unfolding situation, and idealized flashbacks of family moments, as well as the marine figure who though based on a real person, seemed to be written as a representative military figure through whom conservative discussions of revenge and war were weaved into the script. The melodramatic narrative was enhanced by typical Hollywood conventions, such as the dramatic use of light, color, and sound. Substantively, the film reinforces dominant nationalist conceptions of firefighters as heroes, and perhaps of greater and more questionable consequence normalizes the "naturalness" of a war effort springing out of the 9-11 attacks. The film therefore builds on and reinforces the press and State responses to the actual event. With regard to the consumptive experience, the family-focus, similar to that in *Flight 93*, fosters heightened audience projection. Again, this is

central to the building of patriotic sentiment that flows from watching these kinds of historical films.

It is unclear what place this commercial film will ultimately have with respect to long-term September 11th collective memory; however, given Stone's notorious dramatizations of other iconic events and figures, and the rawness with which many Americans still regard 9-11, the movie may (eventually) promote some public discussion about the relationship between popular culture and American history.

A Columbine-Inspired Film

In 2003 filmmaker Gus Van Sant wrote and directed *Elephant*, the only narrative film about Columbine to date. Differing from the Hollywood blockbusters created about Titanic, Pearl Harbor and 9-11, this film employs a decidedly minimalist approach. Though purported to be inspired by the "string" of eight deadly school shooting sprees between 1997 and 1999, and not a recreation of Columbine, the film is clearly inspired by the events at Columbine, if not directly about them. In fact, specific facts from Columbine are incorporated into the film which took two major honors at the Cannes film festival, Palm d'Or and Best Director. Van Sant was influenced by a 1989 film of the same title, in that case the title was meant to evoke an image of the "elephant in the room" that no one addresses. Van Sant named his film *Elephant* after the parable in which people are able to see parts of an elephant, but none are able to see the whole. This is a recurring theme in this haunting film. Van Sant publicly claims that the aim was to make a film devoid of psychological or sociological analysis, a film that did not posit the causes of school killings; however, his film in many ways both reinforces and resists the Columbine meta-narrative spun by journalists and politicians, and contains many assumptions about society.

The film follows several teenagers through a day in their high school, culminating in two male students going on a killing rampage with explosives and automatic weapons purchased via mail order. Three main themes in the film include: how high school is experienced differently by dissimilar kids and peer groups, how high school can be a very difficult and isolating experience, the various social factors that can contribute to school violence. In addition to these themes, the story communicates ideas about gender (though, perhaps unintentionally). Finally, using several techniques, the film reinforces the idea that personal perspective has a dominant role in shaping experience, which extends to the experience a viewer might have while consuming the film and projecting his or her own high school experiences into the story.

Elephant was filmed in a real high school in Portland Oregon. The school's prosaic architecture is characteristic of Columbine High School, and is representative of many suburban public high schools. The cast followed an improvisational technique, where they created much of their own dialogue. There was also relatively little dialogue in the film with many scenes of students in isolation or walking down long and ominous corridors. The minimalist approach to dialogue is significant, as it helps to create a sense of foreboding, and also serves to highlight particular sounds (discussed shortly). Actual high school students were cast in the film, and purportedly encouraged to build dialogue from their own experiences. While the content and filming style are intimately related in an analysis of any film, in this film, cinematic strategies are so closely tied to the content that they can barely be separated.

At its core, *Elephant* is a story about how socially trying high school can be, especially for kids outside of the popular cliques. The film follows several students throughout their day at high school, emphasizing the banal aspects such as walking down hallways and selecting lunch in the cafeteria. Five important cinematic techniques, in no particular order, are used as storytelling devices. First, there are shots of the clouds in the sky shown periodically, at times either in time lapse, to make time appear to be moving quickly, or in time delay, reinforcing the slow real-time feel of most of the movie. The slowing down or speeding up is affected through noises in the background (ranging from background talking to birds to silence), or changes in the color of the sky, and the film in fact ends with a real-time shot of the clouds which, like the title of the film, are a metaphor for how each person interprets reality differently, much the way people see different shapes in the same clouds. This theme is reinforced via the second technique, using "intersection moments" like, at a critical point (right before the killing spree begins), when several characters converge in a hallway, and the perspective of the shot changes, in effect showing the same "time period" (before and after the intersection moment) but from the perspective of several different characters. In other words, one moment is used as a starting-point for showing the same time period in school from the perspective of several different students. Related to this, is the third major cinematic technique, the "remove" from which most of the action is shot. Though the film may appear to be shot from the perspective of each student as he or she walks down a corridor, in fact the camera is positioned slightly behind the student, offering the viewer a "remove" from the "action," as it were. In this way, not only are we engaged in projection as we would be for all film viewing (and historical film viewing in particular), but also from a slightly altered point of view—being positioned as the "observer." This "remove" is especially noticeable when it is briefly suspended, as the two killers plan their attack, and visualize pointing a gun from a first-person perspective, just as in the computer game one of the characters was seen playing earlier. Also related to these "intersection moments," is the fourth major cinematic technique, which is slow motion. During key moments in the film, including the "intersection moments," the film is briefly slowed down (so a hallway passing occurs slowly, a dog jumps and is suspended in midair, an unpopular girl looks off at the sky during gym class). This emphasizes certain moments and characters while further developing the sense that something awful is about to happen.

Finally, the sound design is integral to the interpretation of the script. In addition to the minimalist dialogue, which facilitates the viewer's role as "spectator," music and sound production are vital to the tone and narrative. Classical music is played at various points in the film, including a powerful scene in which one of the two killers plays the piano while his co-conspirator plays a violent "first person shooter" game on his laptop computer. This is important for two reasons. First, as pointed out, it cultivates an ominous tone. Second, it is the only "hobby" portrayed that contradicts official accounts of the Columbine shooters (who reportedly listened to Marilyn Manson and the like). Other sounds are also essential to the narrative. Mundane sounds are at times highlighted, sounding pronounced against what is otherwise a very quiet sound back-drop. For example, a character rolls a book-cart in the library, making an unnerving squeak. The most significant use of this technique, also in the library, is when a character, Michelle, hears the striking sound of a bullet entering a gun chamber, and turns around. The shot is cut, but later, repeated and played out, serving as the beginning of the exceptionally violent killing spree.

The characters in the film all represent stereotypes, such as, the nerd, the artist, the jock, the loner, the shallow popular girls, and so forth. Though the characters are for the most part, presented as one-dimensional, (partly as a result of many characters being depicted in a relatively short time span) the male characters are emphasized, and the female characters are particularly flat. The main female characters are "the nerd," Michelle, who is defined by her unattractiveness (per the cultural standard), and her own insecurity in gym class where she wears long pants instead of shorts like the other girls, and is shown alone and visibly uncomfortable in the locker room. Through this, and other "lonely" scenes, the pain of high school emerges as a dominant theme. The three "popular girls," in front of whom Michelle is uncomfortable, focus solely on boys and shopping, and in a scene mimicking the cult satire *Heathers* (1989), they are shown purging in three adjoining bathroom stalls. Finally, there is the "jock's girlfriend", defined solely by her boyfriend (a central figure in the film whose character comes to signify "the jocks" that the two killers abhor).

The film opens with John, a likeable student, driving to school with his drunken father. This corresponds with the many commentaries that "parental apathy" was a contributing factor to the Columbine shootings, as well as "troubled youth," more generally. However, the only other time parents are shown in the film is when the mother of one of the two killers (the mastermind), serves the two boys a homemade breakfast of pancakes, implying that the killers' parents were at least, to some degree involved in their lives. Alternatively, the film can be read as removing the parents from the subject almost entirely, as they only appear briefly in these two scenes. This reading of the text implies that parents are not a primary part of the school social context in which violence occurs.

Approximately twenty minutes into the film John is walking outside of the school and sees the two killers, dressed in black and army fatigues and carrying duffle bags, heading toward the school. Mimicking precisely what happened at Columbine, the two killers tell John, "get the fuck out of here and don't come back,"[44] to which he responds, "what are you doing?"[45] and is told "the shit's going down."[46] The moment earlier, when John is walking down the hallway approaching the main door, serves as the major "intersection moment", and is repeated several times, from the vantage point of different students. Following them to, and through, that point, is how most of the film unfolds.

The two killers are also shown in school, and at home, (unlike the other characters), with an emphasis on one of the two, who is named Eric after one of the Columbine killers and portrayed as the ringleader. Through following one of the killers, the filmmaker points to the various factors that culminate in violence. At school, the killer is bullied by "the jock." Prior to the killing, he tells his co-conspirator to go for "the best targets . . . the jocks."[47] At home the two killers are shown playing a violent first-person shooter computer game, ordering guns from a website called "guns USA," and watching a black and white Nazi propaganda film that featured Hitler. These were all reported, by the press and special interest groups, to be "causes" of Columbine (which you'll remember occurred on the anniversary of Hitler's birthday). The two boys are also shown in the shower together experimenting sexually, prior to the killing (which was not derived from public speculation about the Columbine killers).

The film culminates in the mass killing rampage. Eventually, the mastermind shoots his co-conspirator and then finds "the jock" and his girlfriend hiding in the cafeteria meat locker. He stands before the slabs of hanging meat, hauntingly recites "eeny meeny miny moe," and points the gun. The film concludes with a shot of the clouds, and an eerie silence.

Though not a "recreation" per se, this minimalist movie about a high school shooting spree clearly evokes Columbine, drawing on specific information and speculation about that event. The film reinforces the idea that guns, video games, and a fascination with Hitler all contributed to the tragedy, but at the same time provides an alternative to the public narrative about "hard" music contributing to the event, instead showing the killers' preferring classical music. With this said, the film ultimately argues that the social system characteristic of suburban high schools promotes feelings of alienation for many different kinds of students, and that school bullying more specifically, was the primary factor precipitating the event. In terms of comparison within the historical film genre, this is the only major fictionalized film surrounding one of the iconic events in this book that expands on and reopens the social analysis and political commentary about the event and its causes, and is also the only one that did not adopt a formulaic melodramatic script.

Documentaries

The distinction between narrative and documentary film is itself largely an artificial construct shaped by the fiction and non-fiction dualism that governs cinema, as discussed earlier. The problematic nature of this dichotomy is nowhere more evident than with regards to the "historical film," and particularly those films with iconic events as their subject matter. In this area, there are two major genres of documentary film: 1) those that claim to "bear witness" for the "historical record," and 2) political documentaries. These broad categorizations are not intended to reinforce the notion that some documentaries "record" an objective truth for future generations whereas other films are purely political by nature. Rather, these categories draw attention to the *assumptions* that circulate about these films, assumptions which impact public consumption, and correspondingly—the film's place within the larger repository of representations constructed around the event. In both instances, it is also important to consider all categories of documentaries about iconic events as memory projects linked to the renegotiation of national identity. These "memory projects" may serve to contribute to, consolidate or challenge the historical record, or may be appropriated in the service of a social, humanitarian, or political cause.

An abundance of Titanic, Pearl Harbor and September 11th documentaries have been produced by American filmmakers. After viewing a large collection of these films, several themes spring forth. First, the majority of documentaries, typically combine newsreels and/or audio-visual news footage, eye-witness testimonials, interviews with the bereaved, and commentary from experts. The convention of a single narrator is often employed as well. This category of documentary film focuses on "bearing witness" as an "authentic" means of adding to or establishing the historical record. Because of the reliance on first-hand accounts, or interviews with those who have otherwise been personally impacted by the event, these films receive a privileged place with respect to trust in the public eye; however, such films nevertheless contain many assumptions about social life. Documentaries of this nature, produced about the events in this book, all reinforce dominant understandings of the event. In this way, they are *implicitly* political with respect to national identity and related issues. Furthermore, documentaries about Pearl Harbor and 9-11 promote patriotic sentiment and are thus, also closely tied to nation-building. This occurs in two ways.

First, documentaries often employ the same conventions that narrative films use. For example, documentaries use music and color to evoke mood, powerful symbolism (such as flags, medals of Honor, and memorial sites), repetition of particular images (such as the Twin Towers being struck and collapsing), and narrative strategies. In terms of the latter, though labeled "documentary", a film can still "tell a story", and often, documentaries about iconic events build their stories in the same sequence as narrative films, offering closure, and at times, morals and/or a foreshadowing of the future (which may involve military action).

Second, extraordinary claims are repeatedly and routinely made in documentary films—claims which reaffirm the historicity of the event, and in ways that are often difficult to challenge as they come from "first-hand experience" or the experience of grief. For example, the following phrases come from Pearl Harbor documentaries: "a crossroads in history;" "defined an entire generation;" "no American adult will ever forget where they were and what they were doing." Additionally, the simplistic hero-villain story is also retold in documentaries, as is the notion that America never loses: "signaled the birth of the world power it is today [referring to the United States];" "millions of men old and young mobbed their local recruiting stations eager to exact revenge against the Japanese;" "Pearl Harbor attack united Americans like nothing before or after;" "The Japanese had awakened a sleeping giant. And that giant did not sleep again until its enemies had been utterly and completely defeated."[48]

Lastly, documentary films are edited and pieced together, a process that narrative film also undergoes. As such, the filmmaker in this and others ways, is able to tell the story he or she wishes to tell, while highlighting ideas that he or she wishes to emphasize.

The iconic imagery, narrative conventions, use of personal testimonials, and selected commentary, place the documentaries made about iconic events on the continuum between fact and fiction, but should not be taken as the former, nor as "neutral."

The second genre of documentary film is the political documentary. These expressly political films seek to explore the social or political issues from which the events flow, and typically resist official interpretations. Michael Moore's academy award winning film *Bowling for Columbine* (2001), categorized as a documentary, is both a political appropriation itself, as well as a resistive text that challenges the dominant interpretations of Columbine. Arguably, the vigor with which Moore's film was attacked by some as being "propaganda," reveals the very conundrum that films with historical subject matter face as a result of the fact-fiction dichotomy from within which they are viewed. I return to this point after briefly summarizing this resistive film.

Bowling for Columbine uses Columbine as a vehicle for talking about a host of issues in American culture, including the country's legacy of racism, Americans' predilection for guns, and it builds on the work of sociologist Barry Glassner's *The Culture of Fear* which argues Americans learn to fear "the wrong things" (such as one-on-one crime instead of corporate crime or pollution).[49] Moore also explores the Columbine shootings from several vantage points, interviewing performer Marilyn Manson, bringing Columbine victims to K-Mart to (satirically) return the bullets lodged in their bodies, and placing the Columbine shootings in the context of suburban school killings across the United States as well as the larger history of violence of which America, the nation, is a part (including footage of the Twin Towers being struck on 9-11). This film is a resistive text that counters dominant ideology while raising a host of social and political questions about the culture in which Columbine, and other violent acts, occur.

The major critique of the film is that it is not "factual" and through editing and selective focus, Moore is said to be spinning left-wing ideology as if it were "documentary." Though the film certainly has a progressive or "liberal" point of view with regards to social issues such as gun control and the like, the film did manage to fill a void, namely that of meaningful analysis or public discourse, one that you would think would have been filled—while the country was under the democratic leadership of Bill Clinton, and hence, one could argue that *Bowling for Columbine* raised issues that were otherwise not being addressed publicly. The more interesting issue pertains to Moore's use of "dramatic license," prompting criticism that the film is rife with factual errors and "trick editing." Of course, this critique hinges on the notion that there *are* factually accurate and complete accounts of social reality and that it is these accounts that documentaries are supposed to represent. Again, this is an erroneous belief. *Bowling for Columbine* unsettles the questionable fact-fiction distinctions upon which historical texts are judged and makes a case for explicit social analysis in "documentary" films as opposed to disavowing one's place within a film. In this respect, in addition to being resistive, the film is also reflexive.

Commodities

Iconic events are not only the subject of films, but may be the subject of plays, songs, television programs, poetry, and so forth. Additionally, the mythology surrounding an iconic event may be embedded in a range of objects for public display, auction, or sale. These objects, like other pop culture representations, are also a part of an event's repository of collective memory where particular myths or ideas are further reduced. Though popularly thought of as historical objects or memorabilia, these items are best understood as "memory-objects," constituted by social processes of remembering, forgetting, and commodification. These objects become part of the process by which an iconic event permeates the culture over time—they become signs of how an event has been interpreted and historicized and depict the role of the citizen as "within" or "having a piece of" national history. Memory-objects may emerge in relation to one another, contain each other or be a constituent part of each other. For example, books and memorabilia items sold in conjunction with a film's release are linked to that cinematic project. The resurgence of public interest in the event, flowing from the film, may however, create the production of event commodities for many years to come—at this point, the presence of books and products in the society may create yet another round of interest in the event for a new, younger audience who did not necessarily experience the film's release (let alone the lived historical experience of the event). Websites that sprout up in conjunction with renewed interest in an event may be maintained for years after a film's release, and these new "sites of memory" prompted by a film, may thus exist long after it.

Some memory-objects are an integral part of a larger memory-project. For example, national memorial sites for Pearl Harbor, (and that which may occur for 9-11), have "gift shops" that sell products associated with the event. The Titanic Historical Society also has this kind of store, as well as a museum which houses many Titanic objects. The store sells the very kind of items that satisfy, and contribute to, the public's fascination with the event, while allowing "Titanic buffs" to feel they are purchasing a part of the very history that has captured their personal imagination. For example, the store sells many books and the like, but more interestingly, offers reproduced documents including, among other items: Titanic tickets, advertisements, maps, floor plans, drawings, passenger rosters, crew rosters, registration and inspection certificates, the chilling wireless messages, photographs, the inquiry transcripts, and letters to and from the White Star Line (some bearing the line's official seal). Many of these items are identified as simulations of the real documents.

In addition to the production of commodities in the memorabilia genre, some events promote the sale of preexisting items that were not necessarily always linked to the event, but become equated with it. Perhaps the most obvious recent example is the American flag post-September 11th. As it became the symbol immediately available for those coming to terms with 9-11, the flag also became a widely sold commodity appearing in many sizes for home use, car antennas, and on bumper stickers, pins and other less conventional forms. Wal-Mart reported a nationwide 1,800 percent increase in the sale of flags, compared with a year earlier.[50] The flag, and related patriotic sentiment, also cropped up in fashion, and soon department stores were filled with sequin-studded and other adorned T-shirts and fashion items bearing the image of the American flag and/or messages such as I Love NYC, I Love the NYC PD, I Love the NYC FD and so forth. The prevalence of these items also encouraged the production of T-shirts, bumper stickers and the like with counter-culture messages, bearing the image of the American flag and statements about dissent. Again, these items all bore preexisting images but became associated with September 11th and its aftermath. Some iconic events do not inspire the production of commodities per se, but nevertheless impact commercial culture. Though the events at Columbine High School did not cause the production of new commodities, many products linked to school security, from metal detectors to clear backpacks, saw major spikes in their sales.

While memorials, special organizations, and constructed collective sentiment may offer the citizen "access" to the material of the past, in addition to, or in lieu of such institutionalized projects, commodities often develop in relation to blockbuster films. The development of commodities in relation to commercial films is not exclusive to iconic events. Action and children's films have a history of producing related products such as action figures, dolls, T-shirts, and lunchboxes. Recently, the production of film-related commodities has been most noticeable with respect to *Titanic* and *Pearl Harbor*.

During the release of *Titanic* a range of related commodities entered the market. Major bookstores prominently displayed Titanic books in store windows and on displays in the front of stores. Some bookstores created special Titanic sections. This prompted new editions of many out-of-print or low circulating books. For example, Marshall Everett's 1912 book re-circulated in a special 1998 commemorative edition with the modified title *Story of the Wreck of Titanic*. Furthermore, the spate of new Titanic books shows a sudden resurgence of interest in the event, illustrating the effect a film may have on the production of new scholarship. The film induced historians and social scientists to revisit the event, which is ironic, considering the contempt with which most scholars and critics wrote about the film for its use of melodrama.

Along with books, chain bookstores sold reprinted copies of some 1912 newspapers that initially reported the tragedy. These newspapers sold for approximately $5.00 per copy and were displayed near store registers (point-of-sale) next to current newspapers. A citizen could walk around a shopping mall grounded in the happenings of 1997 and then pass a bookstore window display and be confronted with a piece of 1912 history. This brush with the national past is fragmented, partial, fleeting, and always linked to present experience.

A similar phenomenon occurred with the release of *Pearl Harbor*. Books on the subject flooded stores, including books with reprinted newspaper headlines from the days following the event. These books however, had a shorter shelf-life than Titanic books. Days after the 9-11 attacks, Pearl Harbor books were removed from prominent displays, and moved to the bargain shelves. The effect of September 11th on the ultimate failure of Pearl Harbor books is speculative, as the movie was far from a hit.

In the case of Titanic, many material products including puzzles, games, maps, postcards, jewelry, salt and pepper shakers, etc., also cropped up as a result of the success of the film. Many of these items reinforced Titanic myths about gender and social class, while also reaffirming the primary historical figures of the story. For example, a 1997 Titanic puzzle sold by the Milton Bradley Company containing eighteen images, served to create an overall picture of the event. It depicts several people including Captain Smith, a crew officer, Molly Brown, John Jacob Astor, and Madeleine Astor. In addition to a resurgence of interest in the Titanic event, there were also many products available that were derived directly from *Titanic*, the film, not the event. Most famously, there were many replicas of the "heart of the sea" necklace, available in two permutations: precious gem stones (where a sapphire replaced the blue diamond) and costume versions. Other items, such as broaches, were also modeled after "the heart of the sea." These memory-objects represent a complete departure from the empirical record of the event, and instead are linked to the event solely through the film. In other words, these items are explicitly created from fictional inspiration but are inextricably bound to the event, via people's memory *of the film*.

The history-emptying processes involved in creating these kinds of commodities associated with iconic events, can ultimately conceal or at least confuse the struggles over social meaning that are embodied in the object, so that all that appears to remain, is myth.

Conclusion

Popular culture plays a pivotal role in the creation and endurance of iconic events. Films, for example, may serve to reinsert an event into the public consciousness long after its passing or at a time when national identity is being renegotiated. Through the consumptive processes in which viewers engage in anticipation and projection, films made about iconic events create new memories of the event, while also reinforcing or challenging earlier interpretations. These exercises in collective memory-building, though often not given their due credit with respect to impact on public perception, become a part of the "public history" of iconic events.

Initial press interpretations, particularly with regard to tragic events, are often taken as "just the facts" reporting. Consequent political appropriations may fly under the radar as citizens become so used to associating the event with a few issues or concepts that the use of an event for a directed end may go unnoticed. Films however, as well as other commercial or popular interpretations, have the potential, at their best, to ignite a public discourse about the very conundrum on which *all* historical narratives are based. As Kaes explains, historical film can expose "the irresolvable dual status of historical narratives, as document and fiction."[51] As evidenced in the review of both narrative and even documentary film, the study of historical film raises questions about the fact-fiction dichotomy that informs public perception of historical representations. Because they explicitly blend fiction with non-fiction, a study of historical films underscores the lager problems associated with historiography.

It is not surprising that iconic events become the subject of cinematic interpretation. Not only are these events that have at one time or another captured the public's imagination, and by extension are assumed to have mass appeal (translation, box office potential), but the earlier interpretations that shaped collective memory of the event created the very material that reverberates in cinematic representation. In particular, in films, personalities are often collapsed into composite characters.[52] This was evident in all of the narrative films reviewed, particularly *Titanic, Pearl Harbor,* and *Elephant* in which the representative types were fictional creations. More specifically, classic melodramatic distinctions between heroes and villains abound in historical films.[53] From the outset, iconic events are narrated as classic good versus evil stories producing central figures of exceptionally positive or negative qualities. This is the stuff of American cinema, making iconic events fruitful subject matter, not necessarily because of the nature of a particular event itself, but rather, because of how it was represented. Furthermore, those in the industry, or financially supporting it, who have an interest in keeping the memory of a particular event in the forefront of the public domain, are likely to invest time and capital in the production for such films.

Given their prominent place in the historical record as "watershed moments", the relationship between historical commercial films and issues pertaining to national identity should not be underestimated. For example, *Pearl Harbor* and the commodities related to it, brought the event back into the public arena, and did so by reaffirming the dominant American narrative. *Titanic* on the other hand, served to confer meaning on an event that was no longer central to the society's view of its past, but once again through popularization, came to be thought of as a defining moment. Differing from the straightforward allegiance to the official story as seen in *Pearl Harbor*, *Titanic* displayed reverence for some long-held myths while serving to dislodge and even reverse others. In these films, the melodramatic scripts which were read by many critics as being implicitly "unhistorical,"[54] actually facilitated the public's (re)connection to the "historic" event. In this regard, Marcia Landy writes, "Films employing a fictional format . . . using melodrama in ways that can create an affective relation to events, re-animating a sense of a past that is becoming increasingly remote in time."[55] Bear in mind that what films about Titanic, Pearl Harbor and 9-11 all have in common is their explicit mixing of fiction and nonfiction, while their makers claim to be creating "authentic" accounts of the events. Again, the apparent contradiction is only such if one assumes that fiction cannot serve the narrative in ways that are consistent with the nation's view of its past, whether utopian or resistive. The two September 11th films about United Flight 93 both employed, to varying degrees, conventions of melodrama to aid the storytelling process, as did *World Trade Center*. Elsaesser explains that melodrama is a narrative form that is consistent with mourning and can represent the trauma attached to some events in ways that could otherwise not be captured.[56] Reading the United Flight 93 films through this lens can help contextualize the differences between these two films, as well as the similarities. While *United 93* showed a stronger fidelity to the "empirical record," could it not be viewed that the melodramatic family-driven *Flight 93* was more consistent with the mourning and grieving experienced by many in the nation, also a truthful part of how many Americans think about and remember 9-11?

Rejecting the assumption that there is a single factual account available (of any of the events in this book), it is my contention that the different films, some that are admittedly less factual but evoke relevant emotions, and others that stick closer to the empirical records available sometimes at the expense of the "humanity" of the experience, elicit different (and partial) kinds of "truth."

Though some scholars, Sobchack for example, treat the observation that history has become a commodity, as a "view of the cynical,"[57] in fact, there is no escaping this truth. Historical events, and our ideas about them, are embedded in products and other artifacts that circulate in commercial culture. This does not, however, mean that history is *only* a commodity. Certainly, in the case of iconic events, commodifying the event, which entails a reductive process, is *a part* of how the event circulates in the society over time. It is not the only way. These objects can offer insight into both the producer's current view of the past, and also the series of collective memory practices that came before, and invariably left traces within the artifact.

Regardless of how one conceptualizes the properties of historical films and other commercial forms with historical subject matter, it is through popular culture that new generations may become invested in particular events, or parts of those events, and that they may come to endure as being significant. Furthermore, the visceral memories that films help produce in consumers, opens up a space where dominant narratives can be fortified, contested or subverted, revealing the contingency and partiality on which historical narratives are built.

Notes

1. Roy Rosenweig and David Thelen, "The Presence of the Past: Popular Uses of History in American Life," *Humanities: When Stones Speak: Communicating Across the Ages* Special Issue 20, no. 1 (January/February1999): 15-16.

2. Anna Reading, *The Social Inheritance of the Holocaust: Gender, Culture, and Memory* (New York: Palgrave Macmillan, 2002), 77-8.

3. John R. Gills, *Commemorations: The Politics of National Identity* (Princeton, N.J.: Princeton University Press, 1994), 7.

4. Marcia Landy, *The Historical Film: History and Memory in the Media* (New Brunswick, N.J.: Rutgers University Press, 2001), 7.

5. Trevor B. McCrisken and Andrew Pepper, *American History and Contemporary Hollywood Film* (New Brunswick, N.J.: Rutgers University Press, 2005), 2.

6. Debbie Lisle and Andrew Pepper, "The New Face of Global Hollywood: Black Hawk Down and the Politics of the Meta-Sovereignty," *Cultural Politics* 1, no. 2 (April 2005): 135-136.

7. Robert D. Romanyshyn, *Technology's Symptom and Dream* (New York: Routledge, 1989), 19.

8. McCrisken and Pepper, Contemporary Hollywood, 1.

9. George Lipsitz, *Time Passages: Collective memory and American Popular Culture* (Minneapolis: University of Minnesota Press, 1990).

10. Julia Kristeva, *Language – The Unknown: An Initiation into Linguistics* (New York: Columbia University Press, 1989), 315.

11. *Apollo 13 Collectors Edition*, DVD, directed by Ron Howard (Universal City, Ca: Universal Home Video, 1998).

12. Paul Grainge, *Memory and Popular Film* (Manchester, N.Y.: Manchester University Press, 2003), 3.

13. Grainge, *Memory and Popular Film*, 4.

14. McCrisken and Pepper, *Contemporary Hollywood*, 2.

15. McCrisken and Pepper, *Contemporary Hollywood*, 2.

16. Simon Mills, *The Titanic in Pictures* (Chesham: Wordsmith Publications, 1995).

17. Mills, *Titanic in Pictures*.

18. (Titanic Historical Society)

19. Steven Biel, *Down With the Old Canoe: A Cultural History of the Titanic Disaster* (New York: W. W. Norton and Company, Inc., 1996).

20. Of course, another reading of Ida Straus' decision, as noted by many suffragists shortly after the sinking, is that she was asserting her equality with her husband—a narrative that would make her story about gender equality and not marriage. Furthermore, other interpretations may take her age into account and imagine that she opted to let a younger person take her place, or perhaps someone with young children to raise (as there were reports by survivors of single women who gave their seats to mothers). These readings of her story take her choice outside of the discourse of marriage altogether.

21 The Titanic Historical Society headquarters are located in Indian Orchard, MA.

22. Donald Lynch, *Titanic: An Illustrated History* (New York: Hyperion, 1992), 198.

23. Lynch, *Illustrated History*, 201.

24. Lynch, *Illustrated History*, 201.

25. Lynch, *Illustrated History*, 208.

26. Lynch, *Illustrated History*, 208.

27. Lynch, *Illustrated History*, 208.

28. Lynch, *Illustrated History*, 208.

29. *Titanic*, directed by James Cameron (Hollywood, Ca: Paramount, 1999).

30. *Titanic*, Cameron.

31. Mark Engelhart, "Review of Pearl harbor Theatrical Release," 2001, *http://www.amazon.com/gp/product/B00003CXTG/qid=1153242423/sr=8-1/ref=pd_bbs_1/103-1147873-1211029?%5Fencoding=UTF8&v=glance&n=130* (July 1, 2006).

32. Howard W. French, "Pearl Harbor in Japan: Love or War," *New York Times,* 22 June 2001, 3(A).

33. Victoria James, "Japan Snores Through Pearl Harbor," 2001, *http://www.newstatesman.com/200107230025* (July 1, 2006).

34. Kristeva, *Language – The Unknown*, 316.

35. Linda Sunshine and Antonio Felix, *Pearl Harbor: The Movie and the Moment* (New York: Hyperion, 2001) 55.

36. Sunshine and Felix, *Pearl Harbor, 55.*

37. French, "Pearl Harbor in Japan," 3.

38. French, "Pearl Harbor in Japan," 3.

39. Peter Hatfield, "Japan's Date with Pearl Harbor," *BBC News. http://news.bbc.co.uk/2/hi/asia-pacific/1399970.stm* (July 1, 2006).

40. James, "Japan Snores," 1.

41. French, "Pearl Harbor in Japan," 3.

42. "11' 9" 01 – September 11," *Artificial Eye. http://www.artificial-eye.com/dvd/ART240dvd/main.html* (June 21, 2006)

43. The preceding paragraph contains quotes from *Flight 93*, directed by Peter Makle (United States: A&E, 2006).

44. *Elephant*, directed by Gus Van Sant (United States: HBO Video, 2003).

45. *Elephant*, Van Sant.

46. *Elephant*, Van Sant.

47. *Elephant*, Van Sant.

48. All quotations from this paragraph are accredited to *Pearl Harbor a Documentary: A Day of Infamy, December 7, 1941* (Eugene, O.R.: Dastar Corp./Marathon Music and Video, 2001).

49. Glassner, Barry. *The Culture of Fear: Why Americans are afraid of the wrong things.* (New York: Basic Books, 1999).

50. Lincoln, Yvonna S and Norman K. Denzin. *9/11 in American Culture.* (Walnut Creek: Alta Mira Press, 2003), 277

51. Anton Kaes, "The Presence of the Past: Rainer Werner Fassbinder's The Marriage of Maria Braun," in *The Historical Film: History and Memory in the Media*, ed. Marcia Landy (New Brunswick, N.J.: Rutgers University Press, 2001).

52. McCrisken and Pepper, *Contemporary Hollywood*, 5.

53. Landy, *The Historical Film*, 8.

54. Landy, *The Historical Film*, 11.

55. Landy, *The Historical Film*, 9.

56. Thomas Elsaesser "Subject Positions, Speaking Positions: from *Holocaust our Hitler, and Heimata to Shoah and Schindler's List*," in *The Persistence of History: Cinema, Television, and the Modern Event*, ed. Vivian Sobchack (New York: Routledge, 1996).

57. Vivian Carol Sobchack, *The Persistence of History: Cinema, Television, and the Modern* Event (New York: Routledge, 1996), 6.

Chapter Six

The Significance of Iconic Events

This book explores the social, political, and market forces that shape the meanings and enduring significance of events deemed iconic in American culture. Though vastly different with respect to scope, breadth/depth of effect, and the nature of the tragedy itself, Titanic, Pearl Harbor, Columbine, and September 11th have all, to varying degrees, captured the public's imagination. By studying representations of these iconic events over time, from their initial representation to political appropriations and commercial adaptations, broader processes of collective memory as well as the central dilemmas of historical research, are revealed. Foremost, as these events are all labeled and later remembered as major markers in the history of the nation, not only of a singular nature (which may be factually so), but also as "turning points" (a quality with which the events are *imbued*), the processes of collective memory through which they are interpreted, are intertwined with cultural processes of national identity formation. As a result, these events are integral to the public's perception of the past, and by extension, the present and future—within a shifting global context in which the effects extend beyond (imagined) borders. Iconic events have become a vehicle through which "nation" is articulated, and so too are these events critical to the renegotiation of that identity, at times via purposeful political challenge, or resistance within popular culture. Additionally, by examining event representations over time and across interpretive realms, the relationship between historiography and cultural memory work—including the fundamental problem inherent in the construction of an empirical record—emerges. Specifically, the

187

fact-fiction dichotomy that guides the public perception of any rendering of events is revealed (and displaced) through the study of iconic events, a project that illustrates the partiality of all empirical accounts.

The Represented, Representational, and Pop Culture Stages of Interpretation

As stated in chapter one and reviewed throughout the book, the iconic events under discussion have all undergone hyper-representation, been appropriated into ongoing political agendas, transformed into commodities, and adapted into popular entertainment. More specifically, this book considers three interpretive phases through which event narratives are derived, reified, and/or contested.

Figure A

Interpretive Phase	Myth Construction	Effect of Interpretation
Initial Interpretive Processes (Press and State Responses)	A Meta-Narrative with Mythical Concepts Develops	The Represented Event
Directed Political Uses	Mythical Concepts Appropriated and Transplanted into other Agendas	Representational Event
Popular Culture Adaptations	Myth further Reduced	Event is Reinserted into the Public Domain, via Commercial Culture

The Represented Event
The first interpretive stage identified in this book culminates in *the represented event*, which is the repository of journalistic event representations that serve to mediate later representations. The process itself is not unique as all major current events undergo an initial and at times intense process of representation, where journalists (or the press more broadly) attempt to communicate information about an event to the public. While delivering information, the press signals

the relative importance of the event via the account itself, the historical or social context provided, the choice of metaphors offered, the language used, and also the space reserved for the reporting of the event. Events that become iconic in the culture experience representation outside of the bounds of "normal" reporting, and through this process, start to acquire mythic status.

There are two primary methods that journalists employ when conveying the exceptional nature of an event, one having to do with space and the other with language and context. The first technique relies on the event being afforded a monopoly of the journalistic space. As seen by comparing Titanic and Pearl Harbor newspaper representations with later Columbine and September 11th representations in multi-media, while the avenues available for accomplishing this end have changed dramatically during the past century, the overall process remains the same. The enormity of Titanic for example, was imparted via a monopoly of newspaper space. Stories filled newspapers, cover to cover. In this respect, headlines were also bigger and bolder than usual. What journalists deem "hard news" was also consistently juxtaposed with "human interest" stories, making the purported "humanity" of the event a part of the reporting from the outset, fostering an emotional dynamic between the public and the event based on the construction of a shared traumatic experience.

In contemporary society, where print, television and Internet news all circulate information about the same event, the monopoly of space as well as the duration of time afforded are together known as "saturation coverage." This type of coverage allows the event to occupy unprecedented space in the public sphere, itself signaling the perceived importance of the event. Additionally, and with great consequence, the multi-media in which events are projected, particularly television news which is carried largely by extraordinary images that break through "clutter," the public is not only bombarded by the event itself, but often by evocative, memorable, and tragic images that may impact people on deep psychic levels. The danger with respect to public perception of the event, is the belief that "seeing is believing." In this way, and as stated in the beginning of chapter five, citizens may feel that moving imagery, whether television or cinema, "makes the event more real." Despite these assumptions, when considering the looped coverage of several selected scenes from Columbine as well as that of September 11th with the Twin Towers being struck and then the buildings crumbling, one must question how "real" it is to "bear witness" to such horrific moments on a loop, for days and even weeks or months.

In both print and media culture, journalists signal the social importance of an event, in part via this domination of the ever-increasing journalistic landscape. In chapter one it was assumed that in this "represented" stage the press mark the event with singularity and a "turning-point" quality; however, it is now clear that these are in fact related but also distinct phenomena. The events in this book, and many others such as the Challenger explosion, the Oklahoma City bombing, Watergate, or the assassination of J.F.K., are singular in nature—as was the Shirtwaist Factory Fire. In terms of scope and at times, the genre, these events *are* historically unique. However, noting the singularity of the event, up until that point in history at least, does not necessitate that the event be imbued with a "turning point" quality which is in fact what defines the event as a watershed moment in the history of the nation—from which other social or political changes should then "naturally" flow. In other words, once defined as a critical moment, a rift is then created in the public record, creating the idea of "before and after" the event, prompting a myriad of responses including formal commemorative action. The press does not operate alone in this construction of national memory.

As collective memory scholars have noted with regards to the different facets of the historical record, iconic events are clearly another point at which the relationship between the press' reporting and the "official" state response to tragedies, reveals itself. Perhaps most clearly seen with respect to September 11th, the press is complicit in the process by which the state an the event with national significance, thereby creating an opportunity to alter national priorities and policies, purportedly as a result of the event. In addition to providing a nearly limitless platform from which the state can communicate their version, the press creates an aura around an event, via adherence to resonant storytelling conventions and nationalistic frameworks. Consider for example the current of patriotism, with its specified meaning that circulated in the culture after 9-11, concurrent with journalistic accounts and the state's official response.

The amount of space designated for representations of a particular event does not alone mark the event. The second method journalists employ is the choice of language, including superlatives, figures of speech, and historical context. Here too, the press can actually serve the state, as made clear by the overuse of Pearl Harbor as a lens through which to view September 11th[1] which arguably reinforced the administration's spin on it and ultimately helped depoliticize the roots of the event by labeling it an incomprehensible "surprise." This is also an example where the intersections of the press and state narratives serve to reinforce dominant, and even traditional, conceptions of national identity. With the exception of Shirtwaist, which could have served as a prompt for the reevaluation of national identity with respect to burgeoning philosophies of capitalism and technological and market changes brought about by mass production, all of the events in this book became focal points through which the renegotiation of national identity occurred, or was thought to have occurred. In the case of Titanic, consider two examples. The press response to Titanic, which emphasized the role gender was assumed to play in the tragedy, served as a platform from which a challenge to the Women's Suffrage Movement would be launched (and then itself resisted through another level of appropriation). Another example, explored in the work of Slavoj Zizek, is that through the sinking of Titanic, European society experienced its own death as it was in a rapid state of trans-formation, undergoing a paradigm shift, with regard to rigid social class distinc-tions, embodied in the fantasy ship.[2] Therefore, the event provided an opportu-nity with which to come to terms with larger changes already occurring.

Returning to the larger issue of how the press narrates current events, be-yond marking the event in the ways discussed, which often includes legitimizing the official story and thus becoming a constituent part of it, the contingency of the historical record itself is evident by the data presented in chapter three. From the outset, a range of conventions, assumptions, stereotypes, and state pressures, help mold the flow of information in particular ways, revealing the tenuous (at best) relationship between the press and its often assumed role in the execution of democracy. Here, the particular conventions employed, are paramount. In their reporting of Titanic, Columbine, and September 11th, and to a lesser de-gree Pearl Harbor, journalists drew heavily on biblical good versus evil scripts, complete with heroic and villainous figures, and in some cases also using the mythical archetype of the martyr. These long-standing mythical concepts served as models that informed the reporting of these events. Shirtwaist, the only event that was not narrated using this framework, was never successfully transplanted into political discourses (outside of worker health and safety advocacy). In all of the positive cases, the event meta-narrative created by the press, centered on these simplified mythical concepts which were then taken and transplanted into other political projects.

With this said, watching the event narratives created by the press being co-opted into explicitly political agendas is the point at which the relationship be-tween iconic events and political culture fully emerges.

The Representational Event

Though the press sets the stage for an event to acquire special stature in the cul-ture, the over-representation of an event itself, complete with extreme statements and imagery, does not alone make an event endure in the public space. Major events, particularly those that are traumatic, are bound to receive (for national, commercial and other reasons) extensive coverage including displacing other national or international stories; however, what is not normative is the inten-tional directed political use of events. It is this process of appropriation, as well as the commercializing and memorializing of events (and their narratives), that make the event iconic in a sustained way.

Through the political stage of interpretation, the event becomes "representa-tional," meaning, a vehicle for purposes outside of itself. It is at this juncture, the critical representational stage, that the intent motivating hermeneutic (meaning-making) activities explicitly changes. Many ideas can circulate via the event but in order to do so must have sponsors or backers who consolidate, organize and disseminate their interpretation. Not all sponsors have the same persuasive voice in the culture, influenced by capital, technologies of mass communication, other interest groups and powerful lobbies, and where the sponsor sits relative to current administration favor. These sponsors, at times already established special interest groups like the Pro-Life lobby or NRA, activate the repository of collective memory already established by journalists, the state (and any other early interpreters) for their own purposive end. These groups create what is referred to as a "memory project" within collective memory literature. The activation of an event's collective memory may appear natural given the over-exposure the event has already received in the culture as well as the social and political ideas that have already been normalized during initial reporting and government press conferences (such as "women and children first" in the case of Titanic, which fueled the public's consumption of an anti-suffrage Titanic discourse). Despite appearing natural, in fact many of the political uses of iconic events serve to appropriate the event into political projects to which they are not directly linked. Consider for example, the public service announcement that opens this book, in which September 11th was implanted into a conservative anti-drug campaign that had existed for over twenty years. In the introduction I posed the question, with regard to this political appropriation: should we be concerned?

The issue, as seen in chapter four in particular, is the *extent* to which these appropriations occur and moreover that they seem to appear *natural* by those positioned to accept them as such. By studying how these appropriations transpire, we can denaturalize this process in order to expose the exploitation or power plays underscoring these very intentional efforts. Of note, the time delay from which representations could circulate within print culture, allowed counterculture or otherwise resistive groups (with access to the means of communication), the opportunity to inject themselves into the discourse, posing resistance, and creating a mass-mediated dialogue of sorts. Though in the mass media era resistance to dominant stories occurs more swiftly, via the Internet, podcasting, and other sources, resistive efforts are at times subsumed within larger waves of sentiment created in dominant media. Nonetheless, from Titanic to September 11th it is clear that the appropriation of event narratives into political discourses, with which they have no inherent link, creates a space for alternative politics to circulate. In other words, resistive politics are fueled by dominant appropriations. Therefore, despite concerns regarding the co-opting of shared trauma experiences, on the positive side this act (potentially) opens a space for public discourse, where multiple viewpoints may then circulate. It is nevertheless important to bear in mind that not all perspectives do circulate, or do so with the same support system backing them, or that resistive narratives, are by extension always relegated to "response" with dominant appropriations usually having the luxury of "initiation." This also has an affect on the way the dialogue will ultimately be read by the public.

The process by which some events are appropriated into political campaigns, and the extent to which groups resistive to those uses of the event are able to circulate their own narratives, is underscored through the comparison of the Shirtwaist Factory Fire to the other events. This comparison ultimately reveals that the development of distilled mythical concepts (heroism, martyrdom, etc.) within a resonant good versus evil narrative, is integral to later political appropriations where it is really these reduced over-identified concepts that are transplanted into other arenas—concepts which may then be again appropriated (as in the case of chivalry with respect to Titanic and Suffrage). This process of directed political usage is important because it is via this process that social power is executed from more directions, via over-determined moments in national history.

Pop Culture Adaptations

Popular culture plays a vital role in the collective memory of the national past, and iconic events provide a focal point through which to see these processes unfold. In particular, historical films serve collective memory in several ways including, signaling the perceived importance of a particular event, reinserting it into the public's consciousness, creating new narratives and images pertaining to the event (which may legitimize or subvert the dominant narrative), and animating segments of the society to reinvest their energies into the event and our ever-changing record of it. In some cases, as evidenced by Titanic, it is the release of a film that grabs hold of the public's imagination long after the effects of the event have passed. Furthermore, the film can become not only a means to alter the public's perception of the historical event, but due to the time-lag, also a chance to record the society's own perception of its changed values. In the case of 1997's *Titanic*, the film created new images of the event, as well as public interest, but could also be read, through its sharp reversal of the gender and class stereotypes that comprised earlier representations, as a vehicle for noting some of the social changes that have occurred in the culture (irrespective of Titanic sinking). In other words, when an event has been represented over a long period of time, new interpretations can serve as a mechanism through which the society can trace and record a host of social changes in a way that appears informal—because the most visible objective is the creation of a new narrative about the contained event not the culture as a whole.

Iconic events translate easily into film screenplays, as seen in chapter five. This cannot be assumed to result from the nature of the "pure" event, though certainly tragedies are dramatic, but alternatively, as a result of how the event was formerly represented.[3] All of the events in this book that did become iconic within the culture were reported in very particular good versus evil formats. These ways of understanding and then remembering the event are the stuff of

Hollywood. The initial press narratives that communicate ideas about the event to the public therefore influence later cinematic representations (in addition to political appropriations). The role journalists and their sponsors play, within the context of collective memory is consequently significant in numerous ways and over time.

As films reinsert events into the public sphere, two issues emerge. First, what is the nature of films with regard to dominant collective memory and national identity? Second, without simply rejecting them, how can we evaluate historical films given their use of fiction?

Narrative and documentary films play a major role in the reconstruction of collective memory. With new information, changed cultural values, and updated means of expression, films may serve to reinforce, challenge and/or subvert widely held assumptions about the past. They also reach large diverse audiences, thereby becoming part of public history. The composite characters that represent contingents of a given population, and are also used to symbolize idealized versions of heroism and its counterpart, serve as the moral compass in historical films—relaying ideas about how the audience should feel about the event and its central figures. These representative types, developed from seeds planted in early press accounts, are a conduit for the nation-building that occurs via historical films. In other words, as central, collapsed characters (that may or may not derive from fiction), guide films such as *Titanic*, *Pearl Harbor*, and *Flight 93*, they offer the audience a version of right and wrong. However, given the historical subject matter on which the films are based, combined with its appropriation(s), these characters actually offer the public a *nationalist moral compass*.

The main themes in historical films, as well as the sequencing (and narrative closure in particular), contribute to a reconstruction of national identity. In this regard, Grainge has argued that Hollywood has been integral to the "codification of the cultural past"[4] and Sobchack explains that historical films narrate "coherent moral tales"[5] which are central to the idea of "nation." As many film and memory scholars have noted, this is certainly true with respect to *Pearl Harbor* which reaffirmed America's official story and simultaneously managed to make the United States appear victorious (a recurring theme in the nation's view of itself as a superpower), by ending with America's successful retaliatory raid. Moreover, despite claims that the film dignified the Japanese, only the Americans in the film were afforded subjectivity, a point not lost on the Japanese audiences who had seen a "softer" version of the movie. Though *Flight 93* and *United 93* offer different windows onto the experience of that September 11th flight, both films affirm, and reinsert into the public consciousness, the dominant narrative of heroism swiftly spun out of those events. All of these films also call on viewers to engage in heightened processes of projection and anticipation, both of which, but particularly projection, fuel nationalistic or patriotic sentiment—essential to the ongoing forging of national identity. Additionally, as is the case with *Pearl Harbor*, both United 93 films fail to grant the attackers subjectivity, thus rendering the assaults outside of political culture. In this way these films further legitimized the dominant press and state interpretation which uniformly depoliticized the event. Significantly, these September 11th films were both released during and at a point which the Iraq War was waning in public support and therefore may, by effect if not design, have served to figuratively "bring Americans back" to initial 9-11 feelings—as discussed in chapter four, feelings which were, from the outset, conflated with the otherwise unlikely Iraq War.

While some films reestablish dominant identity conceptions linked to particular events, others may promote a renegotiation of collective memory and possibly national identity. These films, or aspects of them, may resist dominant versions of the past and seek to demystify past events, or, "decode" the unitary view held to date. This can occur in different ways as evidenced by *Titanic*, *Elephant* and *Bowling for Columbine*, which span American filmmaking as a Hollywood blockbuster, independent film, and documentary, respectively. Regarding collective identity, *Titanic* traces changes in cultural notions about gender and social class by privileging the perspective of fictional characters Rose and Jack, over others. Furthermore, the film, though sharply criticized for historical inaccuracies and its explicit use of melodrama, ultimately did challenge the historical record, including the Senate Inquiry which failed to find misconduct on the part of the crew. *Elephant* and *Bowling for Columbine*, are also resistive, but differ in that both films, one through a fictional plot-line and one via documentary/editorializing, revisited an iconic event in order to explore the social and political issues from which it flowed, issues which had been largely marginalized in the mainstream. In these ways, the films not only address the validity of the historical record, but also create further social projects out of this contestation. Because of their large audiences, films are an important medium for resistive narratives and politics in general to circulate.

Given their mixing of fact and fiction, a criticism of all of the films under discussion, how can films about iconic events be assessed?

Many of the films reviewed in chapter five have been criticized for relying on fiction and melodrama in their storytelling; however, as this book attempts to highlight, all historical records, including journalistic accounts and government responses, employ cultural techniques of narrative, weighted language, selected historical metaphors and so forth, and thus are not "pure" accounts of the event either. Therefore, it seems more effective to judge particular historical films based on the part of the event story they tell, as opposed to how they measure up to an oversimplified conception of nonfiction versus fiction. What's more, film is the interpretive form that most clearly exposes the falsity of the fact-fiction dualism. With their explicit mixing of fact and fiction, films, ironically, represent an honesty with regard to larger sociological questions pertaining to historical representation. In this vein, historical films reveal the contingency upon which all historical narratives are built, and moreover, that historical records are actually the outcome of memory work, which always involves remembering and forgetting.

The analysis in chapter five shows that films may employ fiction and melodrama in different ways and with different outcomes. Additionally, the process of anticipation and projection which characterize the consumptive experience of historical film is intertwined with the varied uses of fiction and melodrama which these films often rely on. The use of fictional composite characters in *Titanic* and *Pearl Harbor* allows anticipation to build while the melodramatic storyline in which these characters operate fosters viewer identification with *particular* characters, a consumptive process that itself has been scripted. The idealized characters in *Titanic* offer a modernized view onto the Titanic experience, and therefore Rose, with her spirited rejection of traditional femininity and Jack with his ability to transcend a crumbling class system, are relatable to contemporary audiences, allowing viewers to project themselves more easily into the script. More than being relatable, these characters are so totally idealized, that they simultaneously appear banal and larger-than-life, much like the mythology surrounding the event and those who died during it. Pearl Harbor follows a similar pattern with regard to the consumptive experience but goes even further by denying the Japanese soldiers subjectivity, that which makes them human, while devoting the first half of the epic film to building subjectivity in the representative American soldiers—the contrast being stark. This prompts audience identification with the Americans (the soldiers who merely respond, not the officials who execute social power). This identification with the Americans stationed at Pearl Harbor facilitates the projection of one's self into those roles, thus building patriotism into the consumptive experience. Here it is clear that not only is the text nationalist, but so too are the methods used to encourage the public's *ingestion* of the text.

Similarly to *Pearl Harbor*, the television movie *Flight 93*, with its dramatic family-focused storyline, also fosters audience identification and projection, serving to fuel patriotic sentiment. Though the characters are derived from real people, and not fictional constructs, the use of melodrama alone allows a very similar consumptive experience and relationship to national identity construction. *United 93* creates higher levels of anticipation and less projection and is perceived as more authentic with regard to the empirical record. Nevertheless, the diminished subjectivity afforded the passengers serves to link them as "Americans," resonating with press and state responses to the event. Therefore, though accomplished differently, *United 93* also fosters projection though not with individual characters but rather the constructed identity category "American." This too is part of nation-building.

Given the traumatic nature of iconic events, these films also serve the public in ways connected to the human condition. The explicit use of fiction and/or melodrama in historical films can obscure or expose the humanity of the event. With an older event, like Titanic, the strong emotional connection between the viewer and fictional characters allows the consumer to be touched by some trace of trauma, as the society at the time was. As Elsaesser notes, this kind of script can facilitate the grieving process.[6] *United 93* revealed the trauma a citizen might experience knowing that anyone could have been on that plane, while *Flight 93* created a space to take in some of the loss that real, particular families experienced. In these ways, though the experience is entirely constructed, the tools of fiction can bring the consumer closer to the *feeling-states* conjured by the event.

Finally, as seen in *Elephant*, fiction can be used to impart social meanings, or as a means of posing the social questions a society must routinely ask itself, a process that serves as part of how a society reinvents itself, itself an integral component of progress. In this vein, film can be an effective forum for resistance and also provide a screen on which to reflect, challenge and transform social norms and values. Like the other iconic event films, *Elephant* also inspires projection, though in a different manner. The focus on many characters, versus one or two, allows audience members to identify with any one or more, out of several archetypal high school characters. The process of projection builds more slowly, enabled by the slight "remove" filming technique used to shoot the long (lonely) hallway walking scenes, fostering a slightly paused and therefore thoughtful projection (at least in terms of a reasonably plausible consumptive experience)

As films and other pop culture forms ignite an interest in an event, and offer citizens a space to experience some of the emotions linked to the event, it is not surprising that commodities emerge. Whether associated with a film or some other site of memory, there is great market potential for products linked to iconic events. These events occupy a special place in the public imagination and it is this fascination that creates the market for these products, of which the major categories are: memorabilia, political, and off-shoot commodities. The memorabilia genre feeds the idea that citizens can "own a piece of history" (reducing historical events to the simplified idea embedded in a given object). The popularity of these items therefore depends on the stature of the event in the public sphere. Politically charged commodities can grow out of specific political appropriations or might result from an intense initial interpretive process (such as in the case of the terrorist trading cards that flooded the Internet shortly after September 11th). While some political products reveal themselves as such (consider expressly political T-shirts), others contain ideas derivative of the legitimized official story. By these, I mean products bearing representations that have been deeply conflated with the event itself, so much so that they appear to embody something about the event itself and may not at first glance appear to be political in nature. For example, the "United We Stand" bumper stickers that circulated after September 11th promoted a particular patriotic vision and political agenda but may not have been widely perceived as political tools. The last major commodity genre is comprised of off-shoot commodities, which are those pre-existing products that experience spikes in popularity as a result of channeling the effects of the event or the social and political spin coming out of the event. Clear back-packs, appearing more visible in the market after Columbine, are an example.

Though spanning several major genres, the commodities associated with signature events, share commonalities. First, they all appear emptied of the struggles over meaning that resulted in the reduced object in the first place. Additionally, the purchase of such products implies that history can, at least in one respect, be objectified and owned. These items also engage the consumer in the execution of a memory-act, incorporating the buyer as an integral part of ongoing collective memory work. Finally, the obvious critique that arises regarding the commercialization of national history and the like, assumes that other kinds of representations are not commercialized to the same extent, which may be a mistake given the institutional context in which journalists operate. Moreover, it is precisely this assumption which implicitly places more authority in other, perhaps textual, representations. In other words, these kinds of assumptions may inadvertently end up privileging "official" accounts.

Future Research

This book considers the place of iconic events in American culture, and some of the forces and interpretive activities that shape their ever-changing meanings. There are other avenues explored in the tremendous literature on collective memory that also impact the space that particular events may occupy. In this vein, there is a great body of literature on memorialization and commemoration. This too, is an important aspect of how some events become legitimized as turning-points, and come to occupy both physical and symbolic space in the society. Also, particularly important given the stretch of catastrophic natural disasters over the past several years, our understanding of iconic events would be strengthened by studies focusing on the interpretive and commemorative activities surrounding natural disasters. In light of Hurricane Katrina which devastated the Gulf Coast, complete with a well broadcast, botched emergency aid plan, perhaps such studies will continue to emerge. As the events in this book are all contained, a study of sprawling or diffuse events would also extend our current body of knowledge. Particular events, such as the Holocaust and Rwandan Genocide, deservedly, receive considerable attention from collective memory scholars; however, other events could benefit from additional investigation with respect to the multiple interpretive realms that mark our memory of the event.

This work suggests that iconic events do not just "happen"; they are created out of a confluence of extraordinary events. The efforts of many interested parties, or "communities of memory," converge through their seizure of traumatic moments in the history of the nation. Some of their narrative practices coalesce into a meta-narrative of the event—one that is widely circulated in all available media. In this way, these events are integral to the renegotiation of group identity, as well as serving to record the negotiation process itself, at times in cinematic form. Though these selected events become vessels for the execution of social power, they also serve as focal points through which a society may engage in complex questions pertaining to identity, image and change. As they capture the public's imagination in powerful ways, so too can iconic events serve as sites through which to rupture dominant memories of the past.

Notes

1. Betty H. Winfield, Barbara Friedman, and Vivara Trisnadi, "History as the Metaphor Through Which the Current World Is Viewed: British and American Newspapers' Uses of History Following the 11 September 2001 Terrorist Attacks," *Journalism Studies*, 3, no. 2 (April 1, 2002).

2. Slavoj Zizek, "Titanic-Le-Symptome," *L'Ane* 30 (April-June 1987): 45.

3. This must be considered in scholarly studies of historical films which often do not account for representations of the event outside of film, and in this way may naturalize the assumption that the event itself inspired the making of the film. This is indeterminable.

4. Paul Grainge, *Memory and Popular Film* (Manchester, N.Y.: Manchester University Press, 2003), 4.

5. Vivian Carol Sobchack, *The Persistence of History: Cinema, Television, and the Modern* Event (New York: Routledge, 1996), 9.

6. Thomas Elsaesser "Subject Positions, Speaking Positions: from *Holocaust our Hitler, and Heimata to Shoah and Schindler's List*," in *The Persistence of History: Cinema, Television, and the Modern Event*, ed. Vivian Sobchack (New York: Routledge, 1996).

Selected Bibliography

"7 December 1941: Tora, Tora, Tora!." *Osprey Essential Pearl Harbor.*
http://216.168.37.48/FMPro?DB=osehph.FP3&FOMAT=/scribe/osehph/ose
hphfmtday.html&ReferenceNumber=OSEHPH343&-Max=1&-Find (January 20, 2006).

"8 December 1941: A Day Which Will Live in Infamy." *Osprey Essential Pearl Harbor.*
http://216.168.37.48/FMPro?DB=osehph.FP3&FOMAT=/scribe/osehph/ose
hphfmtday.html&ReferenceNumber=OSEHPH344&-Max=1&-Find (January 20, 2006).

"11' 9" 01 – September 11," *Artificial Eye. http://www.artificial-eye.com/dvd/ART240dvd/main.html* (June 21, 2006)

"Analysis: What is the NRA." *BBC News.* 2000.
http://news.bbc.co.uk/2/hi/americas/332555.stm (May 15, 2006).

Apollo 13 Collectors Edition, DVD, directed by Ron Howard (Universal City, CA: Universal Home Video, 1998).

Barczewski, Stephanie. *Titanic: A Night Remembered.* New York: Hambledon and London, 2004.

Barthes, Roland. "Myth Today." Pp. 93–149 in *A Barthes Reader,* edited by Susan Sontag. New York: Hill and Wang, 1982.

Baty, S. Paige. *American Monroe: The Making of a Body Politic.* Los Angeles: University of California Press, 1996.

BC Cycle, 16 April 2004.

Bellah, Robert. N., and Richard Madsen. *Habits of the Heart: Individualism and Commitment in the American Life.* New York: Harper and Row, 1985.

Biel, Steven. *Down With the Old Canoe: A Cultural History of the Titanic Disaster.* New York: W. W. Norton and Company, Inc., 1996.

Binder, Amy. "Constructing Racial Rhetoric: Media Depictions of Harm in Heavy Metal and Rap Music." *American Sociological Review* 58, no. 6 (December 1993): 753–67.

Blackwell, Alice Stone. "Suffrage and Life–Saving," *Woman's Journal* 43, no. 17 (April 27, 1912): 2.

——. "The Lesson of the Titanic," *Woman's Journal* 43, no. 17 (April 27, 1912): 2.

Boorstin, Daniel J. *The Image: A Guide to Pseudo–Events in America.* New York: Harper and Row, 1964.

Boston Globe, 2 May 1999.

Bowling for Columbine Special Edition, DVD, directed by Michael Moore (Santa Monica, CA: MGM Home Entertainment, 2003).

Brockmeier, Jens. "Introduction: Searching for Cultural Memory." *Culture & Psychology* 8, no. 1 (March 2002): 5–14.

Brooks, Brian S. and George Kennedy. *News Reporting and Writing* (5th ed.). New York: St. Martin's Press, 1996.

Butler, Daniel Allen. *UNSINKABLE: The Full Story of the RMS Titanic.* Mechanicsburg, Pa.: Stackpole Books, 1998.

Cameron, Kenneth. *America on Film: Hollywood and American History.* New York: Continuum, 1997.

"Charting School Violence," *Columbine Angels* April 28, 2006, *http://www.columbine-angels.com/Violence_Chart.htm* (March 20, 2006).

"Columbine Killing Took 16 Minutes." *BBC News.* *http://news.bbc.co.uk/2/hi/americas/749966.stm* (May 15, 2006).

"Columbine Memorial." *Columbine Memorial. http://www.columbinememorial.org* (April 19, 2006).

Cummings, Scott. "September 11, 2001 Timeline" *The Patriot Resource History: September 11, 2001.* 2001–05. *http://www.patriotsource.com/wtc/timeline/sept11c.html* (March 23, 2006).

Davie, Michael. *Titanic: The Death and Life of a Legend.* New York: Henry Hold and Company, 1988.

Dayan, Daniel and Elihu Katz. *Media Events: The Live Broadcasting of History.* Cambridge, Mass.: Harvard University Press, 1992.

Denver Post, 26 March 1911.

Denver Post, 16 April 1912–21 April 1912.

Denver Post, 21 April 1999–23 April 1999.

Der Derian, James. "9/11: Before, After, and in Between." Pp 170–90 in *Understanding September 11*, edited by Craig Calhoun, Paul Price and Ashley Timmer. New York: The New Press, 2002.

Dorr, Mrs. Rheta Childe. "Women and Children First." *Woman's Journal* 43 no. 18 (May 4, 1912): 141.

Drehle, David Von. *Triangle: The Fire That Changed America.* New York: Atlantic Monthly Press, 2003.

Edkins, Jenny. "The Rush to Memory and the Rhetoric of War." *Journal of Political and Military Sociology* 31, no. 2 (Winter 2003): 231–50.

——. *Trauma and the Memory of Politics.* Cambridge, U.K.: Cambridge University Press, 2003.

Elephant, directed by Gus Van Sant (United States: HBO Video, 2003).

Engelhart, Mark. "Review of Pearl harbor Theatrical Release." 2001,
http://www.amazon.com/gp/product/B00003CXTG/qid=1153242423/sr=8-1/ref=pd_bbs_1/103-1147873-1211029?%5Fencoding=UTF8&v=glance&n=130 (July 1, 2006).

"Excerpts From Trial Testimony in the Triangle Shirtwaist Fire Trial." *University of Missouri–Kansas City School of Law.*
http://www.law.umkc.edu/faculty/projects/trials/triangle/triangletest1.html (April 12, 2006).

Fentress, James and Chris Wickham. *Social Memory.* Cambridge, MA: Blackwell Publishers, 1992.

Flight 93, directed by Peter Markle (United States: A&E, 2006).

Gamson, William A. and Andre Modigliani. "Media Discourse and Public Opinion on Nuclear Power: A Constructionist Approach." *American Journal of Sociology* 95, no. 1 (July 1989): 1–37.

Gans, Herbert J. *Democracy and the News.* Oxford: Oxford University Press, 2003.

Gills, John R. *Commemorations: The Politics of National Identity.* Princeton, NJ: Princeton University Press, 1994.

Gracie, Archibald. *Titanic: A Survivor's Story.* Chicago: Academy Chicago Publishers, 1996.

Grainge, Paul. *Memory and Popular Film.* Manchester, NY: Manchester University Press, 2003.

Griffin, David Ray. *The New Pearl Harbor: Disturbing Questions about the Bush Administration and 9-11.* Northampton, MA: Olive Branch Press, 2004.

Hall, Stuart. "Notes on Deconstructing the Popular." 227–340. in *People's History and Socialist Theory*, edited by Rapael Samuel. London: Routledge and Kegan Paul, 1981.

Hatfield, Peter. "Japan's Date with Pearl Harbor," *BBC News.* 2001.
http://news.bbc.co.uk/2/hi/asia-pacific/1399970.stm (July 1, 2006).

Hutton, Patrick H.. *History as an Art of Memory.* Lebanon, N.H.: University Press of New England, 1993.

Irwin-Zarecka, Iwona. *Frames of Remembrance: The Dynamics of Collective Memory.* Somerset, NJ: Transaction Publishers, 1994.

James, Victoria. "Japan Snores Through Pearl Harbor." 2001.
http://www.newstatesman.com/200107230025 (July 1, 2006).

Sut Jhally. Speaking on the Tough Guise: Violence and the Social Construction of Masculinity, on November 3, 2003, to Stonehill College.

Jones, Wex. "Woman and Children First." *The Woman's Protest* 1, no. 1 (May 1912): 6.

Kamuda, Edward S. "Titanic Past and Present." *Titanic Historical Society.* 2005.
http://www.titanichistoricalsociety.org/articles/titanicpastandpresent1.asp

Kristeva, Julia. *Language – The Unknown: An Initiation into Linguistics.* New York: Columbia University Press,1989.

Landy, Marcia. *The Historical Film: History and Memory in the Media.* New Brunswick, NJ: Rutgers University Press, 2001.

Laroche, Louise. "A Haitian French Family Which Traveled in Second Class Aboard Titanic." *Titanic Historical Society.* 2005.

http://www.titanichisttoricalsociety.org/people/louise-laroche.asp (January 20, 2006).

Leonard, Mary. "Million Mom March' Against Guns on Mothers Day, May 14." *Common Dreams.org. http://www.commondreams.org/headlines/032900-01.htm* (May 15, 2006).

Lewis, Justin; Sut Jhally and Michael Morgan. "The Gulf War: A Study of the Media, Public Opinion and Public Knowledge." *Department of Communication. http://www.umass.edu/communication/resources/special_reports/gulf_war/i ndex.shtml* (March 23, 2006).

Lincoln, Yvonna S and Norman K. Denzin. *9/11 in American Culture.* Walnut Creek: Alta Mira Press, 2003.

Lipsitz, George. *Time Passages: Collective memory and American Popular Culture.* Minneapolis: University of Minnesota Press, 1990.

Lisle, Debbie and Andrew Pepper. "The New Face of Global Hollywood: Black Hawk Down and the Politics of the Meta-Sovereignty." *Cultural Politics* 1, no. 2 (April 2005): 135–36.

Lynch, Donald. *Titanic: An Illustrated History.* New York: Hyperion, 1992.

Manoff, Robert K. and Michael Schudson.. *Reading the News: A Pantheon Guide to Popular Culture.* New York: Pantheon Books, 1986.

McCrisken, Trevor B. and Andrew Pepper. *American History and Contemporary Hollywood Film.* New Brunswick, NJ: Rutgers University Press, 2005.

"Million Mom March Concludes on National Mall." *CNN.com Transcripts. http://transcripts.cnn.com/TRANSCRIPTS/0005/14/sun.02.html* (May 15, 2006).

Neal, Arthur G. *National Trauma and Collective Memory: Extraordinary Events in the American Experience.* Armonk, NY: M.E. Sharp, 2005.

——. *National Trauma & Collective Memory: Major Events in the American Century.* Armonk, NY: M. E. Sharp, 1998.

New York Times, 26 March 1911–28 December 1911.

New York Times, 12 April 1912–16 April 1912.

New York Times, 8 December 1941–10 December 1941.

New York Times, 22 June 2001–17 September 2001.

Nora, Pierre. " Between Memory and History: Les Lieux de Memoire." *Repre- sentations,* 26, Special Issue: Memory and Counter–Memory (Spring 1989).

Peacock, James. "Memory and Violence." *American Anthropologist,* 104 no. 3 (September 2002): 961-63.

Pearl Harbor a Documentary: A Day of Infamy, December 7, 1941 (Eugene, OR: Dastar Corp./Marathon Music and Video, 2001).

"Pearl Harbor, Hawaii, Sunday December 7, 1941." *The History Place. http://www.historyplace.com/worldwar2/timeline/pearl.htm* (January 20, 2006).

"Pearl Harbor Timeline." *Osprey Essential Pearl Harbor. http://www.essentialpearlharbor.com/osehphtime.html* (January 20, 2006).

Pellegrino, Charles. *Ghosts of the Titanic.* New York: HarperCollins Publishers, Inc., 2000.

Prance, Gordon W. and Donald M. Goldstein and Katherine V. Dillon. *Dec. 7 1941: The Day the Japanese Attacked Pearl Harbor.* New York: McGraw–Hill, 1988.

Reading, Anna. *The Social Inheritance of the Holocaust: Gender, Culture, and Memory.* New York: Palgrave Macmillan, 2002.

Romanyshyn, Robert D. *Technology as Symptom and Dream*. New York: Routledge, 1989.

Rosenstone, Robert A. *Revisioning History: Film and the Construction of a New (Past*. Princeton, NJ: Princeton University Press, 1995).

Rosenweig, Roy and David Thelen. "The Presence of the Past: Popular Uses of History In American Life," *Humanities: When Stones Speak: Communicating Across the Ages*. Special Issue 20, no. 1 (January/February 1999): 15–16.

Ross, Marc H. "The Political Psychology of Competing Narratives: September 11 and Beyond." Pp 303–20 in *Understanding September 11*, edited by Craig Calhoun, Paul Price and Ashley Timmer. New York: The New Press, 2002.

Saphire, William B. "The White Star Line and The International Mercantile Marine Company." *Titanic Historical Society*. 2005.
    http://www.titanichistoricalsociety.org/articles/titanicpastandpresent1.asp

Schudson, Michael. "Deadlines, Datelines, and History." 79–108 in *Reading the News: A Pantheon Guide to Popular Culture*. edited by Robert K. Manoff and Michael Schudson. New York: Pantheon Books, 1986.

——. *Watergate in American Memory: How we Remember, Forget, and Reconstruct the Past*. New York: Basic Books, 1992.

Schwartz, Barry. "Memory as a Cultural System: Abraham Lincoln in World War II." *American Sociological Review* 61, no. 5 (October 1996): 908–27.

"September 11, 2001 attacks timeline for the day of the attacks." *Wikipedia, the Free Encyclopedia*. May31,2006.
    http://en.wikipedia.org/wiki/September_11%2C_2001_attacks_timeline_for _the_day_of_the_attacks (March 23, 2006).

Slackman, Michael. *Target: Pearl Harbor*. Honolulu: University of Hawaii Press: Arizona Memorial Museum Association, 1990.

Sobchack, Vivian Carol. *The Persistence of History: Cinema, Television, and the Modern Event*. New York: Routledge, 1996.

"Some Mothers See Million Mom March For Gun Control as Personal Memorial." *CNN com Transcripts*,
    http://transcripts.cnn.com/TRANSCRIPTS/0005/14/sm.07.html (May 15, 2006).

Spurling, Sly. "Trenchcoat Scapegoat Superstar," *Rock Out Censorship Incident Updates* 2003, *http://www.theroc.org/updates/mm-denver.html* (22 March 2006).

Star Tribune, 22 April 1999–11 May 1999.

Storey, John. Cultural Studies & The Study of Popular Culture: Theories and Methods. Athens, GA.: University of Georgia Press, 1996.

Strauss–Levi, Claude. *The Savage Mind*. Chicago: University of Chicago Press, 1966.

Sturken, Martita. "Memorializing Absence." Pp 374–85 in *Understanding September 11*, edited by Craig Calhoun, Paul Price and Ashley Timmer. New York: The New Press, 2002.

Sunshine, Linda and Antonio Felix. *Pearl Harbor: The Movie and the Moment*. New York: Hyperion, 2001.

"The Morning of December 7, 1941 at Pearl Harbor, Oahu, Hawaii." *Pearl Harbor.*
   http://projects.pisd.edu/webmastering/vines/pearl_harbor/contents3.html (January
   20, 2006).
"The Pacific War: A World War II Special Feature." *War Times Journal.*
   http://www.wtj.com/articles/pacific_war/articles/pearl_harbor.htm (January 20,
   2006).
"The Wreck of the Titanic." *The Common Cause* 4. no. 159 (April 25, 1912): 1.
"Timeline of Events: September 11–18, 2001." *Teachervision.com.* 2005–06.
   *http://www.teachervision.fen.com/war/unitedstates/6825.htmlhttp://www.te
   achervision.fen.com/war/united-states/6825.html* (March 23, 2006).
"Timelines, Images, and Graphics from the September 11, 2001 Attacks on the World
   Trade Center in NYC and the Pentagon in Washington." *September 11th News.com.*
   2001–03. *http://www.september11news.com/AttackImages.htm* (March 23, 2006).
Titanic, directed by James Cameron (Hollywood, Ca: Paramount, 1999).
"Titanic Myths." *The Titanic Historical Society.* 2005.
   http://www.titanichistoricalsociety.org/articles/titanicmyths.asp (January 20, 2006).
Toland, John. *Infamy: Pearl Harbor and its Aftermath.* Green City: NY: Doubleday,
   1982.
"US Moms Protest Against Guns." *BBC News.*
   http://news.bbc.co.uk/2/hi/americas/747619.stm (May 15, 2006).
Varisco, Daniel Martin. "September 11: Participant Webservation of the 'War on Terror-
   ism.'" *American Anthropologist* 104, no. 3 (September 2002).
"Votes for Women to the Rescue." *Woman's Journal* 43, no. 17 (April 27, 1912) 1.
Wade, Wyn Craig. *The Titanic: End of a Dream.* New York: Penguin Books, 1979).
Wertsch, James V. *Voices of Collective Remembering.* Cambridge, U.K.: Cambridge
   University Press.
White, Hayden. *Metahistory: The Historical Imagination in Nineteenth Century
   Europe.* Baltimore, Md.: Johns Hopkins University Press, 1973.
*White Star Line, Royal & United States Mail Steamers Olympic and Titanic 45,000 Tons
   Each the Largest Vessels in the World* (Liverpool, U.K.: Liverpool Stationery Com-
   pany, 1911) 3–5.
Williams, Patricia J. "Diary of a Mad Law Professor: Smart Bombs." *The Nation* 268 no.
   21 (June 7, 1999): 10.
Winfield, Betty H. Barbara Friedman, and Vivara Trisnadi. "History as the Metaphor
   Through Which the Current World Is Viewed: British and American Newspapers'
   Uses of History Following the 11 September 2001 Terrorist Attacks." *Journalism
   Studies,* 3, no. 2 (April 1, 2002): 289–300.
Winocour, Jack. *The Story of the Titanic as Told by its Survivors.* New York: Dover Pub-
   lications, Inc., 1960.
Zelizer, Barbie. Covering the Body: The Kennedy Assassination, The Media, and the
   Shaping of Collective Memory. Chicago: University of Chicago Press, 1992.
——. and Stuart Allan. *Journalism After September 11.* New York: Routledge, 2002.
Zizek, Slovaj. *Desert of the Real: 5 Essays on September 11 and Related Dates.* New
   York: Verso, 2002.
——. "Titanic-Le-Symptome." *L'Ane* 30 (April–June 1987): 45.

About the Author

Patricia Leavy, Ph.D. is Associate Professor of Sociology at Stonehill College in Easton, MA. She is also the Founder and Director of the Gender Studies Program at Stonehill College. She is coauthor of *The Practice of Qualitative Research* (Sage Publications, 2006) and *The Practice of Feminist Research: A Primer* (Sage Publications, 2007). She is co-editor of *Approaches to Qualitative Research: A Reader on Theory and Practice* (Oxford University Press, 2004) and *Emergent Methods in Social Research* (Sage Publications, 2006). She is also the editor of *Method Meets Art: Social Research and the Creative Arts* (forthcoming, Guilford Publications). She has published articles in the areas of collective memory, mass media, popular culture, body image, and methodology and is regularly quoted in newspapers for her expertise on popular culture and current events.